edited by
Tarrell Awe Agahe Portman
Chris Wood
Heather J. Fye

THIRD EDITION

Critical Incidents in SCHOOL Counseling

AMERICAN COUNSELING
ASSOCIATION
6101 Stevenson Avenue • Suite 600
Alexandria, VA 22304
www.counseling.org

THIRD EDITION

Critical Incidents in SCHOOL Counseling

American Counseling Association
6101 Stevenson Avenue • Suite 600
Alexandria, VA 22304

Associate Publisher   Carolyn C. Baker

Digital and Print Development Editor   Nancy Driver

Senior Production Manager   Bonny E. Gaston

Copy Editor   Juanita Doswell

Cover and text design by Bonny E. Gaston

Library of Congress Cataloging-in-Publication Data

Names: Portman, Tarrell Awe Agahe, editor. | Wood, Chris (Christopher Todd) editor. | Fye, Heather J., editor.
Title: Critical incidents in school counseling / edited by Tarrell Awe Agahe Portman, Chris Wood, Heather J. Fye.
Description: Third edition. | Alexandria, VA : American Counseling Association, [2019] | Includes bibliographical references.
Identifiers: LCCN 2018047343 | ISBN 9781556203473 (pbk. : alk. paper)
Subjects: LCSH: Educational counseling. | Student counselors. | Critical incident technique.
Classification: LCC LB1027.5 .C248 2019 | DDC 371.4—dc23
LC record available at https://lccn.loc.gov/2018047343

Dedication

We dedicate this work to our mentors and friends, who have supported us throughout our professional journeys.

To our loved ones—Dr. Gerald Portman, my partner, who has enriched my life journey and cared for me as no other.
—Tarrell Awe Agahe Portman

To Danica, Charlotte, Grace, and Molly—with tremendous love and gratitude. Every day of my life is better because of each of you.
—Chris Wood

To Eric, my extended family, and CES mentors—I am thankful for your love, generosity, and support along the way.
—Heather J. Fye

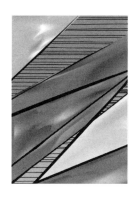

Table of Contents

Preface   xi

About the Editors   xiii

About the Contributors   xv

Acknowledgments   xxix

Chapter 1
  Introduction   1
    Chris Wood, Heather J. Fye, and Tarrell Awe Agahe Portman

Part I   Who I Am as A Counselor

Chapter 2
  I Never Thought I Would Be in This Position
  as a Supervisor!   9
  Incident
    Cindy Wiley
  Responses
    Sandra A. Loew, Patrick R. Mullen, and W. Bryce Hagedorn

Chapter 3
  Is This Really What I Went to School For?   19
  Incident
    Lawrence E. Tyson
  Responses
    Franciene Sabens and *Amy Upton*

Chapter 4

When Is There Time for Me? How Do I Cope?   29

Incident
Lacey Ricks

Responses
Karen Moore Townsend and Yvonne Ortiz-Bush

Chapter 5

What About One's Religious Beliefs?   37

Incident
Tomeka McGhee

Responses
Zachary Michael Pietrantoni and Diana L. Wildermuth

Part II   What I Do as a Counselor

Chapter 6

Who Will Advocate If I Don't?   47

Incident
Emilie E. Shaver

Responses
Jolie Daigle and Debbie Grant

Chapter 7

How Did All of This Come Into My School?   55

Incident
Cheryl Lynn Spaulding Sewell

Responses
Tori Charette and Sandra (Sandi) M. Logan-McKibben

Chapter 8

Suicide: Who Are You Going to Call?   65

Incident
Judith A. Harrington

Responses
Christy W. Land and Carolyn Stone

Chapter 9

What Do I Do When My Supervisor Lacks Supervision?   75

Incident
Claire Merlin-Knoblich

Responses
Sarah I. Springer, Christine Hennigan Paone, and Melinda M. Gibbons

Chapter 10
We're Counseling as Fast as We Can!
Trapped in the Cracks of the System 83
Incident
Kenya Bledsoe

Responses
Jolie Daigle and LaWanda Edwards

Chapter 11
When It Rains, It Pours!
Where Do I Begin to Help? 91
Incident
Tiffany Stoner-Harris

Responses
Sophie Maxis and Jonique Childs

Part III How I Serve as a Counselor

Chapter 12
Now That I Stand Up, How Do I Survive? 103
Incident
Matthew J. Beck

Responses
Darcie Davis-Gage and S. Kent Butler

Chapter 13
Prepared and Not Prepared:
Which Culture Decides? 113
Incident
Na Mi Bang

Responses
Joel M. Filmore and Erin Lane

Chapter 14
Not Enough Books and Too Many Students 121
Incident
Maiko Xiong

Responses
Norma Day-Vines and Tina Anctil

Chapter 15
Blowing Up in Science Class or
Getting Trapped in the System 127
Incident
Rafe McCullough

Responses
Tim Poynton and Anita Young

Chapter 16
What Do I Need to Know, and How Can I Get the Answers? Needs Assessment From a "Not Nosy" School Counselor
135

Incident
Jennifer Sharp

Responses
Brandie Oliver, Tom Keller, Nick Abel, and Richard E. Cleveland

Chapter 17
She's Come Undone! Alternatives for Amy?
145

Incident
James Gondak

Responses
Linda Foster and Bradley T. Erford

Chapter 18
Did You Bring a Suicide Note?
153

Incident
Tracy L. Jackson

Responses
Malik S. Henfield and Laurie A. Carlson

Chapter 19
Professional Dilemma: Unteachable Teacher?
159

Incident
Jason Durrell

Responses
Richard E. Cleveland and Laurie A. Carlson

Chapter 20
But She's Going to Be Famous! Addressing Attendance Concerns in Third-Culture Students
169

Incident
Sebastien Laroche

Responses
Jared Lau, Chris Wood, and Caroline A. Baker

Chapter 21
Assessment: Case of the Ninth-Grade Gap
181

Incident
Justin R. Fields

Responses
Christopher A. Sink, Richard T. Lapan, and Catherine Griffith

Chapter 22

**"Other Than That, Mrs. Lincoln,
How Was The Play?" Career Development**   193

Incident
Allison List

Responses
Wendy Hoskins, Katrina Harris, and Cass Dykeman

Part IV   What I Can Do to Make a Difference as a Counselor

Chapter 23

**I Need to Know About
Adverse Childhood Effects**   205

Incident
Jodi L. Saunders

Responses
*Amanda Dreisbach Rumsey, Catherine Y. Chang, Tom Keller,
Brandie Oliver, and Nick Abel*

Chapter 24

The "We" in Cyberbullying   213

Incident
Stephannee Standefer

Responses
Brandie Oliver, Nick Abel, Tom Keller, and Chris Janson

Chapter 25

Ambassador Between Two Nations   221

Incident
Lisa Grayshield

Responses
*Heather J. Fye, Chelsey Windl, Nick Abel, Tom Keller,
and Brandie Oliver*

Chapter 26

How Can We Be Stronger Together?   233

Incident
Laura L. Gallo

Responses
Carrie A. Wachter Morris and Susannah M. Wood

Chapter 27

Am I Biased Too? Bias-Based Bullying   241

Incident
Cassandra A. Storlie

Responses
Jodi L. Saunders, Rhonda M. Bryant, and Beth A. Durodoye

Chapter 28
      When Systems Fail, What Is Next?   247
      Incident
          Robin Alcala Saner

      Responses
          Meredith A. Rausch and Danielle S. Bryant

Chapter 29
      **Please Help Me, but Don't Tell Me
      How to Raise My Child**   257
      Incident
          Anna Viviani

      Responses
          Sondra Smith-Adcock and Lourdes M. Rivera

Chapter 30
      **How Can We Work Across the Road
      If We Aren't Included?**   265
      Incident
          Dawnette Cigrand

      Responses
          Eric R. Baltrinic and Tarrell Awe Agahe Portman

      References   273

Preface

The first edition of *Critical Incidents in School Counseling* (Calia & Corsini, 1973) was published the year the United States began withdrawing troops from Vietnam, the U.S. Supreme Court outlawed state bans on abortion (*Roe v. Wade*), the World Trade Center opened in New York, the Watergate scandal extended to the White House, and an oil crisis caused gas rationing across North America. In the realm of education, Section 504 of the 1973 Rehabilitation Act was implemented as the first civil rights statute designed to prohibit discrimination against individuals with disabilities. The U.S. Supreme Court ruling in *San Antonio Independent School District v. Rodriguez*, however, set the stage for decades of inequity in school financing and subsequent educational quality. School counselors reading articles in the journal *School Counselor* found titles such as "Youth and the Occult" (Grey, 1973), "Career Education: The Counselor's Role" (Brown, Feit, & Forestandi, 1973), "Integration Is More Than Just Busing" (Weinrach, 1973), and "Hand Scheduling Versus the Computer" (Marlette, 1973). Sample topics in Calia and Corsini's text included the following: unwanted teen pregnancy; race relations; discerning mental illness, narcolepsy, or school phobia; cultural conflicts between school and family; the school counselor's role in the promotion of college; trade vs. college degree; how to handle a discrepancy between parents' perception of their child and the child's poor performance as a student; and ethical dilemmas regarding school confidentiality, school policies, and/or the law.

The purpose of the first edition of the text was to offer to school counselors, and school counselors in training, what textbooks did not; to meet the authentic needs of school counselors by providing a "practical" opportunity for learning. By presenting cases (critical incidents) and subsequent responses by expert consultants, the editors hoped to bridge the gap between theory and professional practice.

This original intent is consistent in the second edition, and now the third edition. Although the training for school counselors has improved dramatically over the years and the profession now has better guides to professional practice, including a code of ethics (American School Counselor Association [ASCA], 2016) first published in 1984 and a national model for comprehensive school counseling programs (ASCA, 2012a), the need to help professional school counselors learn to critically reason through a wide array of specific incidents in unique professional contexts remains.

Obviously, the current world is very different than the one in 1973 or even 2000. In 1973, there were no mobile phones, personal computers, or the internet. Even since 2000, the explosion of social media seems to have created a different reality for youth. In 2000, just 6% of kids indicated they had been a victim of cyberbullying (Finkelhor, Mitchell, & Wolak, 2000), but by 2004, the number had risen to 42% (Wolak, Mitchell, & Finkelhor, 2006). Surprisingly, although the culture of today's youth may seem vastly different from that in 1973 or 2000, the critical incidents that concern school counselors seem surprisingly similar. The third edition of *Critical Incidents in School Counseling* includes themes that are similar to those in the previous editions: ethical questions, gangs, drug use, academic motivation, angry parents/families, and situations that don't seem to easily lie within the topics addressed by school counseling textbooks.

Many of the elements of this edition are also consistent with those of previous editions. Each *critical incident* is approximately the same length as in the previous editions; and, similarly, each *response* is equivalent in length to the *responses* published in the previous two editions.

About the Editors

Tarrell Awe Agahe Portman, PhD, is the dean of the College of Education at Winona State University. She is a licensed school counselor, mental health counselor, and teacher, with over 35 years in education. She was one of two school counselor educators appointed to sit on the National Board for Professional Teaching Standards School Counseling Standards development committee. Dr. Portman has served the profession as president of the Association for Counselor Education and Supervision and president of the Association for Multicultural Counseling and Development. She has received numerous awards and recognitions over her career and was the first recipient of the Mary Smith Arnold Anti-Oppression Award from the Counselors for Social Justice division of ACA. Her research and publications focus upon school counseling and counseling issues among American Indians. She has served on editorial boards for the *Professional School Counseling, Journal of Multicultural Counseling and Development*, and *The Journal of Humanistic Counseling*.

■ ■ ■

Chris Wood, PhD, is an associate professor in the Counselor Education program at the University of Nevada, Las Vegas. Dr. Wood has previous experience as a high school counselor, a counseling/guidance department chair, a counselor/group leader at a residential youth facility for troubled teens, and a career counselor at an alternative school serving grades 7–12. Dr. Wood was the editor for the journal *Professional School Counseling* for 6 years. Dr. Wood has been the principal investigator or faculty research associate on research teams that were awarded over $3 million in state and federal grants. He has had over 30 conference presentations and 30 publications, including articles in *Professional School Counseling*, the *Journal of Counseling & Development*, the *Journal of College Counseling, Counselor Education and Supervision, Career Planning and Adult Development Journal,* and *The Elementary School Journal.* Chris Wood was coeditor for the fifth and sixth editions of the National Career Development Association publication, *A Counselor's Guide to Career Assessment Instruments.* Dr. Wood was honored with the American Counseling Association Fellow Award in 2017.

■ ■ ■

Heather J. Fye, PhD, is an assistant professor at the University of Alabama. She is a certified K–12 school counselor and licensed professional counselor. Dr. Fye has worked in the mental health and school settings for 13 years. She has previously worked in child protective services, at a nursing home, in the elementary school setting, at an outpatient counseling clinic serving youth and their families, and at a college counseling center. Her research, publications, and presentations primarily focus on school counselor wellness, stress, coping, burnout, creativity in counseling, and implementation of the American School Counselor Association National Model. She has over 30 professional presentations on these topics and has been published in the *Journal of Counseling & Development, Measurement and Evaluation in Counseling and Development,* and *Professional School Counseling.* Dr. Fye and her colleagues were awarded the Association for Assessment and Research in Counseling MECD Patricia B. Elmore Award for Outstanding Research in Measurement and Evaluation in Counseling and Development in 2015 and the American Counseling Association Research Award in 2016 for their research on school counselor burnout.

■ ■ ■

About the Contributors

Nick Abel, EdD, is an assistant professor of school counseling at Butler University. He is keenly interested in training future school counselors to implement comprehensive school counseling programs in an equitable, data-driven manner. Before entering counselor education, Mr. Abel worked for almost 9 years as a professional school counselor and has experience at both the elementary and high school levels.

Tina Anctil, PhD, is the associate dean for academic affairs in the Graduate School of Education at Portland State University. Dr. Anctil has been a practicing rehabilitation counselor for over 20 years and continues to provide clinical supervision to pre-licensure counselors through her private practice. Her research explores career development with adolescents and adults with disabilities.

Caroline A. Baker, PhD, is an associate professor and director of the counseling program at the University of Wisconsin—River Falls. Dr. Baker teaches school counseling courses including cultural and ethical foundations, practicum, and career. Her primary research focus has included understanding the experiences of students of color in graduate programs and the scholarship of teaching and learning in counselor education.

Eric R. Baltrinic, PhD, is assistant professor of counselor education at The University of Alabama. Before obtaining his doctorate, Dr. Baltrinic worked as a chemical dependency, outpatient, school-based, and home-based mental health counselor for nearly 20 years. His research interests and related publications include teacher in counselor education, supervision, co-occurring disorders, and counseling adolescents.

Na Mi Bang, PhD, is an assistant professor of school counseling at the University of Central Arkansas. She has provided workshops and lectures for counselors on the topic of career counseling and counselors' professional development. Dr. Bang has conducted diverse studies, using quantitative and qualitative methods, on the concerns and needs of counselors in their career path, career-related variables, and multicultural career counseling.

Matthew J. Beck, PhD, is an assistant professor in the Department of Counselor Education at Western Illinois University—Quad Cities. Dr. Beck worked in public education for 12 years as a teacher and professional school counselor at the elementary, middle, and high school settings in Illinois. His research interests are informed by his school counselor practice, which encompasses how school counselors, administrators, and schools can provide an optimal school climate that fosters academic, career, and social–emotional success of LGBTQ students.

Kenya Bledsoe, LPC-S, NCC, NCSC, is a doctoral student in counselor education and supervision at The University of Alabama. She is the interim executive director at College Admissions Made Possible (CAMP). Ms. Bledsoe is a 2017–2018 National Board for Certified Counselors (NBCC) Minority Fellow and a Chi Sigma Iota (CSI) International Leadership Fellow.

Danielle S. Bryant, PhD, is an adjunct professor of school counseling at California State University—Bakersfield. Dr. Bryant is a professional high school counselor in southern California. For more than a decade, she has provided individual and group counseling to diverse student populations in diverse school communities covering topics related to academic, career, personal, social, and emotional development.

Rhonda M. Bryant, PhD, is associate vice president of student life and dean of students at the University of the Pacific. She holds state and national counseling credentials in school counseling and mental health counseling. She has published articles and book chapters on school success, leadership, and counselor supervision. Dr. Bryant also mentors and coaches newly inducted counseling professionals.

S. Kent Butler, PhD, LPC, NCC, NCSC, joined the faculty at the University of Central Florida (UCF) as an associate professor in 2007. He currently serves as the faculty advisor to the Chi Sigma Iota International Honor Society (http://www.csi-net.org/). Outside of UCF, Dr. Butler has served as the 2011–2012 president of the Association for Multicultural Counseling and Development (AMCD) and currently serves as the AMCD Governing Council representative (2015–2018) for the American Counseling Association (ACA).

Laurie A. Carlson, PhD, Colorado State University. Dr. Carlson is a former school counselor with a specialty of counseling LGBTQ youth. Laurie is coeditor of *Critical Issues in Counseling Children*, published by ACA.

Catherine Y. Chang, PhD, is a professor of counseling and psychological services at Georgia State University. She has conducted over 100 presentations, workshops, and keynote addresses and has authored/coauthored more than 80 publications, including one edited book. Dr. Chang's primary areas of interest include social justice and advocacy, multicultural counseling competence, supervision, and counseling implications related to Asian American and Korean American clients.

Tori Charette, EdS, is a school counseling intern at the University of Florida, Gainesville.

Jonique Childs, PhD, NCC, is an assistant professor at the University of Massachusetts Amherst. Dr. Childs's work experience includes serving various individuals from different ethnic backgrounds. Her work experiences within school and clinical mental health settings has allowed her to serve adolescents, high school students, undergraduates, graduate students, and older adults.

Dawnette Cigrand, PhD, is chair of the Department of Counselor Education, Winona State University. She has multiple years of experience as a teacher and school counselor. She is actively engaged in school counseling advocacy issues at the state level.

Richard E. Cleveland, PhD, is a school counseling program coordinator in the counselor education program at Georgia Southern University. After serving as a full-time school counselor, Dr. Cleveland decided to pursue a doctoral degree at Seattle Pacific University.

Jolie Daigle, PhD, LPC, is a professor in the Department of Counseling and Human Development Services at the University of Georgia. Dr. Ziomek-Daigle teaches the clinical core courses such as interpersonal skills, counseling children and adolescents, psych diagnosis, play therapy, and internship. She is the 2014 recipient of the 2014 Association for Counselor Education and Supervision (ACES) *Counseling Vision and Innovation* award and is currently a service-learning fellow at the University of Georgia.

Darcie Davis-Gage, PhD, University of Northern Iowa. She brings 10 years of varied counseling experiences to the classroom. She worked as a counselor in a variety of mental health agencies, which included a partial hospitalization program, a women's mental health agency, a college counseling and advising center, and private practice. Dr. Davis-Gage's research interests are in the area of group counseling, creativity and flow theory, and diversity issues related to counselor education and practice.

Norma Day-Vines, PhD, Johns Hopkins University. She has published widely on counseling strategies for working more effectively with culturally and linguistically diverse children and adolescents, with a special emphasis on African American youngsters. Dr. Day-Vines has also worked with a collaborative team of researchers to examine the impact of school counselors and school counseling programs on student academic outcomes and college decisions using large national longitudinal datasets (e.g., Educational Longitudinal Study 2002; ELS 2002).

Beth A. Durodoye, EdD, Georgia Southern University. Dr. Durodoye's research spans topics in the area of multicultural counseling. She has authored or coauthored publications emphasizing multicultural counseling competencies as well as social justice and advocacy counseling. Dr. Durodoye currently sits on the Elders Council of the *Journal of Multicultural Counseling and Development* and is a former associate editor of the *Counseling and Values* journal.

Jason Durrell, MA, is a school counselor in the Olentangy Local School District in Delaware, Ohio.

Cass Dykeman, PhD, is an associate professor of counselor education at Oregon State University. He earned his doctorate in counselor education from the University of Virginia and his Master of Education in school counseling from the University of Washington. Before becoming a counselor educator, Dr. Dykeman served as a school counselor in Seattle, Washington. Dr. Dykeman has served as the principal investigator for two federal grants and is the author of numerous books, book chapters, and scholarly articles in the area of counseling. A complete listing of Dr. Dykeman's scholarly work can be found at https://scholar.google.com/citations?user=OCvKsKUAAAAJ&hl=en.

LaWanda Edwards, PhD, ALC, NCC, is an associate professor in counselor education at Alabama State University—Montgomery.

Bradley T. Erford, PhD, LCPC, NCC, LPC, LP, LSP, is a professor in the human development counseling program of the Department of Human and Organizational Development at Vanderbilt University. He has authored or edited more than 30 counseling books. His research specialization falls primarily in development and technical analysis of psycho-educational tests and outcomes research and has resulted in the publication of more than 75 refereed journal articles, more than 125 book chapters, and 15 published tests. Dr. Erford has received numerous awards for his scholarship and service to the counseling profession.

Justin R. Fields, PhD, is a professional school counselor at Denton High School in Denton, Texas. He also has experience as a lecturer in counselor education programs. Dr. Fields works in an urban high school setting, partnering with students, parents, administrators, and community members to address issues related to academic achievement, personal/social wellness, and college and career readiness. His research interests include school counselor training programs, college and career readiness, and first-generation college students.

Joel M. Filmore, EdD, LCPC, is an assistant professor and program coordinator for the mental health counseling program at Springfield College Milwaukee. He is the 2017–2018 president of the Association for Lesbian, Gay, Bisexual & Transgender Issues in Counseling (ALGBTIC). Dr. Filmore received his doctorate in counselor education from Northern Illinois University's CACREP (Council for Accreditation of Counseling & Related Educational Programs)-accredited counseling program along with a graduate certificate in quantitative research methods.

Linda Foster, MS, is a core faculty member in the MS in Clinical Mental Health Counseling program. Dr. Foster has worked as a licensed professional counselor for more than 10 years at the elementary, middle, and high school levels and has been a counselor educator for 12 years. She has served on local, state, national, and international counseling and editorial boards. Dr. Foster has presented various topics at the state, national, and international levels and has published numerous articles in peer-reviewed journals, as well as several book chapters.

Laura L. Gallo, PhD, is an assistant professor in the Department of Counselor Education at Boise State University. She was a high school counselor in Marion, Iowa, for 10 years and recently graduated from the University of Iowa. Dr. Gallo has extensive experience in suicide prevention in K–12 schools as well as leading social–emotional support groups for high school students. She is also on the editorial review board for the *Professional School Counseling* journal.

Melinda M. Gibbons, PhD, is a professor of counselor education and the PhD program coordinator at the University of Tennessee. She previously worked as a high school counselor and currently focuses her research on career development for underserved populations and school counseling best practices. Dr. Gibbons oversees several federal grants that support career and postsecondary awareness for rural Appalachian youth.

James Gondak, MEd, is a school counselor in Anne Arundel County, Maryland. Mr. Gondak works both in a traditional comprehensive high school and in an alternative evening high school with at-risk students, many of whom have recently immigrated. He has served on his county's crisis response team, supervised school counseling interns, and is the coordinator of the Maryland College Application Campaign at his school.

Debbie Grant, MA, NBCC, LPC-S, works as a therapist in the New Beginnings program at Hoover High School in Hoover, Alabama. She has been a counselor for 33 years and is a licensed professional counselor supervisor, a national board-certified counselor, and a certified rehabilitation counselor. Prior to her move to Hoover High School in 2007, she served nearly 13 years as a counselor educator.

Lisa Grayshield, PhD, is an assistant professor of counseling and educational psychology at New Mexico State University. Dr. Grayshield is a member of the Washoe Tribe of Nevada and California. Dr. Grayshield is an avid proponent of Indigenous Ways of Knowing (IWOK): the incorporation of ancient and traditional forms of knowledge into academic endeavors.

Catherine Griffith, PhD, is an assistant professor in the Department of Student Development at the University of Massachusetts Amherst. Dr. Griffith is an associate director of the Ronald H. Fredrickson Center for School Counseling Outcome Research and Evaluation (CSCORE). Her primary interests include the development of affirming interventions with LGBTQ youth, the ethical and legal aspects of school professionals' use of social media, and the overall contribution of outcomes research in school-based settings.

W. Bryce Hagedorn, PhD, LMHC, NCC, AMC, QCS, is the program director of counselor education at the University of Central Florida. Dr. Hagedorn has served the counseling profession for such organizations as the ACA, the Association for Counseling Education and Supervision (ACES), the Association for Spiritual, Ethical, and Religious Values in Counseling (ASERVIC), CACREP, and the International Association of Addictions and Offender Counselors (IAAOC). His research in addictions, addicted family systems, the integration of spirituality and counseling, and counselor development have led to numerous publications and presentations.

Judith A. Harrington, PhD, SLPC, LMFT, is a faculty member in the Department of Counseling of the University of Montevallo Graduate School in Birmingham, Alabama.

Katrina Harris, PhD, is an assistant professor in residence in the Department of Educational & Clinical Studies, University of Nevada, Las Vegas. She has served as the internship coordinator in the counselor education program for the past 7 years and works closely with community mental health agencies and the local school district to provide and facilitate field experience placements for practicum students and interns. Dr. Harris's research interests include self-advocacy, mentorship, homeless youth, cultural competence, and the recruitment and retention of faculty of color.

Malik S. Henfield, PhD, is an associate professor and school counseling program coordinator at the University of San Francisco. Dr. Henfield received a BA in biology from Francis Marion University, an MEd and EdS in K–12 school counseling from the University of South Carolina, and a PhD in counselor education from The Ohio State University.

Wendy Hoskins, PhD, is an associate professor in the Department of Educational & Clinical Studies, University of Nevada, Las Vegas (UNLV). Previously, she served as a school counselor in the K–12 setting and as a career counselor at a technical school. She continues to serve the school counseling profession as the school counseling program coordinator at UNLV.

Tracy L. Jackson, PhD, is the school counseling supervisor for the Loudoun County Public Schools, Loudon County, Virginia. For the past 11 years, she has served as a school counseling central office administrator. She has experience as an elementary, middle, and high school counselor and department chair. She currently is a Recognized ASCA Model Program (RAMP) reviewer and editorial review board member for the American School Counselor Association. Dr. Jackson has been an adjunct instructor at Regent University, Old Dominion University, Syracuse University, and George Mason University.

Chris Janson, PhD, is an associate professor and the director of the Center for Urban Education and Policy, University of North Florida. Before his work in academia, Dr. Janson was a public school teacher and counselor. His publication topics include explorations of school counselor leadership and collaboration. He was on the national leadership team of the Community Learning Exchange, a Kellogg Foundation initiative designed to build collective leadership capacity within historically marginalized communities.

Tom Keller, EdD, is the director of school counseling at Butler University. He was a high school counselor and director of guidance for 10 years. He has served as president of the Indiana School Counselor Association and was on the board of directors for the National Board for Certified Counselors (NBCC). He also is a consultant and chairs CACREP teams for universities seeking national accreditation.

Christy W. Land, PhD, is an assistant professor in the Department of Clinical and Professional Studies, University of West Georgia. She is an experienced school counselor turned counselor educator. Her skills include research, cognitive–behavioral therapy, group therapy, crisis counseling, and student counseling. Dr. Land is a strong health care services professional, with a PhD focused in counselor education/ school counseling and guidance services.

Erin Lane, PhD, is an assistant professor of counselor education at Western Illinois University. Dr. Lane has over 10 years of experience in education as a teacher, administrator, and school counselor. She spent the last 5 years of her career as a school counselor serving the needs of gifted students in her district.

Richard T. Lapan, PhD, is a professor and chair of the Department of Student Development in the College of Education, University of Massachusetts Amherst. Dr. Lapan is a professor, counselor educator, and psychologist committed to transforming the profession of school counseling from an ancillary support service to a comprehensive program central to the academic, personal development, and social justice/ diversity mission of every school.

Sebastien Laroche, PhD, is a school counselor in the Department of Defense Education Activity (DoDEA). Before working for DoDEA, Sebastien was a counseling intern at Highline High School in Burien Washington working with at-risk youth in grades 9–12. Currently, Dr. Laroche is a school counselor at Sullivans Elementary School, located in Command Fleet Activities, Yokosuka, Japan, where he supports the development of over 1,200 military-connected students in kindergarten through fifth grade.

Jared Lau, PhD, NCC, LPC, is an assistant professor in the CACREP-accredited counselor education program at the University of Nevada, Las Vegas. He teaches and supervises students in school counseling and clinical mental health counseling. Previously, Dr. Lau worked as a high school teacher abroad, where he also served as a cultural consultant for the Okinawa Prefecture Board of Education, and also served as a high school counselor in the southeast United States.

Allison List, MA, is a student–parent facilitator for GEAR UP, at the University of Nevada, Reno. She previously served in public education for 13 years, and for 7 of those, she was an elementary and middle school counselor. Ms. List was nominated for the Nevada State Counselor of the Year award for the 2016–2017 school year.

Sandra A. Loew, PhD, is a professor of counselor education at the University of North Alabama. She has experience counseling in schools, family counseling centers, and private practice. She was the School Counseling Program coordinator and taught the school counseling courses for 10 years. Currently, Dr. Loew is the chair of the department and, every semester, spends over 10 hours in local schools working with school counselors to stay aware of recent developments.

Sandra (Sandi) M. Logan-McKibben, PhD, NCC, NCSC, ACS, is a clinical assistant professor of counselor education in the Department of Leadership and Professional Studies, Florida International University. Before earning her doctorate, Dr. Logan-McKibben worked as an elementary and middle school counselor; was the district-level Tobacco Use, Prevention, and Education (TUPE) coordinator; and was a site supervisor for practicum and internship students. Her specific research interests include school counseling supervision, counseling children and adolescents, and professional issues in counselor education.

Sophie Maxis, PhD, is an assistant professor of school counseling at the University of North Florida. She is a former school counselor and high school math teacher, and she has served in a university–school partnership that aimed to increase the number of racially diverse, first-generation students who access and successfully complete college. Dr. Maxis currently prepares school counselors for urban contexts, with emphases on community-based practices, social justice, and advocacy for historically marginalized student groups in schools.

Rafe McCullough, PhD, NCC, LPC, is an assistant professor of educational leadership in the school counseling program at Lewis & Clark College in Portland, Oregon. Previously, Dr. McCullough was a middle school counselor. He served on the Professional Education Advisory Board for school counseling at Seattle University for 5 years and recently served on the Multicultural Competency Revision Committee for the Association of Multicultural Counseling and Development.

Tomeka McGhee, PhD, is an assistant professor and clinical placement coordinator at Walden University. She is a licensed professional counselor, global career development facilitator, and independent contractor. She conducts children's clinical assessments and supports two rural school systems through pro bono group counseling services for grades 1–4, 7, and 8. She was the governance chairperson of her county's Children's Policy Council, which assesses children's needs, and develops community plans to collaboratively address those needs, and remains a member.

Claire Merlin-Knoblich, PhD, is an assistant professor in the Department of Counseling, University of North Carolina Charlotte. She is a former school counselor and received her PhD in counselor education and supervision from the College of William & Mary. Dr. Merlin-Knoblich's research focuses on multicultural education and school counseling, with an emphasis on prejudice reduction in K–12 schools. She also studies flipped learning in counselor education.

Carrie A. Wachter Morris, PhD, is an associate professor in the Department of Counseling and Educational Development at the University of North Carolina—Greensboro. She coordinates the school counseling track. She is past-president of the Indiana School Counselor Association and served on the school counseling advisory board to the Indiana Superintendent of Public Schools. Dr. Morris served as president of the Association for Assessment and Research in Counseling and a member of the editorial boards of *Counselor Education and Supervision* and *Professional School Counseling*.

Patrick R. Mullen, PhD, is an assistant professor of counselor education and the faculty director for Project Empower in the College of William & Mary School of Education. He teaches graduate students in the master's and doctoral counselor education program, with a focus on school counseling. Dr. Mullen is a national certified counselor, a national certified school counselor, and an approved clinical supervisor. Dr. Mullen's general research areas include school counseling, counselor education and supervision, and counseling children and adolescents.

Brandie Oliver, EdD, is assistant professor of school counseling in the College of Education, Butler University. She was a middle school counselor and a grief counselor, and she has experience counseling at all developmental levels. She has served as president of the Indiana School Counselor Association and continues to serve on the board. Ms. Oliver is dedicated to the training, development, and supervision of school counselors who strive to be change agents in preschool–grade 12 education.

Yvonne Ortiz-Bush, PhD, is an assistant professor in the Advanced Educational Studies Department at California State University—Bakersfield. Her previous professional experience includes serving as an elementary and junior high school counselor in ethnically diverse school settings. Dr. Ortiz-Bush also worked as a mental health clinician for a school-based special education mental health program.

Christine Hennigan Paone, PhD, currently coteaches at Monmouth University. Her experience includes mental health counseling and teaching in both the high school and higher education settings. Dr. Paone's research interests include counselor preparation and development.

Zachary Michael Pietrantoni, PhD, is an assistant professor in counseling education at California State University, Sacramento. Dr. Pietrantoni was an elementary school counselor, and, as an counselor educator, is active in teaching, publishing, and presenting research related to school counselor multicultural development. He an editorial board member for the *Journal of School Counseling* and on the advisory council for the Evidence-Based School Counseling Conference.

Tim A. Poynton, EdD, is an Associate Professor in the Department of Counseling and School Psychology, University of Massachusetts Boston. He was a school counselor at a school serving grades 6–12 and a senior research fellow at the Ronald H. Frederickson Center for School Counseling Outcome Research & Evaluation. Mr. Poynton is also the developer of the EZAnalyze data analysis tools, designed to assist school counselors in data collection and analysis.

Meredith A. Rausch, PhD, is an assistant professor in the College of Education at Augusta University. Before teaching, she enjoyed working in a number of clinical counseling settings, including outpatient day treatment, field work with children who endured abusive situations, elementary and high school settings, and on-site crisis work. She focuses her current research on underserved populations.

Lacey Ricks, PhD, is an assistant professor of counselor education and college student affairs at the University of West Georgia. She has 7 years of experience working in school settings. Dr. Ricks's areas of focus are poverty, disabilities, counselor self-care, social justice, narrative therapy, identity development, advocacy, and diversity.

Lourdes M. Rivera, PhD, is an associate professor at Queens College. Her work has focused on the career development and college and career readiness of students in grades 6–12 and preparing school counselors to effectively address these needs. Working with teachers and administrators, Dr. Rivera developed and implemented a career development and college and career readiness program for students attending an early college high school.

Amanda Dreisbach Rumsey, PhD, Clemson University. Her clinical background includes over 20 years of school and mental health counseling with adolescents and their families in a variety of programs, including outdoor residential treatment, wilderness therapy, and hospital settings, as well as rural, suburban, and urban school settings. Dr. Rumsey's primary areas of interest focus on adolescents, trauma, and school counseling, with an emphasis on training needs and skill acquisition in the areas of suicide intervention, trauma, and multiculturalism.

Franciene Sabens, MSEd, LPC, NCC, is a counselor at Carbondale Community High School. She was the Illinois 2014 High School Counselor of the Year. She is coauthor of the 2014 Developmental Counseling Model for Illinois Schools and blogs at SchoolCounselorSpace.Blogspot.com. Ms. Sabens also serves on her state association board and is involved with school counseling related initiatives at the state and national levels.

Robin Alcala Saner, MA, is an assistant professor of counselor education at Winona State University. She was a practicing school counselor for the Rochester Public Schools for 22 years, working with students in grades 7–12 and acting as chair of the district leadership team for 5 years. Ms. Saner is a member of the Southeast Minnesota School Counselors Association Board of Directors and is currently a part of the Minnesota Reach Higher Team.

Jodi L. Saunders, PhD, is an associate professor and the director of child advocacy studies at Winona State University. She is the director of the Child Advocacy Studies Program. Before entering academia, she was a rehabilitation and mental health counselor for over 15 years, with 12 years in K–12 schools. Dr. Saunders is a foster parent and court-appointed special advocate (CASA) and also has numerous publications in the fields of counseling and advocacy.

Cheryl Lynn Spaulding Sewell, PhD, received her doctorate from the University of Georgia. She is a professional school counselor at Fowler Drive Elementary School.

Jennifer Sharp, PhD, NCC, is an assistant professor of counseling at Northern Kentucky University. She is an experienced school counselor and supervisor. Dr. Sharp is recognized for her work on incorporating character strengths in the classroom.

Emilie E. Shaver, MA, NCC, is a residence life coordinator at the University of Alabama at Birmingham. Before her current position, Ms. Shaver worked in areas of K–12 education as well as nonprofits. She works as an advocate for the Prison Rape Elimination Act crisis response line.

Christopher A. Sink, PhD, NCC, LHMC, is a professor of counseling and human services at Old Dominion University. Dr. Sink spent many years in high school and postsecondary counseling. He is on the editorial board of several major counseling journals and served as editor for *Professional School Counseling* and *Counseling and Values*. Among other areas of interest, his numerous publications and nationwide school district consulting focus on comprehensive school counseling and accountability issues.

Sondra Smith-Adcock, PhD, is an associate professor of counselor education at the University of Florida. She has taught in both the school counseling and clinical mental health programs. Her counseling experience includes working with children and families from the preschool to the high school years. Dr. Smith-Adcock has authored more than 40 publications on counseling topics, with an emphasis on counseling children and adolescents.

Sarah I. Springer, PhD, is an assistant professor in the Department of Professional Counseling, Monmouth University. Before her role as a counselor educator, Dr. Springer worked as an elementary and high school counselor for close to a decade. Dr. Springer developed and continues to maintain an online school counselor consultation and peer supervision group and regularly presents on related topics. Her research interests and scholarly work include counselor development, supervision, and group work.

Stephannee Standefer, MA, LCPC, is the program director of The Family Institute at Northwestern University—Evanston. She was a preschool–8th grade parochial school counselor and a clinical counselor/manager of clinical services at a large behavioral health hospital, where she led groups of all ages addressing various topics in addition to providing individual counseling to youth and adolescents. Ms. Standefer has provided consultation and community training regarding parenting, partnering, and family issues.

Carolyn Stone, PhD, is a professor in the College of Education & Human Sciences, University of North Florida. She has worked in education for over 40 years, focusing on transforming school counseling. Dr. Stone has numerous awards as recognition of her expertise and respect among school counseling professionals.

Tiffany Stoner-Harris, PhD, is an assistant professor in the Department of Counselor Education, Western Illinois University. She teaches the school counseling practicum and internship courses. Her prior experiences include early intervention counseling with children from birth to age 5 and their families, and counseling school-age children and adolescents in both individual and group counseling capacities in schools, community centers, and youth correctional settings. Dr. Stoner-Harris currently serves as an elected school board member in her local community.

Cassandra A. Storlie, PhD, is an assistant professor in the School of Lifestyle Development & Educational Sciences at Kent State University. Her research includes the career development of marginalized populations, specifically Latinos/as, and leadership in the counseling profession. Dr. Storlie has counseling experiences in elementary and alternative school settings and has coedited a special issue in school counseling for the *Journal for Counselor Preparation and Supervision* in 2016.

Karen Moore Townsend, PhD, is a professor of counselor education at the University of North Alabama. She was a professional school counselor in a K–12 public school and has taught secondary English, history, and Russian language. Dr. Townsend is a member of the Alabama School Counselor Association, having served as postsecondary vice president, and is also a member of the Alabama Association of Counselor Education and Supervision board, as well as the Riverbend Mental Health Foundation board.

Lawrence E. Tyson, PhD, is an associate professor of counselor education at the University of Alabama at Birmingham (UAB). Dr. Tyson has been at UAB for the past 20 years and is the school counseling advisor. Before arriving at UAB, Dr. Tyson served as president of the Florida School Counselor Association and president of the Florida Counseling Association. After arriving at UAB, Dr. Tyson served as president of the Alabama Association for Counselor Education and Supervision, was a reviewer for *Professional School Counseling,* and was one of the original trainees for ASCA's National Standards implementation. Dr. Tyson currently serves on numerous local school counseling advisory committees.

Amy Upton, PhD, NCC, NCSC, is an assistant professor in the Department of Professional Studies, University of South Alabama. Dr. Upton worked previously as a school counselor for 16 years, serving as a department chair during her last 3 years. Her research interests are around professional identity, school counselor preparation, school counseling program development, and development of resiliency in young people.

Anna Viviani, PhD, is an associate professor and program coordinator at Bayh College of Education, Indiana State University. She has 15 years of clinical mental health counseling experience in a variety of settings and has taught graduate and undergraduate courses at the master's level in clinical mental health and school counseling programs. Dr. Viviani has presented at local, state, regional, and national conferences on childhood sexual abuse, counselor preparation, and supervision and training issues.

Diana L. Wildermuth, PhD, NCC, LPC, is an assistant professor of counseling at Temple University. She was a high school counselor and counseling department chairperson in a southeastern Pennsylvania for 14 years. Dr. Wildermuth has an extensive background in mental health, sports counseling, research methods, and diverse learners in the school setting. Her research interests include multicultural counseling and the role of the school counselor with English-language learners.

Cindy Wiley, EdS, LPC, is with the Shelby County Schools in Birmingham, Alabama. She was a high school teacher, counselor, and the counseling supervisor of Shelby County Schools in the Birmingham area. She holds an MA in counseling from the University of Alabama at Birmingham and an educational specialist degree in counseling from the University of Alabama.

Chelsey Windl, BA, is a graduate assistant at Winona State University. She is pursuing her master's degree in school counseling.

Susannah M. Wood, PhD, is an associate professor at the University of Iowa. She teaches school counseling and counselor education and supervision courses. Dr. Wood is an experienced school counselor. Her research interests encompass preparing school counselors for their practice, with a focus on serving the gifted population, in collaboration with other educators and professionals.

Maiko Xiong, PhD, is a school counselor in Central Valley, California. Dr. Xiong currently works as a school counselor serving students in kindergarten through grade 6, a career counselor at a community college, and an adjunct professor in a clinical counseling program.

Anita Young, PhD, is an associate professor of counseling and human development at Johns Hopkins University. She has extensive experience in the field of education as a teacher, school counselor, school administrator, and district school counselor supervisor. Dr. Young's research interests are school counselor leadership, examining best school counseling practices, and using accountability strategies to close achievement and opportunity gaps for all students. She is coauthor of *Making DATA Work and School Counselor Leadership: The Essential Practice.*

Acknowledgments

This project owes a debt to the many school counselor educators who have used the previous editions and will use this book as an instructional tool. Your continued teaching improves our field and the lives of others. To the school counseling professionals who daily serve in the trenches to improve the lives of children and our society, whose purpose is to help people face the very incidents included in this book; and to the school counseling students striving to learn as much as possible about decision making and real-world incidents, who will serve on the frontlines in schools with the greatest national asset—our children. To the authors who contributed to this book, your insight, patience, and perseverance made this project possible.

A special place in our acknowledgments is given to the work of the authors of the first and second editions of *Critical Incidents in School Counseling*. Dr. Paul Pedersen was one of the early pioneers to consider creating a teaching text for counselor educators to use in preparing future counselors. His work has been replicated in many critical-incidents texts focused on specific counseling specialties. Dr. Larry Tyson joined Paul on the second edition and started work on this edition of *Critical Incidents in School Counseling*. We are grateful for Dr. Tyson's selfless efforts; without him, this project would never have come to fruition. In addition, we were honored to work with great leaders in the field. I am thankful for their contributions to the field of school counseling over their career journeys.

A heartfelt special "thank you" goes to Carolyn Baker at the American Counseling Association, whose professionalism, patience, and commitment to this project were never ending. We, as professional counselors, are made better because of her support and dedication. We are also grateful to Chelsey Windl, a graduate assistant at Winona State University, for her tireless help.

Chapter 1

Introduction

Chris Wood, Heather J. Fye, and
Tarrell Awe Agahe Portman

New to This Edition

There are several things that distinguish this third edition from previous versions of this text. One is the overall structure and organization. Whereas in previous editions the structure was based upon the incident topics, we started with topics as a structure to organize the incidents. Specifically, guided by professional accreditation/training standards, we asked authors to create incidents and respond to them within the topical framework of the 2016 Council for Accreditation of Counseling & Related Educational Programs (CACREP) Standards (CACREP, 2015). This structure resulted in 30 incidents for this edition.

Previous editions of the text had authors of the *incidents* posing several questions for the *response* authors to address. We kept this format but added a few enhancements for the reader. We asked the authors of responses to include a list of resources that would be helpful for professional school counselors. The inclusion of resources such as textbooks, websites, and other tools for school counselors increases the utility of this text for both the school counselor in training and the practicing professional school counselor.

The addition of supplemental learning activities is also an enhancement to the new edition of the text. We asked the authors of *responses* to incidents to include individual/class assignments, discussion topics, and/or small-group exercises that could be used in courses for school counselors in training or as professional development for practicing professional school counselors. The intent of adding learning activities was to provide applied, practical learning opportunities for the reader(s) for self-directed professional development.

Also, to enhance practical learning and ensure meaningful examples, we used different criteria for soliciting the authors of both (a) the critical incidents and (b) the responses to critical incidents. With a focus on relevance to practice, we set the *practicing professional school counselor* as the ideal individual to author a critical incident. Moreover, we set the standard for respondents as *counselor educators with school counselor experience* and a primary professional identity focused on training school counselors. With this inclusion criteria, we generated a list of "school counseling experts" and matched the training standard to the expertise of specific individuals. To generate the critical incidents, we contacted former students and sent out a call on school counselor electronic mailing lists. Using this selection criteria resulted in a collection of authors committed to quality practice in professional school counseling.

It is possible that many of the authors in this text were the students in the educational contexts described in the first edition of this text and/or received their graduate training during the timeline of the second edition. As noted earlier, some of the same conundrums face school counselors today. The first edition of *Critical Incidents in School Counseling* was published at a time that would soon see the first U.S. president to resign from office. This third edition of the text is published at a time following signs of progress, including the first African American U.S. president and the first woman running for president as the nominee of a major party (as well as Michelle Obama, the only first lady to speak at a national school counseling conference and to honor the school counselor of the year in a ceremony at the White House). However, it is still a world in which students are exposed to violence and bullying in greater capacity than in previous generations and in which school counselors continue to battle educational and socioeconomic inequities and injustices, as have the generations of school counselors before them.

By noting some comparisons between current and previous editions of the text, we do not mean to suggest that the profession of school counseling has not grown. Since 2000, multiple editions of the American School Counselor Association (ASCA) National Model and the expansion of respective professional associations have resulted in an unprecedented level of resources and support for the school counseling profession. Although some of the themes continue from previous editions of this text, the critical incidents reflect contemporary concerns of today's professional school counselors and the sociopolitical world of their students. We hope the present edition honors this unique group of deeply committed individuals who strive to make the world a better place by helping a diverse range of students and their families—often one critical incident at a time.

—Chris Wood

Teachable Moments

The classroom is a place where the expected and unexpected moments in learning occur. I may plan a lecture based on the chapter readings/topic and objectives, include corresponding discussion and/or experiential activities, and expect a particular learning outcome. However, from my experiences with students, learning often occurs in unexpected ways, in those moments of spontaneous inspiration and interaction. In other words, those moments when I step away from the teaching plans and really observe and listen to what students are saying is when the learning happens. The moments are teachable. They may occur in or out of the classroom. They cannot always be pre-planned: Sometimes, they just happen.

The term *teachable moments* is often used in health care settings to refer to patients' health behavior change. Teachable moments are defined as those naturally occurring events that leads to individuals making a change (Cohen, Clark, Lawson, Casucci, & Flocke, 2011). McBride et al. (2008) added to this definition by noting that teachable moments occur within social and interactional dimensions; in this case, within the classroom setting. Teachable moments are not created in isolation; they emerge through a collective experience. It is important to incorporate teachable moments and consider the context in which they occur when approaching teaching and learning endeavors. Using this textbook in the classroom, especially during a practicum or internship course, provides a medium for those teachable moments to occur both intentionally and spontaneously.

A strong instructor is able to identify teachable moments, even those occurring spontaneously, and apply context for the learning. In these moments, I (as the instructor) learn too. I learn what my students really need from me in their preparation as a school counselor. *Critical Incidents in School Counseling* (3rd ed.) is meant to provide information and pointed examples to help facilitate teachable moments in the classroom. Students can passively review a textbook and listen to lectures. However, how does an instructor promote active learning? The second edition of *Critical Incidents in School Counseling* discussed five critical components of school counselors (Tyson & Pedersen, 2000). The fifth component described the importance of school counselors-in-training to move from theoretical- to practical-based experiences. The third edition continues to provide a manner in which to apply theoretical knowledge to practical knowledge. Students actively apply what they are learning into the context of a practicing school counselor. As an instructor, I do not strive for students to remember everything in our 3-hour, once-per-week meetings. I want them to have the "a-ha" moment when they take away key concepts to remember several weeks, months, or years later.

One may ask: What is the relationship between critical incidents and teachable moments? My response: there is no amount of preparation that fully prepares you for what happens in the classroom or on the job. Educational policies and practices have evolved, along with school counselor roles, over the past 100 years (Gysbers, 2012). Graduate programs often focus on fostering the counseling skills of school counselors-in-training. However, school counselors may engage in various roles. These roles may shift because of the type of school district, grade level, or significant needs of the school. As a helpful tool to explain school counseling program activities, the ASCA (2012a)

National Model details appropriate and inappropriate duties of school counselors (see p. 45).

This textbook provides realistic examples of what school counselors may face on the job. Instructors may use the materials contained in the text to prompt teachable moments to inspire school counselors in the classroom. An additional goal of *Critical Incidents in School Counseling* (3rd ed.) is to help instructors take teachable moments and apply them to their students' needs. I hope you find many teachable moments with your students and are able to reflect, process, and turn those moments into lasting learning experiences that continue to shape the students, school counselors, stakeholders, and the profession.

—Heather J. Fye

Reflective Discussion

My goal for this text was to provide an instructional tool for the professional preparation and development of school counselors. The incidents in the *Critical Incidents in School Counseling* (3rd ed.) are worthwhile in applying the multitude of expectations for case conceptualization, examination of biases, and demonstration of skill acquisition or deficit. The flexibility of the incidents in all of the *Critical Incidents in School Counseling* books allows counselor educators and students the ability to engage in dialogue surrounding many topics.

Reflection is a difficult skill to learn and practice. The content in this book may be used as focused reflection by school counselors for professional development. Each incident can be used to examine the CACREP Standards in practice today. The topics included do not cover every area of concern a school counselor will face; however, we hope that the topics will encourage discussion and reflection that is transferable to the many critical situations a school counselor may encounter.

I love teaching and utilizing reflective teams in my classes. A reflective team allows the counselor to be the focus of attention. The attention is on counselor awareness, knowledge, and skill demonstration. Reflective teams usually follow procedural steps that provide the structure for the learning activity. There are many different models for review in the counseling literature. My preference is for an extended time of approximately 90 minutes, but I have observed this happening in shorter and longer time frames. One example format to consider may include the following steps for reflective work. First, organize a group of three to four peers to serve as your reflective team. Second, identify a clear time frame for the team to meet. This should be in a area where team members can focus and not be interrupted. Third, the counselor of focus is given 15–20 minutes to articulate their incident/case, how they conceptualize the case, and how they would proceed with providing service or determining action. During this focused presentation, the reflective team takes notes but doesn't interrupt the speaker. The key is that the speaker must continue speaking during the duration of the time allotted. When the time has concluded, the fourth step begins. This fourth step allows 5–10 minutes for one designated team member to ask clarifying questions specific to the case while the other team members continue to take notes without interrupting. In the fifth step, open the door for team members to speak about what they heard the counselor of focus share and make statements questioning why certain skills, actions, or determinations were made or missed. The counselor of focus listens to the conversation and takes notes but does not engage in the conversation—even when asked direct questions. This generally continues for about 15–20 minutes. The sixth step mirrors the fourth step: The counselor of focus and the designated team member in step 4 discuss what the counselor of focus reflected on or heard from the reflective team. The other team members do not engage over the 5–10 minutes when this dialogue is occurring. Finally, in step seven, open the conversation to the entire team with free-flowing conversation regarding the incident/case and actions to be taken.

You may be a self-directed learner who will use the incidents and responses to reflect upon your professional conceptualizations of the cases. My suggestion would be to begin with the incident. Read, reflect, read again, and then question your thought processes. What are you using as a structure for critical examination of the incident? What additional information would you like to have? What skill set do you bring or not bring to the case? Then, I would suggest reading the responses and critically examining each. Hypothetically, transfer and apply these incidents and responses to your current context. What would be similar or different? This critical exploration of school counseling practice is necessary for professional growth.

You will find many ways to explore the incidents found in this book. The choice of reading the incidents and providing surface responses or spending time reflecting on the depth within each incident is up to the reader. It may be that each method of use will depend on your development as a counselor and where you are on your career journey. At the end of each chapter, you will find a listing of supplemental readings, resources, and activities. These vary by chapter, but some items overlap. For this chapter, we have compiled resources and readings that can be used for all chapters. Please refer back to these excellent professional resources as you proceed through the text.

—Tarrell Awe Agahe Portman

Supplemental Readings

American School Counselor Association. (2012a). *ASCA National Model: A framework for school counseling programs* (3rd ed.). Alexandria, VA: Author.

American School Counselor Association. (2012b). *ASCA school counselor competencies.* Retrieved from http://www.schoolcounselor.org/asca/media/asca/home/SCCompetencies.pdf

American School Counselor Association. (2018). *ASCA ethical standards for school counselor education.* Retrieved from https://www.schoolcounselor.org/asca/media/asca/Ethics/SCEEthicalStandards.pdf

Association for Multicultural Counseling and Development. (n.d.). *AMCD multicultural counseling competencies.* Retrieved from https://www.counseling.org/resources/competencies/multcultural_competencies.pdf

Cohen, D. J., Clark, E. C., Lawson, P. J., Casucci, B. A., & Flocke, S. A. (2011). Identifying teachable moments for health behavior counseling in primary care. *Patient Education Counseling, 85,* 8–15. doi:10.1016/j.pec.2010.11.009

Gysbers, N. C. (2012). Embracing the past, welcome the future: A brief history of school counseling. In *ASCA National Model: A framework for school counseling programs* (3rd ed., pp. vii–ix). Alexandria, VA: American School Counselor Association.

McBride, C. M., Puleo, E., Pollak, K. I., Clipp, E. C., Woolford, D., & Emmons, K. M. (2008). Understanding the role of cancer worry in creating a "teachable moment" for multiple risk factor reduction. *Social Science Medicine, 66,* 790–800. doi:10.1016/j.socscimed.2017.10.014

Tyson, L. E., & Pedersen, P. B. (Eds.). (2000). *Critical incidents in school counseling* (2nd ed.). Alexandria, VA: American Counseling Association.

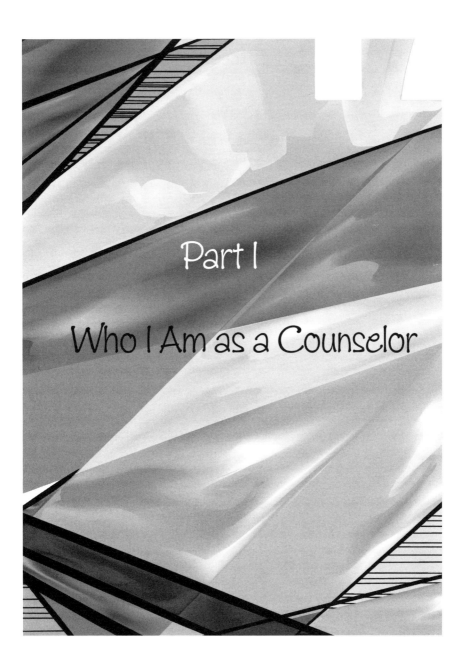

Part I

Who I Am as a Counselor

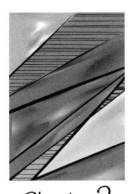

Chapter 2

I Never Thought I Would Be in This Position as a Supervisor!

Cindy Wiley

I am the counseling supervisor of a school district with 34 schools and 53 counselors. My position involves the coordination of district school counseling programs as well as oversight of the assessment program for the district. This incident involves an elementary school counselor who had been diagnosed with major depressive disorder. Although she seemed to function well in her position as a school counselor for several years, during the past 3 years, she showed signs of impairment as her symptoms increased.

Background

In years past, this counselor was a model of excellence. She was recognized as an outstanding counselor, on both the district and state levels. She was often asked to present best practices from her own creative approach to effective counseling at the statewide counseling conference. This counselor was often a mentor to new counselors in our district and was greatly revered as a strong leader in our district.

During the past several years, the counselor seemed to function in her duties, yet her affect changed, and she appeared somewhat melancholy. I noticed that she seemed to be more disconnected from local and state activities and often complained that her job was overwhelming. She asked to be transferred to a school closer to home and was moved to a school where she was the only counselor. Although I was concerned about the workload and her increasing disengagement, she was eager to move closer to home and was energized by the community, which is a high-poverty area with many social needs. The counselor seemed to function as "her old self," and her program grew to be an integral part of the school community. The principal reported that the faculty and parents were thrilled with the focus and direction of the school program.

Incident

In the fall of her second year at her new placement, I began receiving phone calls from the principal who was worried about the counselor. She began missing days for sickness. The principal also reported that she, along with several of her faculty members, were concerned that the counselor seemed more "down" than usual and that the counselor reported having some difficulties focusing in the classroom as well as in parent conferences. I met with the counselor several times, and she discussed the effects from her depression that seemed to be increasing. She had changed medications and was hoping this would help. She continued to miss several days until the end of the semester. This pattern of attendance continued into late February, when she missed an entire week. She did not return and soon called me to inquire about a leave of absence in the hopes that she could work on her coping skills and get her medicine regulated without the added stress of work. She was able to take the rest of the year off and returned to work again in August.

During the first few months back, teachers became concerned that her sadness seemed to have been replaced with a bitterness that began to show up in her dealings with students, faculty, and parents. She talked openly about her depression during parent meetings, and on several occasions, the parents reported feeling that they had spent their time consoling her. The counselor became angry and more despondent during the second semester but was in attendance each day. We continued to get reports from the teachers of inappropriate, "strange" behavior in the classroom. I continued to meet with the counselor and check on her progress with outside resources.

The principal called me one morning to come to the school, because the counselor was acting erratically in her office and then in the classroom. She was very anxious when I arrived, and I found it very difficult to help her calm down. She vacillated between outbursts of anger and crying spells. I decided that she needed to be removed from the situation, and she was sent home on leave for several days. Through phone calls to her, I realized that she was no longer seeing an outside therapist or doctor, and I was unsure as to whether she was continuing her medication.

After discussion with the human resources specialist, I decided to move another counselor to the school to help with the workload. Because the faculty and the students had frequently commented on this counselor's "strange" behavior during classroom guidance lessons, the principal felt that it would be more beneficial for the temporary counselor to continue with classroom guidance lessons and for the other counselor to work with individual guidance as well as testing. This seemed to work well for the counseling program, and the year ended without incident.

During the summer, a decision was made to move the counselor to a school close by, where she would not be the only counselor on staff. I talked to her about her new placement, and she let me know that she felt that this would be a positive move for her. She worked several days at her new placement, but the counselors called concerned about her, reporting that she was very quiet and melancholy. After the first few days, she no longer came to work and did not inform the administration. We continued to try and contact the counselor but were alerted by her family later that week that she had died. The cause of death was not confirmed.

Discussion

Working as the supervisor of an impaired counselor presents several difficult situations. On a professional level, certainly the top priority is the best interest and welfare of the students. Assessing the level of impairment is critical in determining the best placement for the counselor. Whereas nontenured or temporary employees may be removed, it is more difficult when dealing with a tenured employee. Dealing with counselor impairment requires input from several sources, including administration and human resources specialists. Counselors are acutely aware of the signs and symptoms of mental health and are well trained in intervention resources and positive outcomes. Through these interventions, the goal is for the individual to work through the challenges and return to their position. Hopefully, there is a degree of realization in which the counselor acknowledges the need for intervention and is amenable to resources and requirements for return. However, this is not always the case, and stringent methods must be taken to ensure that requirements are met for reentry into classroom guidance and individual counseling. There are also issues of confidentiality and perception when dealing with impairment. Administrators, central office staff, peers, and sometimes parents and students might find it difficult not to discuss the possible obvious behavioral symptoms that surround impairment. These same people might also have a generalized negative perception about mental health and could possibly express these perceptions in harmful ways after the counselor returns to the school.

Questions

1. What could be possible signs of counselor impairment?
2. How do you handle the judgment of others in the school system who are not familiar with impairment and mental health issues and who are also not bound by confidentiality?

3. Is there the possibility of loss of respect when a counselor deals with mental health issues? What steps can you take to help the school community regain respect?
4. How can supervisors effectively intervene to provide intervention services to the counselor while also ensuring quality counseling services for the students?
5. How do you handle the death of the counselor with the students, faculty, and community?

Response 1
Sandra A. Loew

Possible signs of counselor impairment may manifest in several ways. Impairment signs may include changes in behavior, missing work, erratic behavior, and negative interactions with students, teachers, etc. (e.g., rudeness or anger). Because this was a counselor who was a "model of excellence," her change in demeanor could be strong indicators of possible impairment.

While personnel issues are bound by confidentiality, there is the possibility of "gossip," which cannot be controlled. Counselors can invite mental health counselors from the community to do programming in the classroom that increases awareness of mental illness and possibly lessens the stigma related to mental illness. Also, in-service programs and school-wide awareness campaigns can provide information that helps to lessen the shame associated with mental illness and its treatment.

When a counselor suffers from mental health issues, there is the possible loss of respect from people who do not understand or who stigmatize those who have a mental illness. As counselors, we hope that we would get the treatment that we need and show by example that one can have a mental illness and, with treatment, be healthy again. We can model for others how to manage this challenge and normalize the experience and treatment of mental disorders. Dealing with a mental illness effectively is probably the best way to regain respect.

It is important to document those changes in behavior and affect that are seen firsthand and that are reported to the supervisor by others, such as the principal and teachers. This documentation shows a pattern of behavior that has occurred so that the supervisor, the human resources specialist, and the counselor can begin to construct an effective plan. That plan might include continued counseling, medication compliance, or required supervision. In this case, the supervisor allowed the counselor to move to a school closer to home and that seemed to be effective for a time. This supervisor also met with the counselor when she seemed to be struggling again and allowed her time off from work to manage her depression. Given confidentiality constraints in personnel issues, the supervisor's own workload, and the isolation that is inherent in those suffering from mental illness, this supervisor managed this challenging and sad situation as effectively as any human could manage it. From the description, it seems that the supervisor did everything possible to ensure quality counseling services to students.

This counselor's death could be handled in the same way any that other death would be handled in the school community. Providing counseling services to students, teachers, and others in the school who request those services would be appropriate. This counselor was a very positive force in two different schools and was a respected colleague before she became ill; therefore, acknowledging those facts would be helpful for those who are grieving this loss. A death caused by a mental illness (if that was the case) is not different from a death caused by a physical illness. When asked what happened, we might say, "We don't know exactly, but we do know that she had been sick on and off for some time, and she recently died. We are all going to miss her."

Response 2

Patrick R. Mullen and W. Bryce Hagedorn

Impairment is a vital issue in the field of counseling and has been acknowledged as a problem for professional counselors in every scope of practice (Witmer & Young, 1996). Defined as "a significantly diminished capacity to perform professional functions" (American Counseling Association [ACA], 2014, p. 20), impairment occurs when a counselor's functioning is affected in such a manner that client care is jeopardized and an increased risk for doing harm is present (Lawson & Venart, 2005). Furthermore, impairment may result from an assortment of personal concerns that include: (a) substance abuse/dependency, (b) mental illness, (c) traumatic events, (d) vicarious trauma, (e) burnout, (f) life crisis, and (g) physical debilitation or illness (Emerson & Markos, 1996; Lawson & Venart, 2005; Stamm, 2010).

Impairment (which can result from professional burnout and/or compassion fatigue) can manifest in a variety of ways. Lamb and colleagues (1987) stated that impairment can be reflected in counselors who lack the capability and/or exhibit reluctance to: (1) use professional standards as a part of their professional behavior, (2) develop clinical skills at a competent level, and/or (3) manage their emotional state (e.g., stress, dysfunction, or overreaction). From the perspective of burnout as an indicator of impairment among professional school counselors (PSCs), possible signs can include a lack of caring or commitment, the expression of negative attitudes toward students and families, a demonstrated lack of empathy for student situations, physical/emotional exhaustion, feelings of incompetence, and/or the deterioration of one's personal life (Lee et al., 2007; Maslach, 2003). Furthermore, compassion fatigue (sometimes referred to as secondary traumatic stress) can produce feelings of exhaustion, anger, frustration, and depression, most of which are associated with work related to counseling those who have experienced trauma and extreme fear (Figley, 1995; Stamm, 2010).

The PSC discussed in the critical incident experienced and expressed several warning signs of impairment. These included: (a) change in affect to melancholy, (b) withdrawal from local and state activities, (c) complaints about the job, (d) increased absence from work, (e) appearance of being more down, (f) symptoms of depression, (g) bitterness toward students and other stakeholders, and (h) increased anger. At the recognition of these warning signs, the counselor herself or the district supervisor could have acted to intervene.

District supervisors can promote counselors' awareness of their wellness (and thereby prevent burnout, compassion fatigue, and, ultimately, impairment) by encouraging ongoing self-assessment. One example of an available assessment is the Professional Quality of Life Scale, which is available for download and use (see Online Resources) and which provides respondents with indicators of burnout, secondary traumatic stress, and compassion satisfaction.

The act of judging others based on their impairment or mental illness is closely related to the topic of mental health stigma, which is quite prevalent in the general public (Rüsch, Angermeyer, & Corrigan, 2005). To help understand mental health stigma, it is useful to distinguish between public stigma and self-stigma (Corrigan, 2004). Public stigma represents the negative responses expressed by the public regarding the specific circumstances or qualities of a person (Bathje & Pryor, 2011). For example, as the faculty and administrators encountered the increased negativity and erratic behaviors of the PSC noted in the critical incident, they likely sought to distance themselves from her. She was also likely the topic of workplace gossip, which only serves to increase public stigma and distance others from those most needing assistance. On the other hand, self-stigma embodies "the internalized psychological impact of public stigma" (Bathje & Pryor, 2011, p. 162). Therefore, when the PSC encountered her colleagues who were actively distancing themselves from her—as she noticed how their discussions would cease immediately upon her entering the staff lounge—her self-stigma likely increased, which, in turn, negatively affected her mental health. The cyclical nature of stigma can, therefore, exacerbate workplace mental health issues and result in obvious negative outcomes. Workplace interventions to break this cycle are, therefore, necessary for everyone's well-being.

Supervisors and administrators can help reduce public stigma through a variety of methods. One method is to promote sympathy for individuals with mental illness (Bathje & Pryor, 2011). One way to promote sympathy includes the use of "person-first" language. For example, rather than referring to "our depressed school counselor," person-first language would result in a statement such as, "We have a colleague who is struggling with depression." Another way to reduce stigma is to promote mental health awareness initiatives (i.e., the National Alliance on Mental Illness) and combat mental illness stereotypes through educational activities (Brown & Bradley, 2002). An example of an educational program that can help educate community members on mental health issues is Mental Health First Aid, which is an 8-hour course on risk factors and warning signs of mental health concerns. This would be an excellent training to conduct with the school faculty and staff where a colleague once worked who experienced a mental health concern. A final suggested approach to reduce public stigma is to assess and examine the negative biases and beliefs towards mental illness in the workplace. Crowe and Averett (2015) suggested the use of an attitudes continuum with individuals by exploring the range of beliefs toward various mental illnesses. Ultimately, supervisors and administrators must lead the way in reducing public stigma by their careful actions and words that demonstrate compassion and respect for those who struggle with mental health concerns.

A logical connection exists between the issue of mental health public stigma and the respect one receives from their school community. Colleagues who (a) lack knowledge related to mental health concerns and who (b) have limited experience interacting with people who struggle in these areas may likely lose respect for those with mental illness. This is particularly true for those whom they feel should exhibit the most mental wellness: the PSC. Consequently, the efforts noted earlier that are designed to educate and expose school community members to the topic of mental health issues may counteract the loss of respect that occurs. An additional step that can be taken to regain respect is through improving workplace environments to promote interpersonal relationships and teamwork (Young & Lambie, 2007). Supervisors can work with the school administration to plan social or wellness-related events that allow the colleagues to interact in ways that promotes unity. In terms of the school counselors' caseload, supervisors can plan a tiered reentry plan in which the counselors' workload will start off with a smaller caseload with planned increases over short time durations. Therefore, the school counselor starts the reentry process in a manner that supports small successes and builds up to a full-time reentry. School counselors reentering their position can celebrate the small successes with their colleagues and restore their confidence.

School counselors' wellness and mental health are challenged by lack of clarity in job duties, inconsistent job roles, and conflicts in their job expectations (Burnham & Jackson, 2000; Culbreth, Scarborough, Banks-Johnson, & Solomon, 2005; Lambie, 2007; Scarborough & Culbreth, 2008). Therefore, one method of intervention is to provide organizational supports to enhance the work environment for PSCs. Young and Lambie (2007) noted the positive impacts of clarifying the PSC's roles by (a) the development of a district school counseling manual that aligns with the American School Counselor Association's (2012a) National Model, (b) the education of the school administration on the roles typically filled by the PSC, and (c) the offering of professional development activities that pair the PSC with administrators. Ultimately, clarifying the PSC's roles within the school system may help reduce inappropriate workloads and allow counselors to spend more time doing the work that they are best equipped to do.

Next, given that PSCs who do not receive ongoing clinical supervision have increased changes to experience lower states of well-being and higher incidents of impairment (Lambie, 2007; McMahon & Patton, 2000), supervisors who identify impaired PSCs can intervene by offering regular clinical supervision (Young & Lambie, 2007). In the case where impairment is indicated, supervisors should consider the use of supervision models with a specific focus on counselor wellness (see Blount and Mullen [2015] and Lenz and Smith [2010]). Another intervention may include the supervised development and implementation of a wellness plan that includes concrete and achievable goals for the PSC to work toward. In accordance with a wellness plan, supervisors can offer referrals to local mental health counselors to aid the PSC in engaging in personal therapy with the aim of addressing the issues related to their impairment. Finally, if the PSC is unwilling or unable to engage in some of the "encouraged" activities noted earlier, the need for a more formal remediation plan with identified target behaviors with accompanying dates for implementation may be necessary. Such a plan would include the specific behaviors that indicate impairment (e.g., suspected alcohol misuse away from the workplace that is affecting job performance), the intervention that matches each maladaptive behavior (e.g., mandated 12-step group attendance with a signature page for group leaders to sign), and a target date (e.g., over the course of the next 6 months). If the PSC does not comply with the remediation plan, then both the PSC and the supervisor are aware of the consequences and agree to them as indicated in their both signing the remediation plan. Readers should consult with the policies and procedures in their own school districts before pursuing and devising such plans.

The death of anyone in the school affects everyone in the system. When the death is of the PSC (who is "supposed" to mirror optimal mental wellness), this can add additional complications. School counseling supervisors serve a vital role in supporting students, faculty, staff, students' families, and community members during such events. One method of handling the passing of a counselor is to develop and enact crisis response teams (CRTs). The CRTs can address interventions from multiple levels (e.g., regional, district, or school), and the contributors to such teams may vary based on community resources (Knox & Roberts, 2005). More specifically, supervisors can develop a list of experienced counselors, along with other educational stakeholders (e.g., administrative personnel, social workers, and a psychologist) who can be called in from neighboring schools or agencies to serve and support the community that experienced such a loss. Additionally, supervisors can collaborate with local community resources, such as hospice centers and private practitioners, to identify volunteer grief counselors. Obviously, these response teams should be developed before such a crisis occurs and can get involved through hierarchical levels of intervention that include primary prevention, secondary intervention, and tertiary intervention (see Knox & Roberts, 2005). Enacting the district CRT would allow supervisors to place trained counselors and other individuals from helping professions immediately in the crisis zone to deal with the immediate effects of shock and grief. For those who experience prolonged effects, these counselors can refer individuals to local mental health practitioners for continued counseling.

District supervisors can also oversee programs that aim at preventing suicide and preparing schools to deal with crisis. Training manuals (e.g., Brock, Sandoval, & Lewis, 2001; Johnson & Stephens, 2002; Sandoval, 2013) for professional development are available for supervisors to utilize, and the workshops they provide guidance on can address topics such as crisis preparation and prevention, individual and group crisis intervention, and psychological first aid. Additionally, district supervisors can seek advanced training for the CRT members so that they are well prepared to handle crises as they arise, such as suicide in this case. The American Red Cross provides psychological first aid training sessions (among other topics) that offer suggestions on what to do and say during a crisis (see Supplemental Readings and Online Resources).

In summary, some consistent themes came up across these questions regarding steps that district PSC supervisors can take when facing issues related to PSC mental health and impairment. One theme was the use of training or professional development to prevent issues before they occur and to react to problems as they arise. Educational sessions could be used to bring attention to mental health stigmas, aid schools preparing for a crisis, and help individuals heighten awareness for their own well-being. An additional theme found throughout the answers to these prompts was the support of the PSCs as they work through their mental health concerns. This came in the form of providing clinical supervision, the development of a wellness plan, and assistance in finding a source for personal counseling. A third and final theme that arose was the encouragement of strong relationships among school staff. District supervisors for PSCs can facilitate social or wellness events at schools to enhance interpersonal relationships or start initiatives that fight mental health stigmas to support colleagues facing these concerns. In these cases, district supervisors have the opportunity to support PSCs as they work through their impairment and to aid the school community in providing more effective services to students and their families.

Supplemental Readings and Online Resources

Supplemental Readings

American Counseling Association. (2014). *ACA code of ethics*. Alexandria, VA: Author.

Baker, E. K. (2003). *Caring for ourselves: A therapist's guide to personal and professional well-being*. Washington, DC: American Psychological Association.

Hendricks, B., Bradley, L., J., Brogan, W. C., & Brogan, C. (2009). Shelly: A case study focusing on ethics and counselor wellness. *The Family Journal, 17,* 355–359.

Kottler, J. A. (2012). *The therapist's workbook: Self-assessment, self-care, and self-improvement exercises for mental health professionals.* San Francisco, CA: Jossey-Bass.

Kottler, J. A., & Chen, D. D. (2011). *Stress management and prevention: Applications to daily life* (2nd ed.). New York, NY: Routledge.

Lawson, G. (2007). Counselor wellness and impairment: A national survey. *Journal of Humanistic Counseling, Education and Development, 46,* 20–34.

Norcross, J. C., & Van den Bos, G. R. (2018). *Leaving it at the office: A guide to psychotherapist self-care* (2nd ed.). New York, NY: Guilford Press.

Rothschild, B. (2006). *Help for the helper: The psychophysiology of compassion fatigue and vicarious trauma.* New York, NY: Norton Professional Books.

Skovholt, T. M., & Trotter-Mathison, M. J. (2001). *The resilient practitioner: Burnout prevention and self-care strategies for counselors, therapists, teachers, and health professionals.* Boston, MA: Allyn & Bacon.

Online Resources

American Counseling Association's Taskforce on Counselor Wellness and Impairment
http://www.creating-joy.com/taskforce/tf_wellness_strategies.htm

American Red Cross emergency service courses, and psychological first aid
www.redcross.org/ma/boston/take-a-class/emergency-service-courses

Mental Health First Aid Instructor Training
www.mentalhealthfirstaid.org

School counseling supervisors interested in a way to reduce mental health stigma in their communities would benefit from participating in Mental Health First Aid training for adults and youth. As an instructor, school counseling supervisors could offer Mental Health First Aid trainings to school employees along with members of the general public, which would combat the stigmas associated with mental illness. For information on how to become trained as a Mental Health First Aid instructor or to participate in a Mental Health First Aid course, visit their web site.

National Alliance on Mental Illness
www.nami.org

National Hospice and Palliative Care Organization, CaringInfo
www.caringinfo.org/i4a/pages/index.cfm?pageid=1

Professional Quality of Life website and scale access
www.proqol.org

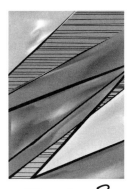

Chapter 3

Is This Really What I Went to School For?

Lawrence E. Tyson

This incident involves an elementary school counselor who works in a small, rural school with one administrator, her principal. The school counselor graduated with her master's degree in school counseling, and this is her first job as a school counselor.

Background

I am a school counselor in a small, rural elementary school of 423 students. There are 15 faculty members and one principal. The principal has been at this school for 3 years; this is also my third year as a school counselor. My principal is extremely pleased with my work; she is aware of our state's school counseling curriculum, which is taken from the American School Counselor Association's (ASCA's) National Model.

I graduated from a university that has a strong school counseling training program and emphasizes the ASCA National Model. School counseling students from this program are comfortable with outcome research, know how to use data in determining effectiveness, and know how to implement a standards-based program. The previous counselor had worked at this school for 25 years and retired last year. The principal was eager to find someone who could "breathe fresh air" into the program. Two teachers in our building have their administrative certification. I do not possess this certification, but I am an associate licensed counselor (ALC), and I am receiving supervision to become a licensed professional counselor (LPC). My goal is to obtain my LPC license in 2 years.

Incident

My principal is often away from the school to attend meetings at the system office. When this happens, she needs to assign someone on campus to "be in charge" while she is away. As stated earlier, two other faculty members hold certifications in administration. However, I believe that my relationship with her and the quality of my work has influenced her decision to ask me to be that person in charge when she is away. She does not place me in this position every time she is off campus, but it is happening more often than I like. In my first year, I was never asked to assume responsibility while she was away. In my second year, it happened about four times—not too many times for it to cause me concern. I was able to juggle my schedule, and I was very happy to provide this service for her. I also must admit, I liked the new responsibility that this assignment gave me. It allowed me to see a new side of administration. Frankly, it also gave me a bit more compassion for what my principal does daily.

The third year has been different. I have been called to be her replacement approximately nine times so far this year. Additionally, my principal and I often have long discussions about the school's direction. These discussions often include the school counseling program, but they also include discussions of faculty and curriculum issues and often just my advice on what she intends to say at faculty meetings. I look forward to these interactions, as I view them favorably because of the respect she has for my opinion and for me as a professional.

Discussion

I have noticed that teachers are starting to treat me differently. During my first year, we would often talk more openly in the hallway, cafeteria, and lounge and at the bus ramp. Sometimes after school, many of the faculty would meet for "happy hour" at a local restaurant. I always enjoyed these after-school social activities because they allowed me to become familiar and bond with them and them with me.

One day, my principal left the building and asked me to be in charge. After I said yes, I reorganized my day, which included cancelling classroom guidance lessons and reporting to the office. On my way to the office, one of the teachers stopped me and asked, "Who was I today?" The question stunned me, as I have never seen myself as other than a school counselor. I replied, "Well, for right now, I'm the acting principal. But she'll be back in 3 hours." The teacher remarked as she was leaving, "Sometimes, it's difficult to tell."

For the next 3 hours, I thought about the teacher's comments. I began to wonder how I was being viewed by the faculty. What did they see as my role, and how did they view me as a professional? It was always difficult to tell teachers that I could not come into their classes for scheduled classroom guidance sessions, but what else could I do? I liked the confidence that my principal had in my administrative abilities, and I did not want to disappoint her. However, I could tell that some of the teachers did not appreciate when I had to cancel classroom guidance time with their students. Additionally, I was beginning to feel that they were a bit hesitant in demonstrating too much disapproval with administration because they did not want me to discuss this with our principal. Who was I becoming?

Questions

1. What's wrong with trying to gain my principal's confidence by agreeing to perform certain tasks other than my school counselor duties?
2. My principal likes me and confides in me. How do I handle this?
3. My school has one counselor and principal. What else are we to do when my principal is off campus?
4. I like the added responsibility that my principal gives me. It shows confidence in my abilities. How do I juggle both?
5. Should I be concerned about how my teachers view me? How do I rectify this if these assignments continue?

Response 1

Franciene Sabens

In reality, every school counselor will have to confront this very question, "Who am I?" For a school counselor, the conflict of "Who am I?" can be of an internal nature and surface because of external pressures, as is evident in this scenario. However, in fact, a school counselor must address and confront any internal conflicts regarding "Who am I?" before the externally presented conflicts may be adequately addressed.

In the 21st century, role ambiguity among school counselors is ever present; as a group, school counselors are still in conflict with how they identify in a school setting. School counselors should first ask the question, "Am I a counselor with an education background or an educator with a counseling background?" Research indicates that some school counselors believe that they are counselors first and educators second, whereas others believe the latter. How do you identify? How do you articulate your professional identity to your administration and staff?

When addressing this underlying question, also consider the following:

1. The history of school counseling
2. Guiding students vs. advocating for access and equity
3. A preventive vs. a reactive focus
4. Aligning work with the National Model
5. What is your main goal in your role as a school counselor?

Once the articulated internal conflict has been addressed, the school counselor can begin to move forward to address any external conflict presented.

While fair-share responsibilities are an important part of the ASCA National Model, and gaining a principal's confidence is important in ensuring a collaborative and supportive relationship, agreeing to perform certain tasks, such as those in this scenario, may compromise the school counseling program as a whole. The principal is traditionally seen as the disciplinarian from a student perspective and as the accountability manager from a teacher's perspective; neither of these roles is synonymous with the role of a school counselor, and both are directly in contrast to the appropriate activities of a school counselor. A school counselor, with the appropriate level of leadership capacity, can gain a principal's confidence without sacrificing the delivery of a comprehensive school counseling program, relationships with building staff, or the ability to advocate for all students with fidelity.

Professional school counselors who seek to gain the confidence of their principal should ask the following questions:

1. What new programs and interventions can I initiate to close the achievement, opportunity, and attainment gaps that exist at my school?
2. How can I take a leadership role on school-wide committees?
3. How can I connect the school counseling program interventions and outcomes with school-wide academic, career, and social–emotional initiatives?
4. How can I collaborate with the administration on school-wide mechanisms (e.g., master schedule, building curriculum, extracurricular activities offered, access to rigorous course work for all students) to create and sustain systemic change assisting all students?
5. How can I best collaborate with families, community organizations, and businesses to create and sustain systemic change regarding all students?

For school counselors, a collaborative and supportive relationship with the principal is essential to program development, growth, and success. Professional school counselors serve as a source of school climate knowledge and expertise, which essentially requires them to have a seat at the table when many administrative discussions take place. While it may feel uncomfortable in some situations to discuss other faculty members with a principal, a school counselor must keep in mind that, if a discussion provides them with an opportunity to advocate for a student or an access or equity concern that could be systematic, the conversation is necessary and within the school counselor's scope of practice. Professional school counselors are in a unique position that allows them the ability to identify the systemic structures in the school that may impede student success; thus, they are poised to offer potential solutions to those who can impose change.

Furthermore, school counselors have an ethical obligation to ensure that the academic, career, and social–emotional needs of the students they serve are being met; sometimes, this requires them to have "those conversations" with principals. In the event that the conversation is centered on what the principal might say at an upcoming faculty meeting, the opportunity for consultation through this capacity is crucial and celebratory, considering that the mission, vision, and goals of the school counseling program should support the school's goals and administrative vision for the school.

A well-planned and executed Annual Agreement and Chain of Command document could prevent this type of situation from occurring on most occasions. Essentially, the Annual Agreement would solidify the focus and understanding of the school counseling department for the year, and the principal would understand that asking the counselor to do anything that did not serve the mutually agreed-upon focus would impede the desired results for the program and compromise the professional school counselor's ability to meet the needs of all students. Additionally, every school has a chain of command, and too often "in smaller school districts," the chain of command progresses from the principal to the school counselor because of a misunderstanding of the role of the school counselor and the purpose of a comprehensive school counseling program, as well as a lack of adequate resources. Professional school counselors should advocate for a more appropriate chain of command that designates the superintendent or a faculty member who holds certification in administration as the "person in charge" when the principal is away. The school counselor could assist the principal in devising and articulating a plan to avoid this type of situation and support the principal in more appropriate ways throughout the transition.

A principal with a true understanding and respect for a comprehensive school counseling program would show just as much, if not more, confidence in the ability of the school counselor if she knew that crucial outcome data was being produced as a result of a comprehensive, data-driven school counseling program. Research supports that principals want school counselors to advocate for their role in the schools and to take on leadership roles to create systemic change. It appears as if the principal in this scenario is pleased with the work of the school counselor within her role as a school counselor, not in the acting principal role. Although the school counselor may like the responsibility the principal gives her, it is outside of her scope of duties. The school counselor should focus her skills, time, and abilities on making sense of outcome data and using the data to create an effective, standards-based school counseling program that meets the needs of all of her students. Finally, the school counselor in this case must accept the realization that taking on the role of the principal, on occasion, may limit or curtail her effectiveness in providing an effective school counseling program. A teacher's negative view of a school counselor can impede the success of the school counseling program. In delivering a comprehensive school counseling program, school counselors must seek the input and expertise of teachers and coplan and codeliver program activities with them. It is essential, then, that school counselors do everything within their capacity to establish and maintain a positive working relationship with faculty members and repair relationships when conflicts arise, noting, however, that some relationships have more potential than others and knowing where to focus effort.

In this scenario, if the school counselor continues to be assigned to the role of the principal, it may be advantageous for her to initiate a private conversation with the teacher who expressed concern, to discuss her perspective and garner the teacher's support to request a change in the chain of command. During this time, it would also be wise for the school counselor to articulate her own vision for her role, so the teacher can better understand how the position in which she is being placed is also in direct contrast with her own vision of the role of the school counselor. Research indicates that teachers are supportive of school counselors performing the duties asserted in the ASCA National Model. Without the ability to collaborate effectively with each member of the school community, the school counselor decreases her ability to facilitate an optimum counseling program.

Response 2

Amy Upton

For school counselors, this is often a common incident. Elementary schools are often smaller in size, with less staffing and fewer administrators. Administrators in schools often do not fully understand what a school counselor is trained to do. They may rely too heavily on them, with a misperception of their abilities, educational attainment, and flexibility with their schedules.

School counselors have struggled for many years with being tasked with noncounseling duties that limit a professional school counselor in implementing a comprehensive school counseling program and meeting the needs of the students and the school. The ASCA (2012a) National Model provides a brief list of appropriate and inappropriate duties and activities for school counselors: Assisting with a principal's tasks is identified as part of the inappropriate duties (see p. 45 for the full list). School counselors may advocate for and assume leadership roles that are appropriately aligned with the themes of the ASCA (2012a) National Model, including counselors as leaders, advocates, collaborators, and systemic change agents. Additionally, the best way to gain the confidence of an administrator is to demonstrate your ability to work within these themes while implementing a comprehensive school counseling program aligned with the mission and vision of the school (ASCA, 2012a).

The school counselor in this incident may be flattered that the principal likes and confides in her. Although people often seek to be liked and acknowledged by others, it is more important that others can trust in the school counselor's ability to provide a school counseling program aimed at meeting the needs of the students and the school community. One way to address this while maintaining the open relationship that this school counselor has with the principal is to speak very honestly with the principal, expressing her appreciation of her trust but also asserting that it is very important to maintain a position of trust with the teachers as well. She should express that she is more than willing to share her perspective in areas of her expertise but would prefer to exclude faculty issues as a part of this dialogue. Functioning in the dual capacities of counselor and quasi-administrator can have negative consequences on the relationships with students, teachers, and parents, as well as perhaps being unethical (ASCA, 2010b).

Small schools with limited administration and faculty do create challenges when an administrator is out of the building. It is the responsibility of the principal to develop a plan, before being out of the building, as to how her responsibilities will be handled. In this school, there are two teachers in the building with administrative degrees who could share the responsibilities while delegating certain tasks to the office manager. Although juggling the added responsibility of taking on administrator duties can be invigorating and rewarding, the school counselor is already stretched to provide the programmatic components of the school counseling program within a school of 423 students. Stretching yourself further only negatively affects the services that students receive as well as your sense of professional self-efficacy.

School counselors need a sense of the professional identity they must reflect to administrators, students, parents, and teachers. A school counselor's primary role is to provide school counseling services to the students, assisting them in the academic, personal–social, and career domains. As consultation and collaboration with teachers is a large component of a school counselor's job, consideration must be given to how teachers view the school counselor and the school counseling program. Teachers need to view the school counselor as a professional who partners with them in helping the students to be successful. They do not need to feel that there is an evaluative quality to the interactions. Teachers will not feel comfortable coming to a school counselor if they feel that they cannot trust him or her. Additionally, if you are cancelling scheduled classroom guidance on a frequent basis, teachers will question your commitment to providing school counseling services to the students and then will be less likely to make referrals to you or to cooperate with your desire to push into the classroom for classroom guidance in the future. As advocating for the profession, our programs, and our identity as professionals often is the responsibility of school counselors, working to ensure that teachers view the school counselor as a professional dedicated to the success of the students should be paramount.

Professional school counselors should know their roles, understand their purpose and identity, and advocate for the profession. As so many challenges can arise in the professional life of a school counselor, it can be beneficial to seek out consultation or supervision from other school counselors. Reaching out to colleagues in your school district as well as contacting a local university or your alma mater may provide opportunities for supervision or consultation. Additionally, joining professional associations can strengthen your school counseling network, help you to navigate your professional world, and support you in your role.

Supplemental Readings, Online Resources, and Supplemental Activities

Supplemental Readings

Deposes, J. A., & Andrews, M. F. (2006). *School counselors as educational leaders.* Boston, MA: Houghton Mifflin.

Dollarhide, C. T., & Miller, G. M. (2006). Supervision for preparation and practice of school counselors: Pathways to excellence. *Counselor Education and Supervision, 45,* 242–252.

Henderson, P., Cook, K., Libby, M., & Zambrano, E., (2007). "Today I feel like a school counsellor!" Developing a strong professional school counsellor identity through career experiences. *Guidance & Counseling, 21,* 128–142.

Hermann, M. A., Remley, T. P., Jr., & Huey, W. C. (2010). *Ethical & legal issues in school counseling* (3rd ed.). Alexandria, VA: American School Counseling Association.

Ponec, D. L., & Brock, B. L. (2000). Relationships among elementary school counselors and principals: A unique bond. *Professional School Counseling, 3,* 208–217.

Wilkerson, K. (2006). Peer supervision for the professional development of school counselors: Toward an understanding of terms and findings. *Counselor Education and Supervision, 46,* 59–67.

Online Resources

American Counseling Association
www.counseling.org

American School Counselor Association
www.schoolcounselor.org

The Education Trust
http://www.edtrust.org

NOSCA: National Office of School Counselor Advocacy
(The College Board)
https://nosca.collegeboard.org/

Supplemental Activities

- Complete the American School Counselor Association (ASCA) School Counseling Leadership Specialist Training.
More details are available at http://www.schoolcounselor.org/school-counselors-members/professional-development/school-counseling-leadership-specialist-training.

- Create a free account on the Center for Excellence in School Counseling and Leadership (CESCaL) website (http://www.cescal.org).

- Review the available Management Agreements (Annual Agreements), and draft an Annual Agreement based on the ASCA National Model (2012a) guidelines that aligns with the perceived role as a school counselor.

- Review the CAFE School Counselor Evaluation tool outlined on pp. 7–15 in *101 Solutions for School Counselors and Leaders in Challenging Times* (Chen-Hayes, Ockerman, & Mason, 2014).

- Write about how counselors can incorporate the indicators into their school counseling practice and use them to improve their school counseling leadership capacity.

- Review the "Enhancing the Principal-Counselor Relationship Toolkit" from the College Board's National Office of School Counselor Advocacy, as well as accompanying publications and documents available at http://nosca.collegeboard.org/research-policies/principal-counselor-toolkit.

- Discuss how counselors might initiate a conversation with their principal regarding using the tools presented to strengthen their relationship and improve student and program outcomes.

- Take a few moments to reflect on your school counseling program and the roles and duties you perform. Think about the roles and duties that your principal performs, and imagine that you were tasked with performing both sets of duties. Reflect on what this would mean for you professionally.
  a. How do you think that would affect your daily work?
  b. How do you think it would affect your relationship with students, parents, and teachers?
  c. Why do you feel that it would have this impact?
  d. Share your thoughts and reactions with a partner.

Chapter 4

When Is There Time for Me? How Do I Cope?

Lacey Ricks

This incident involves a middle school counselor who works in a low-income, rural school with approximately 350 students in grades 6–8. The school counselor has been working within this school for 5 years and is originally from this community.

Background

I am a school counselor in a low-income, rural middle school. There are approximately 20 faculty members in my school, and most have worked here for 5 or more years. We (the faculty members and I) are like a close-knit family, since many of us went to school here and returned after receiving our professional degrees. Many of my students are children or family members of individuals I went to school with, and I see them in multiple settings.

The previous school counselor retired after working for 38 years in this school system. Although the school counselor built strong relationships with students and community members, her practice was not aligned with the American School Counselor Association (ASCA) National Model (ASCA, 2012a). Upon entering the school system, I began trying to incorporate the ASCA National Model into the school environment. Some of the activities or programs that I have incorporated include classroom guidance lessons, small counseling groups, a school counseling department leadership team, a school career fair, and a student recognition program. I have also advocated for the role of a school counselor within my school system and worked to clarify my role as a school counselor.

Incident

Because of the small and remote location of our school, school staff and students often develop close relationships. Teachers interact with students at school and at church, community activities, and local facilities. Two days before returning from winter break, a teacher who had worked at the school for 15 years had a heart attack and died in her sleep. I was close with this teacher and was struggling with her death. As a school counselor, I have never had to deal with the death of a faculty member within my school system, especially one that happened so unexpectedly.

Although many of the students found out about the teacher's death before the end of winter break, several did not hear the news until returning to school. Students were saddened to hear the news of the teacher's death, especially those currently enrolled in her classes. Although I did not have a formal crisis plan in place, I instructed the teachers to send students to my office if they were struggling with this loss. I also planned a memorial ceremony for the teacher.

Discussion

When meeting with students, I found it hard not to cry with them as they shared their stories and experiences about the teacher who unexpectedly passed away. Despite the intense reaction to the students' stories, I tried to help them identify ways to express their feelings and identify additional supports. During this time, if the students continued to have emotional difficulty with the teacher's death, they were excused for the remainder of the school day.

Although I was providing support, it seemed as though several students in the school needed additional services to help them process the death of their teacher. For some students, this was their first experience dealing with the death of someone so involved in their lives. I asked teachers to help me identify students in need of additional services. These students were provided small-group grief counseling for 8 weeks.

Questions

1. Why is it important to have a crisis plan in place before an event occurs?
2. What type of resource should be identified in a crisis plan?
3. Who should be involved in a crisis management team?
4. How can dual relationships affect services provided to students and staff?
5. How can I grieve while providing services to others?

Response 1

Karen Moore Townsend

A main goal of a crisis management plan is to provide safety to individuals. Having a procedure in place in the event of an emergency allows students and faculty to know what to expect and how to best address the crisis. A plan also helps parents and community members know what to expect in the event of an actual emergency and helps them know and be better prepared for their roles. The plan helps media know how distribution of information will be handled and who the spokesperson will be. Finally, a crisis plan can assist in meeting state, local, and federal guidelines.

Resources identified in the crisis plan should include site-based resources such as faculty and staff, two-way radios, and community resources such as community and grief counseling agencies, media, and emergency response agencies. In addition, age-appropriate books for bibliotherapy, such as children's grief and crisis literature, could be on reserve and made available through the school library or school counselor's office.

The crisis plan should name the team leader, typically the principal. Other team members might include the vice principal, school counselor, school secretary, high school faculty member, middle school faculty member, elementary school faculty member, and school nurse. The principal should be responsible for overseeing the plan, including calling team meetings, drills, and distributing information to others. The vice principal should assist the principal and may be the media spokesperson. The school counselor's role would include contacting appropriate community mental health agencies, referrals, immediate counseling needs, and post-crisis follow-up needs. The secretary could be responsible for contacting parents, law enforcement, and emergency workers, as well as screening and keeping a phone log of incoming calls. The teachers could be responsible for supervising their respective hall areas and letting the office know, through the use of a two-way intercom system, of any problems or updates about the execution of the plan. The nurse could be responsible for triage and immediate medical concerns. Although the suggestions here place administration at the top of the plan and lists possible roles for various faculty and staff, it is necessary that schools individualize plans to best serve the needs of their school and to ensure that plans are supportive of already developed district, regional, and state plans.

School counselors often have professional relationships and friendships with other staff. In addition, they may have dual relationships with students. According to the ASCA (2010b) Ethical Standards for School Counselors (A.4.a), school counselors are to "avoid dual relationships that might impair their objectivity and increase the risk of harm to students." When such relationships are unavoidable, the school counselor maintains responsibility for reducing potential for harm through measures such as consultation, supervision, appropriate documentation, and informed consent. The American Counseling Association's ([ACA's] 2014) *Code of Ethics* states that when the counselor cannot be objective, he or she is prohibited from engaging in a dual relationship such as counseling friends or family. Therefore, when dual relationships exist, it is imperative for the school counselor to take appropriate actions to ensure staff and student welfare.

Grieving school counselors should take time to engage in appropriate self-care activities while ensuring the welfare of school personnel. Some steps might include seeking personal counseling, consulting, involving other school and community counselors and resources, using the services of grief counselors, teaming with faculty and staff, providing memorial activities, and asking for help.

Response 2

Yvonne Ortiz-Bush

The ASCA National Model (2012a) encourages school counselors to be proactive in designing and implementing a comprehensive school counseling program. The Model calls for *responsive services* that are intended to address immediate student needs. The death of a teacher in a small rural school will affect the overall school climate as well as students, caretakers, and staff. The current school counselor is to be commended for working to implement systematic change via the ASCA National Model; however, a crisis plan is not in place, and this response is offered.

The development and implementation of a crisis plan to address the death of a teacher is optimal (Sorensen, 1989). Overall, the development of a comprehensive crisis plan allows school staff to deliberate and create responses to possible crisis events before they occur. Without a crisis plan, any response is significantly influenced by the disequilibrium of the collective school environment and individual school personnel (Thompson, 1995). This is especially important in this scenario, given the cohesiveness of the community and the personal impact of the loss on the school counselor. Overall, the distribution and posting of a crisis plan is best practice, as it is more likely to happen when a crisis occurs.

The Center for Mental Health in Schools at UCLA (2008) has produced a downloadable and reproducible document titled *Responding to a Crisis at a School*, which can be utilized in the development of a crisis plan. A crisis plan should outline how the school will address natural disasters, assaults occurring on school property, and the death of a student or staff member. The crisis management team should include school administrators, counselors, psychologists, nurses, teachers, staff, parents, and community mental health providers. The development of a school crisis plan should include school district, school site, and community resources that are readily available and can be accessible and referenced by school personnel at any time. The utilization of school district and school site resources ensures that the emotional and physical needs of each unique educational community are documented and addressed. Community resources include, but are not limited to, law enforcement, disaster relief organizations, and emergency mental health and bereavement services. It is important that the middle school counselor in this scenario is able to link students who might require additional therapeutic services to the appropriate community resources (ACA, 2014; ASCA, 2016).

The school counselor could utilize several readily available resources to coordinate a systemic effort to address this loss. Scholastic's website (http://www.scholastic.com) provides a plethora of information designed to help address a death that occurs in a school setting. The information presented is appropriate for grades 6–8 and includes resources, ideas, and classroom lessons. The National Center for School Crisis and Bereavement website (http://www.schoolcrisiscenter.org) provides videos and downloadable modules for all members of a school community. Cultural sensitivity is discussed, and the school counselor is reminded to be respectful and mindful of how a student's phenomenological worldview may affect their understanding of death and expression of grief. This website also contains a brief video addressing the needs of school staff. It would be helpful for the school counselor to review the professional preparation and self-care module to help normalize and manage her own emotional response.

The school counselor is experiencing the loss of a professional peer and friend while simultaneously providing grief services to a rural school community. Although the school counselor's own grief triggers and experience with loss are unknown, some issues should be addressed. Ethically, it is vital that the school counselor seek support to ensure her own sense of well-being and competency while maintaining professional boundaries and confidentiality (ACA, 2014; ASCA, 2016). This will likely include professional consultation and supervision with other school counselors. If the school counselor finds that her own grief affects her ability to be an effective school counselor, she might also consider seeking mental health and grief services. These services would allow her to further process her own emotional response and implement daily self-care strategies that will support her school counseling role and facilitate avoidance of secondary traumatization. If these services are not available in the immediate area, or if the school counselor feels uncomfortable seeking local services, internet-based mental health counseling and grief services might be a good option to address intrapersonal needs.

Supplemental Readings, Online Resources, and Supplemental Activities

Supplemental Readings

American School Counselor Association. (2013). *The school counselor and safe schools and crisis response* [Position statement]. Retrieved from https://www.schoolcounselor.org/asca/media/asca/PositionStatements/PS_SafeSchools.pdf

Fox, M., & Brown, K. (1994). *Tough Boris*. Orlando, FL: Harcourt.

Heegaard, M. (1988). *When someone very special dies*. Minneapolis, MN: Woodland Press.

Jackson-Cherry, L., & Erford, B. T. (2014). *Crisis assessment, intervention, and prevention* (2nd ed.). Upper Saddle River, NJ: Pearson Education.

Nicholson, J. I., & Pearson, Q. M. (2003). Helping children cope with fears: Using children's literature in classroom guidance. *Professional School Counseling, 7*(1), 15–19.

Samuel-Traisman, E. (2002). *Fire in my heart, ice in my veins: A journal for teenagers experiencing a loss.* Omaha, NE: Centering.

Schwiebert, P., DeKlyen, C., & Bills, T. (2005). *Tear soup.* Portland, OR: Grief Watch.

Solsaa, A., & Duncan, K. (2014). Helping students with grief and loss experiences. In R. Byrd & B. Erford (Eds.), *Applying techniques to common encounters in school counseling* (pp. 179–184). Upper Saddle River, NJ: Pearson Education.

Studer, J. R., & Salter, S. E. (2010). *The role of the school counselor in crisis planning and intervention.* Retrieved from https://www.counseling.org/resources/library/VISTAS/2010-V-Online/Article_92.pdf

Online Resources

American School Counselor Association (ASCA)
www.schoolcounselor.org
ASCA's (2016) Ethical Standards for School Counselors describes the school counselor as ethically required to "(m)onitor emotional and physical health and practice wellness..." (B.3.f.). What additional strategies might the school counselor use to manage his or her own grief? What other self-care measures might the school counselor use during this time?

The ASCA website also contains grief resources, including lesson plans for grades K–12, with a specific section addressing loss and the school community.

The Coalition to Support Grieving Students
www.grievingsstudents.org
The website contains grief support modules for all school personnel, family, and community members.

The Dougy Center: The National Center for Grieving Children & Families
www.dougy.org
The Dougy Center has resources for educators to support grief and bereavement following the death of a school community member.

The Healing Place: A Center for Grieving Children & Families
www.thehealingplaceinfo.org
The National Alliance for Grieving Children website at www.nationalallianceforgrievingchildren.org contains the crisis resource "Help for Schools," which includes a community crisis checklist, a guide for teachers of grieving students, and sample community notification letters.

The National Center for School Crisis and Bereavement
http://www.schoolcrisiscenter.org
The website contains grief and crisis resources (i.e., sample documents, articles, webinars, lesson plans, publications, and websites). Downloads include "Guidelines for Responding to the Death of a Student or School Staff."

The National Foundation for Grieving Children, Teens, and Families
    www.alittlehope.org
    The website contains an extensive bibliography for preschool- and school-age children and teenagers. It also includes links to web-based bereavement resources.

Scholastic
    www.scholastic.com
    Their site contains resources about the grieving process for children and teens. It includes a section on the impact of death in schools.

Supplemental Activities

Learning Activity 1: Loss Activity

Draw three large boxes on a piece of paper. Identify each box as elementary school, middle school, and high school. Record a loss that occurred during each phase of your life (one for each box). Note five words to answer each of the following questions:

- What was your emotional response to the loss?
- How did your caretakers respond to that loss?
- What do you think you needed but did not get?
- How will processing your own developmental responses to loss influence your work as a school counselor?
- Discuss your boxes in small groups.

Learning Activity 2: Assignment

Each student must interview a "first responder" and ask them the following questions:

- How are you notified that your services are needed?
- What is your typical emotional and/or physiological response to the notification?
- How long have you been in this position?
- Has your response changed with experience? If so, how?
- What works for you?
- What do you tell yourself to get through crisis situations?
- What would you tell others who must respond to critical situations?

The responses can be documented in writing or visually recorded. Students will have 15 minutes to report on their interview.

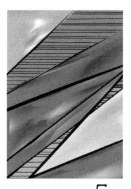

Chapter 5

What About One's Religious Beliefs?

Tomeka McGhee

This incident involves an elementary school counselor who works in a small, southern rural school with one administrator, her principal. She has been the school counselor for 18 years and was previously a special education teacher. She has lived in this rural area for most of her life as the daughter of the chief executive officer of one of the largest companies in the area, yet is naïve and does not possess a strong understanding or inclusion of varying worldviews and cultural understandings, including those within her community.

Background

I am an affluent Caucasian school counselor in a small, southern rural elementary school of over 600 students. The racial demographics of the students are 49% Caucasian, 46% African American, 3% Hispanic, and 2% multiracial. The faculty demographics are 85% Caucasian and 15% African American. Although the school is small, the rural town can span up to a 20-mile radius of farm and pasture land. Most of the families have lived in various subcommunities within the rural town for multiple generations. Many individuals have worked in neighboring city factories, with many individuals having earned a high school degree. In fact, the parents are likely to be first-generation college students. For African Americans, tradition is vital to the existence and functioning of their communities. More specifically, the local church is at the center and heart of community service, support, and family ideology.

Incident

Marvin, an 8-year-old African American male, was referred to my office by his teacher for exhibiting various behaviors during free time, such as the sudden raising of his hands and muttering sounds. As I inquired about the nature of his behavior, he declined to say anything. He told me he could not say anything to me because he was not allowed to talk about God in school. After more prompting, he shared that he had lost his grandmother recently to cancer and was often very sad. He said the muttering sounds are his "prayer language." He agreed to let me call his parents to express my concern for his mental health. I spoke to his mother and told her what was happening. I began to share that overexposure to church practices (i.e., Wednesdays, Fridays, and Sundays) may not be healthy. Furthermore, I stated that a more appropriate approach to his grief would include more scientific activities, such as creating collages and writing letters. The mother was enraged and asked for a meeting with the teacher, principal, and me to which she would bring her husband, pastor, and representatives from the area's ministerial association.

Discussion

I am completely baffled by the mother's response. Throughout my graduate-level school counselor training, I was taught that the behavior he exhibited was an indication of a serious mental illness. I am afraid he will get too deep in this religious thing. His family members talk, act, and dress differently than others in the community. I explained to my principal that I do not want him to become an outcast with his peers or become a fanatic. My principal looked astonished and said we would meet again tomorrow. What did I say?

Questions

1. Why is the mother so upset? Why is she involving the pastor and community ministers?
2. What did I say wrong?
3. What is wrong with wanting to protect Marvin? Isn't that my job?
4. Could I get into trouble? If so, how?
5. Are there other ways I could have handled the religious issue? If so, what are they?

Response 1

Zachary Michael Pietrantoni

The presenting issue in this case study is Marvin's grief about his grandmother's death. However, the focus shifted away from Marvin's grief when he displayed some concerning behaviors to the teacher and school counselor, which prompted a phone call to Marvin's mother; the presenting issue then changed to the school counselor's limited spiritual and religious competence when she expressed concern to Marvin's mother about the family's religious practices, which upset Marvin's mother.

Marvin's mother is upset because the school counselor unintentionally criticized her family's religious practices by stating that "overexposure to church practices may not be healthy" and suggesting that more scientific activities would be beneficial for Marvin's grieving. Marvin's mother more than likely involved her pastor and other community ministers as social and emotional supports as well as spiritual advocates on her behalf. Within this community—in particular, the African American community—the local church is significant for support and family ideology.

The biggest issue in this case study is the school counselor's unintentional criticizing of the religious practices of Marvin's family. The criticism is twofold: criticizing the family's church practices and criticizing the power of spiritual healing for Marvin's grief. The red flag for the school counselor is the limited knowledge of spiritual and religious ideation of Marvin. The teacher and school counselor were quick to define Marvin's hand gestures and prayer language as problematic instead of learning more about what those behaviors meant to Marvin and his family. Spirituality in child and adolescent development is reflective of their cognitive, social, and moral development (Benson, 2004). The church is important to Marvin and his family. There may be numerous explanations as to how and where Marvin learned those behaviors. Children may express spiritual issues around death in many ways (Lambie, Davis, & Miller, 2008), and school counselors should consider the uniqueness of such expressions within the child's developmental level (Sink & Devlin, 2011).

There is nothing wrong with wanting to protect Marvin. The question now becomes, "What are you protecting Marvin from?" The school counselor should be aware of her personal values around spirituality and religiosity and, moreover, how her values and beliefs relate to Marvin and his family's worldview. It appears that the school counselor believes she is saving Marvin from an unhealthy environment.

In addition, it would seem as if the school counselor is also trying to provide the best grief services possible to Marvin. However, the school counselor neglects to acknowledge Marvin's and his family's sense of autonomy. In this case, the sudden raising of his hands and muttering prayer language might be an acceptable practice and a grieving process used in Marvin's family and church.

The school counselor's sense of protection should be helping Marvin to navigate his grief in a culturally sensitive manner. She should address Marvin's spirituality in a way that fosters his personal and social growth (Sink & Devlin, 2011). This would include learning more about Marvin's individual needs and his family's practices. In other words, what does Marvin need to be successful throughout the school day? Furthermore, how does his family grieve? These indicators would help the school counselor as she develops a treatment plan for Marvin. The school counselor should also consider the behaviors that Marvin displays in the classroom. She should focus on protecting Marvin from getting into trouble in the classroom by providing him with a safe environment to address his grief.

The school counselor could get into trouble on several different levels: (a) legal, (b) ethical, and (c) professional. Lambie et al. (2008) noted that stifling religious and spiritual expressions could get school counselors in legal trouble by limiting the student's First and 14th Amendment rights. In addition, the school counselor could receive ethical ramifications from the American School Counselor Association (ASCA, 2016); in noting the unhealthy nature of the family's church practices, she is unintentionally imposing her personal values onto Marvin and his family. Finally, the school counselor may experience professional discipline through her school district for her unintentionally harmful comments.

School counselors should be thoughtful and intentional when addressing spiritual and religious issues (Lambie et al., 2008). Thoughtfulness and intentionality do not imply that school counselors promote their personal spiritual or religious views. Lambie et al. (2008) have suggested a three-step approach to ethical spiritual and religious practice in schools. The three-step approach consists of (a) increased self-awareness of personal and professional beliefs, (b) appreciation of students' spirituality in the counseling process, and (c) tailoring counseling interventions to students' specific needs. School counselors should also seek supervision and consultation when addressing spiritual and religious issues (Sink & Devlin, 2011).

In the case of Marvin, the school counselor approached Marvin's grief in an insensitive way. Marvin's school counselor was unaware of her personal beliefs about spirituality in the grief process, which appeared disrespectful to Marvin's mother and consequently damaged their relationship. The school counselor should have gathered more information about Marvin and his family's spiritual practice and sought supervision before she contacted Marvin's mother.

Response 2

Diana L. Wildermuth

The incident is a clear example of a school counselor whose lack of multicultural competence may be detrimental in aiding a child through a difficult time. School counselors must be able to understand how their beliefs, values, and assumptions affect those whom they serve. The attitude, values, and behaviors that the school counselor has brought to the relationship has resulted in an unfortunate situation that may have a lasting impact on the child and family. It is important that a school counselor is culturally skilled by having knowledge and respecting a student's religious and/or spiritual beliefs and values, as they often affect how the child views the world, the child's psychosocial functioning, and how a child expresses distress (Arredondo et al., 1996). A school counselor has the ethical responsibility to recognize how culture and/or religion relate to a child's daily functioning.

School counselors are not to make value judgments for their students but to understand and accept that students may have a set of beliefs, values, and assumptions that are different from their own. Although separation of church and state remains, it is often difficult to separate religion from a child who is still trying to find his or her place in the world. Making the statement to the principal that this family talks, acts, and dresses differently is insensitive and condemnatory. Furthermore, suggesting that he may become a fanatic with his religious beliefs is inappropriate on the part of the school counselor.

Even though the school counselor may have lived in this rural area, it does not appear as if she understands the significance that the local church plays in the lives of many families, including Marvin's family. Although this appears to be a religious incident, there may also be underpinnings of White privilege that need to be addressed on the behalf of the school counselor.

It is not surprising that the mother is angry with the school counselor in this situation and has every right to be so. For one, she is grieving the loss of her relative and has been told that her religious belief system as a way of coping is not acceptable. A culturally competent school counselor would understand and incorporate the cultural knowledge of how prayer language has aided this child and family in the grieving process. Despite the fact that the school counselor is trained, she is not using a theoretical counseling approach that is most appropriate for school counseling and the issues at hand.

Unfortunately, this school counselor has a false sense of what protecting Marvin is. The school counselor should offer support to Marvin and assist teachers in understanding what is and what is not a culturally appropriate response to grief, creating a safe place for him to express his grief. Additionally, it appears as if the school counselor has not yet recognized her own limitations in counseling and what it means to be culturally competent.

It is quite possible that the school counselor could be in trouble with her administration, as it appears she was passing judgment on this family. However, this could be addressed through additional training in multicultural counseling. This may give her the tools to better handle future situations that may be culturally, ethically, or religiously charged. When counselors have the knowledge, awareness, and skills necessary to meet the needs of diverse populations, it can not only enhance the counseling relationship but also build a better foundation for the future.

The role of the counselor in this situation is to understand what his prayer language means to him and to assist in processing his loss. School counselors need to expand their understanding of others' values. One recommendation for the future would be to become familiar with current research regarding mental health and how it is viewed in different cultures and manifests in various religions. A better way to handle religious situations in the school would be to gain an understanding of the ministerial association and the role it plays in Marvin's life. By contacting the parent, it allows her to know that Marvin is having a difficult time dealing with the loss of his grandmother and that it is affecting him in school; however, the way it was done was not appropriate. It would be more appropriate to partner with the parent to find strategies to help Marvin process his loss by what is culturally acceptable within his family. The school counselor should use a meeting with the parents, administrator, and pastor to plan collectively on how to support Marvin. Additionally, this would be an excellent time to learn more about how prayer language has been his coping mechanism and the role it has played in assisting him to grieve the loss of his grandmother.

Supplemental Readings, Online Resources, and Supplemental Activities

Supplemental Readings

Arredondo, P., Tovar-Blank, Z. G., & Parham, T. A. (2008). Challenges and promises of becoming a culturally competent counselor in a sociopolitical era of change and empowerment. *Journal of Counseling & Development, 86,* 261–268. doi:10.1002/j.1556-6678.2008.tb00508.x

Benson, P. (2004). Emerging themes in research on adolescent spiritual and religious development. *Applied Developmental Science, 8*(1), 47–50.

Chandler, C. K., Holden, J. M., & Kolander, C. A. (1992). Counseling for spiritual wellness: Theory and practice. *Journal of Counseling & Development, 71,* 168–175.

Davis, K. M., Lambie, G. W., & Ieva, K. P. (2011). Influence of familial spirituality: Implications for school counseling professionals. *Counseling and Values, 55,* 199–209.

Dobmeier, R. A. (2011). School counselors support student spirituality through developmental assets, character education, and ASCA competency indicators. *Professional School Counseling, 14*(5), 317–327.

Fowler, J. W. (1981). *Stages of faith.* New York, NY: HarperCollins.

Jordan, A. H., Lovett, B. J., & Sweeton, J. L. (2012). The social psychology of Black–White interracial interactions: Implications for culturally competent clinical practice. *Journal of Multicultural Counseling and Development, 40,* 132–143. doi:10.1002/j.2161-1912.2012.00013.x

Lambie, G. W., Davis, K. M., & Miller, G. (2008). Spirituality: Implications for professional school counselors' ethical practice. *Counseling and Values, 52,* 211–223.

Miller, G. (2003). *Incorporating spirituality in counseling and psychotherapy: Theory and technique.* Hoboken, NJ: Wiley.

Portman, T. A. A. (2009). Faces of the future: School counselors as cultural mediators. *Journal of Counseling & Development, 87,* 21–27. doi:10.1002/j.1556-6678.2009.tb00545.x

Ridley, C. R. (2005). *Overcoming unintentional racism in counseling and therapy: A practitioner's guide to intentional intervention* (2nd ed.). Thousand Oaks, CA: Sage.

Rothman, T., Malott, K. M., & Paone, T. R. (2012). Experiences of a course on the culture of Whiteness in counselor education. *Journal of Multicultural Counseling and Development, 40,* 37–48. doi:10.1111/j.2161-1912.2012.00004.x

Sink, C. A., & Devlin, J. M. (2011). Student spirituality and school counseling: Issues, opportunities, and challenges. *Counseling and Values, 55,* 130–148.

Smith-Augustine, S. (2011). School counselors' comfort and competence with spirituality issues. *Counseling and Values, 55,* 149–156.

Academic Journals for Supplemental Reading
- *The International Journal for the Psychology of Religion*
- *Journal of Beliefs and Values: Studies in Religion and Education*
- *Journal of Spirituality in Mental Health*
- *Mental Health, Religion, and Culture*
- *Psychology of Religion and Spirituality*

Online Resources

American Counseling Association (ACA) Interest Network for Professional Counselors in Schools
http://www.counseling.org/aca-community/aca-groups/interest-networks#Schools

American School Counselor Association (ASCA)
http://schoolcounselor.org/

Association for Multicultural Counseling and Development (AMCD)
http://www.multiculturalcounseling.org/

Association for Spiritual, Ethical, and Religious Values in Counseling (ASERVIC)
http://www.aservic.org/

Greater Good: The Science of a Meaningful Life
http://greatergood.berkeley.edu

Supplemental Activities
Educational Activity: Spirituality Panel

Create a panel of parents and children with various spiritual beliefs. Allow school counselors-in-training (SCITs) the opportunity to ask questions related to spiritual beliefs and counseling needs. Assignments include the following:

- Have SCITs interview a person of a different spiritual belief and then write a reflection paper comparing and contrasting their beliefs with those of the interviewee. SCITs should consider their personal awareness and attitudes about interviewee's spiritual beliefs.
- Research appropriate skills and interventions to use with the interviewee in a counseling session.

Participate in Spiritual Practice

Have SCITs attend a spiritual practice that is different from their own. SCITs can then write a reflection paper on the spiritual practice considering their thoughts and feelings around the practice. In addition, consider the benefits of experiencing the spiritual practice and how this experience might inform future work as a school counselor.

Further Questions for Reflection and Discussion

- What differences do you see between yourself, Marvin, and his family?
- What similarities do you see between yourself, Marvin, and his family?
- What is your reaction to how the school counselor handled the discussion with Marvin and his mother?
- What areas do you see as concerns in this case study?
- How would you address this presenting problem if you were the school counselor?
- How could you use the meeting stakeholders (i.e., teacher, principal, Marvin's parents, pastor, and representatives from the area ministerial association) to facilitate a discussion about grief counseling for Marvin?

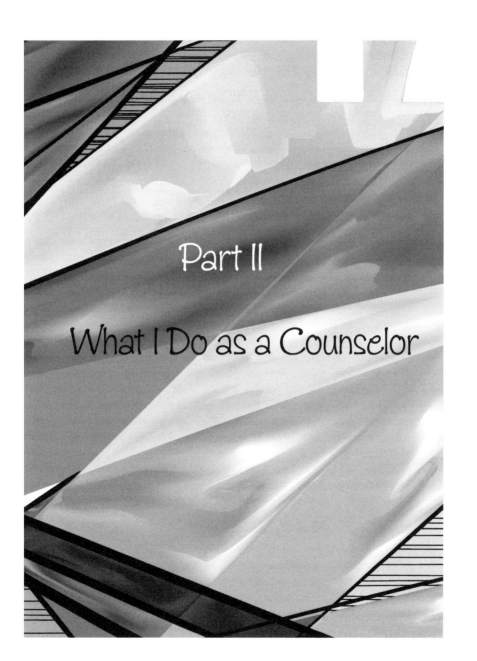

Part II

What I Do as a Counselor

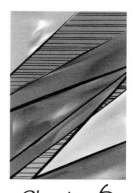

Chapter 6

Who Will Advocate If I Don't?

Emilie E. Shaver

Background

Wallace is the only counselor at a small high school in a rural southern town. He has been working in the school for 6 years and has developed a strong relationship with the administration. As a result, the administration is fully supportive in his endeavors to deliver a comprehensive school counseling program. He has developed a strong relationship with the students and parents within the school. Many school stakeholders are aware that Wallace is gay. However, this is a subject rarely mentioned or even acknowledged by parents or other school faculty. Wallace does not flaunt his relationship with his partner, but he does not deny its existence if the topic is approached. Occasionally, Wallace has had a few students visit his office, wanting to talk about their sexual identity. Having been at the school for several years, he believes that it is a safe time to create a small group for LGBTQ (lesbian, gay, bisexual, transgender, and queer, or questioning) students to meet and share their experiences or the struggles they may face growing up in such a rural area. Wallace believes in the American School Counselor Association's (ASCA's) position on advocacy and indeed sees himself as an advocate for those who have been marginalized.

Incident

Wallace recognizes that there will likely be resistance from the community and parents for the LGBTQ group. Therefore, he sets the meeting time during after-school hours. In his mind, this will allow for more privacy concerning the group, and attendance will be more of a calculated decision for the students. Wallace decides that even though the group will be a small counseling group and not a club, the group will not require parent permission because of the meeting time; also, he believes that high school students can make their own decision as to whether to attend the group. He also is firmly committed to the idea that one's decision to "come out" is a personal right. Asking parent permission for such a group would force interested students to decide whether they should come out to their parents. In the past, the principal often played the part of "peacekeeper" when it came to parent uproar or concern over a controversial topic. Therefore, Wallace is hesitant to approach the principal with the idea of an LGBTQ group. Additionally, Wallace determines that, since the group is meeting after school and his principal has always supported Wallace's work, he will forego requesting permission, and he proceeds to begin the LGBTQ group.

Members are not recruited but enter the group on a voluntary basis. Wallace extends invitations to members of the student body who have disclosed a history of identifying as LGBTQ or who have expressed to him that they are questioning their sexuality. The group is set to meet eight times throughout the spring semester in Wallace's office at 3:15 p.m. The first two meetings come and go without incident. All seven students who attend seem to enjoy and appreciate the safe environment and the comfort of being part a group full of like-minded individuals. Two days after the second meeting, Wallace's principal calls him into his office for a conference with a mother and father who have "stormed" into the school, demanding to speak to the principal. The parents discovered their son has been attending this group and are outraged that they were not even notified of its existence or asked for permission for their son to attend. The parents are not comfortable with their son attending this group, as they are adamant that he is not a member of the LGBTQ community, and they accuse Wallace of pushing his "lifestyle" onto their child. They demand that the principal remove Wallace from the classroom pending a school board ruling on whether Wallace is fit to be a teacher. Wallace looks to the principal for support in defending his action. The principal, realizing the political climate of the town, agrees to consider the matter with both Wallace and the school board.

Discussion

After the parents leave the meeting, the principal asks to meet with Wallace. She expresses her disappointment in Wallace's actions and choices. She recognizes the fact that he has established this group, but she wants to know why she was not informed of its existence. She admits that although she is comfortable with his sexuality and respects that he does not "flaunt it," (a) she is not comfortable with him leading a group on this topic because of parental backlash in such a small community, (b) she believes that she should be informed of such activities, and (c) she believes that parents should give consent for their minor children to participate in after-school activities. She asks him to end the LGBTQ group. The next week when the students arrive for their regularly scheduled meeting, Wallace informs them they will no longer be meeting at the school but instead at his house.

Questions

1. What do you believe Wallace is thinking when it comes to being an advocate?
2. Are there times when being an advocate might not be the most productive route?
3. How might Wallace be jeopardizing his job despite his best intentions?
4. Does having the group meet after school ensure that Wallace did not need parental permission for students to attend the group? Why or why not?
5. What do you think? Did Wallace respect the privacy of the students to be part of this group without their parents' knowledge, or did he disrespect the parents and go behind their backs as guardians?
6. What are the ethical issues with Wallace informing students that they will now be meeting at his house instead of the school?

Response 1

Jolie Daigle

There is no doubt that Wallace has the best intentions in serving as an advocate for the LGBTQ community at his school site. He also shares similar identities (i.e., sexual orientation and rural living) as many of the students interested in the LGBTQ group. However, a few statements Wallace discussed may give cause for hesitation. First, he acknowledged that the group may be controversial with his principal and parents, so he scheduled the group to meet after school. Next, Wallace assumed that parents would find fault with the group and did not consider seeking parental consent. Additionally, he is recruiting only those students who have already identified themselves to him as LGBTQ and did not seek referrals from staff. There are no goals set for the group, and it is not entirely clear whether the group is based on a needs assessment or the counselor's "hunch." After some resistance from parents and administrators, and in stark opposition to their views, Wallace finally agrees for the group to continue meeting at his home instead of the school. After 6 years of working as a school counselor at this school site, Wallace does not seem to value or understand the importance of stakeholders in facilitating a successful school counseling program. Wallace truly believes he is acting on behalf of the students as an advocate, but he is only understanding advocacy on an individual level and not considering advocacy at systemic levels. Wallace is jeopardizing his position as a school counselor by not considering parental consent for the small group, not maintaining open communication with his administrator, and providing counseling services at his home rather than his place of employment.

Remley, Hermann, and Huey (2010) have recommended that school counselors use proactive strategies to increase parent and community involvement and support for school counseling programs. Requesting parent consent or communicating with the parents of children in the group might have garnered support from parents and administrators as the group began. Wallace also should consider gathering statistics, research, and best practices regarding LGBTQ youth and placing this information into summary form, so parents, teachers, and administrators can be knowledgeable and supportive as to why this group needs to meet.

It is also unclear why there is a need for the small group of LGBTQ students to meet. What informed Wallace's decision: data, needs assessment, teacher or parent referral, or student interest? If the school climate has come into question and LGBTQ students are being bullied or marginalized, Wallace may need to think about outreach not just at the individual level but at the school and community level as well. Remley et al. (2010) explained that school counselors function more effectively as leaders of coordinated efforts to influence other school personnel or families to enrich the school environment for LGBTQ youth. If, indeed, bullying or the school climate is a school-wide concern, it would be in the best interest of all students if they received psychoeducational information through classroom guidance programming and if staff offered professional development. On the other hand, should the students need services through a referral-based small group, Wallace should understand the presenting issue of the student. Is the student moving through the "coming-out stages"? Has the student experienced bullying or posttraumatic stress, or is his or her safety being jeopardized? Should efforts be addressed at the individual or system level?

Wallace has organized a small group for students identified as LGBTQ. Is the group designed to be affirming, psychoeducational, and/or skills-based in nature? If allied professions (e.g., school nurse, social worker) will join the group at some point, will students know in advance, and how will confidentiality be managed? The Association for Specialists in Group Work (ASGW, 2000) defines four types of groups: task group facilitation, group psychoeducation, group counseling, and group psychotherapy. Under which category does Wallace's group fall? How will the different goals look for each type of group? Is confidentiality managed differently for each group? How is the group membership managed, as in open and closed, for each category? Is group counseling or group psychotherapy appropriate in the home rather than an office setting?

Newsome and Gladding (2010) discussed several factors when planning small groups in the schools. First, they recommend collaboration with teachers and parents and presenting a rationale as to why the group should meet and students miss instructional time, such as through a needs assessment or summary of referrals. The ASCA's position statement on group counseling (ASCA, 2014c) advises counselors to form group support for students based on the results of survey data or a referral process. Next, the counselor will need to determine the function of the group. Is the group rooted in counseling and therapy or information sharing? Topics for these sessions can be determined from the information gathered on the needs assessment or from participants during the first session. School counselors will then need to plan for the logistics of the group. How many sessions will the group meet? For how long? Will the group time rotate so students do not miss instruction time from one class? If the group continues to meet at Wallace's home, who will be responsible for liability and transportation? Finally, school counselors should recruit students and reach students who may not have received counseling services or been referred in the past. This can be done by placing an information statement in a newsletter, website, or announcement.

Screenings will need to also occur to ensure that members are appropriate for the group and understand group process and confidentiality. Group counseling best practices state that the members of groups should be screened, informed consent should be addressed, the purpose and goals of the group should be carefully explained, and the limits of confidentiality should be understood. ASCA's (2014c) position statement on group counseling also suggests that parent and student consent should be obtained before the start of the group. In terms of group formation, it is not clear whether Wallace carefully screened the members of the group before the start of the group or whether students were asked to sign a consent for confidentiality agreement. Wallace should also keep in mind that national counseling organizations have differing statements on consent (e.g., ASGW and ASCA). ASCA's (2014b) position statement on the school counselor and confidentiality states that a counselor's primary obligation of confidentiality is to the students. However, this obligation must be balanced with the parent's right to guide decision making in their child's life and with certain exceptions such as harm to self, harm to others, or court-ordered/mandated reporting.

Wallace would be positioned well if he were to consult with his administrators, counselors within the school district, the school counseling program's advisory board, and current best practices/research. He is in a very vulnerable and isolated position, and his continued employment may be at risk.

Response 2

Debbie Grant

Being a gay man in the South, Wallace truly understands the complexity of these students' situation. Since students have come to his office to share and discuss their feelings with him, he feels as though it is in the students' best interest to have him serve as their advocate and supporter. He seems to believe that he has been at the school long enough to be "protected" from any pushback from school personnel and parents. He also seems to believe that the after-school sessions will give students confidentiality and keep the group out of the mainstream view of the regular school day. Wallace believes that, as a gay man, he is the perfect choice to advocate for this community of students, regardless of consequences.

In this situation, it appears that Wallace's sexual orientation is counter-productive. (The fact that Wallace, as the students' advocate, is also gay does not provide any additional benefit.) One question to ask would be, "Would the response have been the same from administration and parents if Wallace had been a heterosexual male?" In this case, the fact that he is "close" to the situation may not make him productive as an advocate. Although he certainly understands the situations that the students face each day, his own identity clouds the issue.

As stated, Wallace has now been within this school for 6 years and believes that he has the support from the administration. That being said, he should have shared his thoughts on advocacy and the support group with his administrator to seek guidance and approval for such a group. He placed his administrator in a tough position when the parents arrived to discuss the group and she was not even aware that it had taken place. Wallace knows this is a sensitive subject within a small, rural southern town. He should have considered all the options before scheduling a group at school unbeknownst to his administrator, and now his plan to meet with these students at his home creates even more issues. He is a gay man who is now inviting students from school to his home to discuss issues that are sexual in nature. The school system may see this as insubordination and a clear lack of respect for boundaries and may choose to take disciplinary action against him. Wallace would have been better served by collaborating with a local church or youth center to establish an LGBTQ support group that would not be linked to the school.

As per the ASCA Ethical Standards for School Counselors, A.2.d states that counselors should:

> Recognize their primary obligation for confidentiality is to the students but balance that obligation with an understanding of parents'/guardians' legal and inherent rights to be the guiding voice in their children's lives, especially in value-laden issues. Understand the need to balance students' ethical rights to make choices, their capacity to give consent or assent and parental or familial legal rights and responsibilities to protect these students and make decisions on their behalf. (ASCA, 2010b)

In addition, in accordance with the ASCA ethical standards, counselors should "[r]ecognize that the best practice is to notify the parents/guardians of children participating in small groups (ASCA, 2010b, A.6.b.)."

Wallace was not utilizing "best practice" in not requiring parental consent for this group. Within the ASCA standards focused on responsibilities to parents/guardians, B.1.d. clearly states that counselors should "[i]nform parents of the nature of counseling services provided in the school setting."

I certainly understand that Wallace's intentions were in the right place when he created the group experience for these students. I believe that it is best practice to involve parents in groups, especially those covering value-laden issues. I believe that there are parents who would support their children's participation in the group. Being transparent with the administrators and parents about the group would have been helpful.

In my opinion, this is an extremely poor choice. Wallace is now opening himself up to a number of ethical issues associated with boundaries. The ASCA ethical standards clearly state in A.4.b. that counselors should "[m]aintain appropriate professional distance with students at all times." By having students in his home, he is creating a dual relationship with these individuals. These students now will know Wallace on a more personal level after having been guests in his home. Given that Wallace is a gay man in a small rural community, this type of interaction in his home leaves him open for multiple ethical issues. The ASCA ethical standards describe his responsibility to the community in D.2.d, where it specifies that counselors "[a]re careful not to use their professional role as a school counselor to benefit any type of private therapeutic or consultative practice in which they might be involved outside of the school setting." The group at his house may certainly be considered such a venture.

Supplemental Readings, Online Resources, and Supplemental Activities

Supplemental Readings

Akos, P., Goodnough, G. E., & Milson, A. S. (2004). Preparing school counselors for group work. *The Journal for Specialists in Group Work, 29*(1), 127–136.

Corey, G. (2004). *Theory and practice of group counseling* (6th ed.). Belmont, CA: Brooks/Cole-Thomson Learning.

Furr, S. B. (2000). Structuring the group experience: A format for designing psychoeducational groups. *The Journal for Specialists in Group Work, 25*(1), 29–49.

Singh, A. A. (2010). It takes more than a rainbow sticker! Using the ACA Advocacy Competencies with queer clients. In M. Ratts, J. Lewis, & R. Toporek (Eds.), *Using the ACA Advocacy Competencies in counseling* (pp. 29–41). Alexandria, VA: American Counseling Association.

Stone, C. (2005). *School counseling principles: Ethics and law.* Alexandria, VA: American School Counselor Association.

Online Resources

Centers for Disease Control and Prevention, *LGBT Youth Resources*
http://www.cdc.gov/lgbthealth/youth-resources.htm

The Gay, Lesbian and Straight Education Network (GLSEN)
http://www.glsen.org

Human Rights Campaign
http://www.hrc.org/resources

PFLAG
http://community.pflag.org

Youth Pride Alliance
http://www.youthpridealliance.org

Supplemental Activities

More Reflection Questions

- Did Wallace's sexual identity have an impact on this situation?
- What could Wallace have done to make the situation more comfortable for parents/guardians?
- Is Wallace possibly trying to expand his support of the LGBT community by hosting the group?

Chapter 7

How Did All of This
Come Into My School?

Cheryl Lynn Spaulding Sewell

This incident centers on a local youth sports coach who was involved in a fatal shooting. The event began with the kidnapping of a local adult resident, followed by the shooting and killing of a police officer, and ultimately ended with a manhunt. The events unfolded over several days and were continuously documented by the media. I have been a school counselor for 7 years at the elementary school that services the community directly affected by this tragic event.

Background

The elementary school serves students in pre-K through fifth grade, with a current enrollment of approximately 450 students. The school comprises a diverse population; approximately 50% of the students identify as African American, and 48% identify as Hispanic. Furthermore, 98% of the families qualify for free and reduced lunch rates, indicating the low socioeconomic status of the school community. There are about 60 faculty and staff employed at this elementary school, including one school counselor.

This elementary school is one of 14 in the district. Additionally, there are four middle schools and two traditional high schools. The school district is situated within a small college town and outside of a large southeastern metropolitan area. There are pockets of affluence, as some residents hold faculty and professional positions at the university. However, the community surrounding the university is one of the most impoverished counties in the nation, per capita. Therefore, because of the extreme variations in socioeconomic status, there is a stark divide in the community resources. This translates into a division among racial and ethnic groups and the inherent structure of privilege and oppression.

The community's leisure services department offers many services and activities for children at affordable rates, such as organized sports, summer camps, public parks, and a host of enrichment activities. The majority of the youth leaders and sport coaches are local volunteers, meaning that fathers, brothers, uncles, cousins, and friends are working closely with the young people of the community. Therefore, living in such an intimate community means that dual relationships are common and, most times, inevitable.

Incident

A local African American youth sports coach was involved in a series of crimes that ended with his fatally shooting a White police officer. The coach fled from authorities, prompting a search that lasted for several days. Two times during this search, our school was placed on an emergency lockdown, as he was assumed to be in the neighborhood. Ultimately, the coach was found where several of our students reside.

The apprehension of the coach was broadcast on local news stations. Therefore, some students were anxious because of the close proximity of the publicized events. Other students were unaware of the incident and unaffected. The majority of the students, however, were eager to discuss the details of the events. Specifically, students discussed their personal relationship to the coach and how he had affected their lives. Furthermore, students voiced their opinions of whether the coach's actions were appropriate and justified.

Discussion

Because of the high publicity of the incident, community members formed strong opinions regarding the incident. From a developmental perspective, elementary school-age students may not be mature enough or have the cognitive ability to process events of this magnitude and involving a community figure with whom they may have had a personal relationship. Therefore, young students were mimicking what they heard from the adults in their lives. For example, comments from students included, "That police officer was racist and deserved to be shot," "I would have done the same thing," and "He was a dirty cop and liked to pick on Black folk." In sharing personal reflections, students said, "Man, that was my football coach," and "He was cool." Many of the students and their families believed that he was a role model for the community and justified in his actions of shooting and killing a police officer.

Questions

1. What should be the response of the school and school district in an event like this?
2. What is the role of the school counselor in the response?

3. As a social justice agent, how could a school counselor address the issues of racism without imposing personal assumptions, values, and biases onto students?
4. How does a school counselor prepare young African American boys for the real world of prejudice and oppression without creating a mentality of victimization and justice by violence?

Response 1

Tori Charette

It is the duty of all community members to facilitate healing during a time of crisis. More important, a school must proactively create a culture of conversation and trust to effectively address crisis in schools and in the community. All persons who are responding in this incident must keep in mind that they are serving multiple parties. Family members and close friends of both the coach and the police officer may be seeking support.

When a key community member dies, the school district must take immediate steps to respond to the students and families. In this case, the community coach has affected students in a systemic way. First and foremost, the community will be looking for the school district to make a statement that is unbiased and factual while supporting families of both parties. The school district representative should take time to send a positive letter to students and families in the communities that were affected by the event. In the letter to students, a list of counseling and mental health services in the school and community should be listed. The counselor can also contact both parties to inquire as to what information they would like shared in the school.

The school counselor is uniquely situated to provide systemic support to students and staff. The American School Counselor Association (ASCA) suggests that school administrators and school counselors proactively create a crisis management and response system at the beginning of the year. An emergency phone tree and crisis meeting space and time should be specified in this document. Therefore, the individual(s) identified at the top of the phone tree must call all staff and inform them of the crisis that has occurred in the neighborhood. Additionally, those charged with leading the phone tree should establish a meeting time and space, before school resumes, to discuss action plans for the following day or week. During this initial meeting, the role of the school counselor is to discuss the repercussions that grief has on individuals at all developmental stages, especially children.

Although children may inherently understand the meaning of death, they may struggle to discuss and conceptualize death with adults or peers (Doka, 2000). Death is a subject that is usually surrounded by fear and anxiety. It is most effective to use different media to discuss death with a group of students, instead of directly addressing the situation after a crisis. The school counselor might suggest certain books (e.g., bibliotherapy) that address death or grief. These resources may be used as a read-aloud with students during the week after the death of the police officer and the arrest of the coach. Examples of literature that may be used to facilitate discussion include *Everett Anderson's Goodbye* by Lucille Clifton (1983), or *The Invisible String* by Patrice Karst (2000). These examples are developmentally appropriate for elementary school-age children.

Gurwitch and Schonfeld (2011) have specified the various roles the school counselor must serve in a crisis. School counselors may fill a multitude of roles, including performing triage interventions with those affected by the coach's death. The school counselor's first proactive role in this situation is to recruit other service providers in the community to take part in the response team. Those directly affected by the incident will have the ability to partake in individual counseling sessions with a professional. School counselors should run small groups for students who were intensely affected by this tragedy. When appropriate, the school counselor will take time to respond to students in a large-group setting.

Play therapy is a developmentally appropriate approach to treating children who have experienced trauma. Specifically, the counselor can use prop-based play therapy to evoke students' responses in a nondirective or threatening manner (Goodyear-Brown, 2010). The intent of play therapy is to create a nonthreatening therapeutic environment for children to express their trauma.

School counselors are tasked with the duty of creating a positive school culture that encompasses conversation, tolerance, and acceptance. Singleton (2015) noted that "leadership needs to exercise passion, be engaged in the design and delivery of innovative practice, and demonstrate persistence toward achieving equity at all levels of the system . . ." (p. 254). Schools and communities must first come together to openly discuss racism before any tragedy takes place in the community. School counselors and stakeholders can promote open conversations that provide the opportunity to address issues of racism and inequality. A family–school collaboration can help change perceptions about neighborhoods, teachers, and other school staff, which may lessen inherent racism at the community level.

The school counselor can create opportunities for open conversations during the classroom guidance curriculum and lessons. First, the counselor should have access to a collection of books that include stories of multicultural characters in different socioeconomic settings. Next, the counselor should provide space for students to express their opinions about race in the classroom. When a student's opinion is not recognized, educators are not giving significance to student stories. After stories and opinions have been heard, the counselor can prepare young racial/ethnic-minority students by planning community action with the students. A committee that comprises all stakeholders should be created and aimed to directly address racism on campus and within the community. Tasks that this committee can take on include conducting community meetings, writing letters of grievance, and collaborating with law enforcement to promote positive relationships.

The beginning and end of every school crisis management plan must be based around relationships. Each stakeholder at the school must feel safe and trust the school. Schools and districts must have a crisis plan in place to fully address any trauma or community concerns. It is the counselor's role to follow up with students and families who are directly affected by the shooting. All school staff must cooperate to successfully manage the trauma and crisis that this tragic shooting will bring to the community.

Response 2

Sandra (Sandi) M. Logan-McKibben

Jackson-Cherry and Erford (2010) emphasized that when a crisis occurs on a school campus, school personnel are to respond to the situation professionally. This includes making sure that students and families are provided with the appropriate information and access to school and community resources such as counseling. Additionally, the designated crisis team should follow the crisis plan designed by the school and/ or district, which will allow for efforts to be organized and coordinated effectively to ensure that all stakeholders feel informed, supported, and safe. Such a team typically includes principals; school counselors and psychologists; resource officers; and, at times, outside crisis responders if the situation warrants. At a minimum, this should include gathering the crisis team members for a planning meeting to obtain and verify facts and to decide on how to announce the event and engage in a discussion with students, parents, and community members. On completion of the agreed-upon team activities, a debriefing meeting ought to be held to address the unique needs of the crisis team members and answer any questions that may still be unaddressed. From the school district perspective, it might be helpful for a statement to be made publicly to the media so that community members remain informed just as those associated with the school are informed.

Although the role of the school counselor is vast, one of the main responsibilities is to ensure school safety while children and adults are on campus grounds. Matters of school safety occur through a variety of activities aimed at both prevention and intervention. According to ASCA (2013), school counselors are well prepared to prevent violent incidents, intervene when concerns arise about potential violence, and respond when violence occurs, using various interventions. For instance, in this scenario, a school counselor's prevention efforts may be focused on providing classroom guidance lessons to the elementary students on how to distinguish between making appropriate and inappropriate choices. This would allow students to better understand decision making and how "good people" can still make poor decisions, just as their coach has demonstrated. If it becomes apparent that the clear majority of students are directly affected by the crisis, it may be best to conduct a classroom group crisis intervention (GCI; see Brock, Lazarus, & Jimerson, 2002). On the other hand, school counselors could find themselves providing more individualized support to students and other adults who have been directly affected by the crisis; for instance, the coach's niece and three nephews may attend the elementary school. Of the utmost concern is making sure that efforts are aimed at those in need of assistance rather than being spent on imposing one's personal beliefs and opinions or deliberating about whether the coach's actions were justified.

Given the social context of this crisis, it would be important for the school counselor to carefully address the issues of racism. This could be done by conducting classroom guidance lessons that focus on respect for everyone and embracing one another's uniqueness. It might be quite possible to link these messages to the school's motto or a positive behavior supports and intervention (PBIS) program. For instance, if the school has a focus on being respectful, responsible, and kind, there could be classroom and school-wide activities that focus on being respectful of one another's uniqueness, which includes race and ethnicity. In this manner, it would be possible to educate these elementary students while refraining from imposing personal values, assumptions, or biases. Another opportunity to discuss the community's issues of racism may be in the form of holding a town hall meeting, which could be facilitated in conjunction with a local church, community organizations, and/or the police authorities. This would provide an opportunity for educators and community members to come together to discuss the current barriers and how to make the community a safer environment.

Rather than promoting to students a stance of victimization, school counselors can focus on providing all students with the necessary prosocial skills to be successful citizens within their community and their own lives. For young African American boys, it is crucial that they see beyond just what occurs in their own community. It is important for young boys to feel empowerment from others who recognize their ability to succeed. One example is utilizing community resources, such as volunteers, who can serve as role models and mentors to youth. This could occur through partnerships with neighboring secondary schools, as well as colleges and universities. Another example is offering students and families the opportunity to participate in field trips that promote prosocial skills and college/career readiness.

Although it is important to consider what is developmentally appropriate for elementary students, it is also crucial to make sure that students are well informed and included in conversations. Class discussions about prejudice and oppression can easily be linked to lessons on history and government. Within this context, it is possible to emphasize the learning opportunity that is presented while refraining from promoting a victimization mentality or the use of violence. It is crucial that educators recognize the importance of making a student's classroom congruent to their world in terms of it being a learning environment. As appropriate, bring real-life issues into the classroom and provide the opportunity for rich discussion and dialogue among students.

Although every community—and every school within that community—is different, there is also much commonality. The overall goal in such a school crisis is to make sure that all stakeholders (children, caregivers, and community members) are safe and that communication effectively occurs. The follow-up after such a crisis is imperative. Schools and school districts should regularly be evaluating the effectiveness of the school crisis protocols and procedures to maintain the greatest level of preparedness.

Supplemental Readings, Online Resources, and Supplemental Activities

Supplemental Readings

American School Counselor Association. (2015). *Helping students during crisis*. Available at https://www.schoolcounselor.org/school-counselors-members/professional-development/2015-webinar-series/learn-more/helping-kids-during-crisis

Borum, R., Cornell, D. G., Modzeleski, W., & Jimerson, S. R. (2010). What can be done about school shootings? A review of the evidence. *Educational Researcher, 39*, 27–37.

Brock, S. E., Lazarus, P. J., & Jimerson, S. R. (2002). *Best practices in school crisis prevention and intervention*. Bethesda, MD: NASP.

Center Schools and Communities and Center for Safe Schools. (2018). *Emergency management resources*. Available at http://www.safeschools.info/emergency-management/emergency-management-resources

Gerler, E. R. (2004). *Handbook of school violence*. New York, NY: Haworth Reference Press.

Goodyear-Brown, P. (2002). *Digging for buried treasure: 52 prop-based play therapy interventions for treating the problems of childhood*. Madison, WI: Sundog.

Harris, T., & Taylor, G. (2012). *Raising African-American males: Strategies and interventions for successful outcomes*. Lanham, MD: Rowman & Littlefield Education.

Mercy Corps. (2018). *Helping children through crisis: 10 tips for parents and caregivers*. Available at http://www.mercycorps.org/helping-children-through-crisis-tips-parents-and-caregivers

National Child Traumatic Stress Network. *School personnel*. Available at http://www.nctsn.org/resources/audiences/school-personnel/crisis-situation

National Parent–Teacher Association. (n.d.). *Discussing difficult situations with your children*. Available at http://www.pta.org/programs/content.cfm?ItemNumber=985

New York University Child Study Center. (2006). *Caring for kids after trauma, disaster and death: A guide for parents and professionals* (2nd ed.). Available at https://www.preventionweb.net/files/1899_VL206101.pdf

PBS Parents. (2018). *Talking with kids about news.* Available at http://www. pbs.org/parents/talkingwithkids/news/

Poland, S. (2007, March/April). By the numbers. *ASCA School Counselor Magazine,* 37–39.

Scholastic. (2018). *Resources for responding to violence and tragedy.* Available at http://www.scholastic.com/teachers/collection/resources-responding-violence-and-tragedy

U.S. Department of Education. (2007, January). *Practical information on crisis planning: A guide for schools and communities.* Available at http://www2.ed.gov/admins/lead/safety/emergencyplan/crisisplanning.pdf

van der Kolk, B. (2014). *The body keeps the score: Brain, mind, and body in the healing of trauma.* New York, NY: Viking Penguin.

Werner, D. (2014). Perceptions of preparedness for a major school crisis: An evaluation of Missouri school counselors. *Journal of School Counseling, 12*(3). Retrieved from http://jsc.montana.edu/articles/v12n3.pdf

Online Resources

American School Counselor Association
http://www.schoolcounselor.org/

Institute of Race Relations: Tackling Racism through Education
http://www.irr.org.uk/news/tackling-racism-through-education/

National Association of School Psychologists school safety and crisis resources
http://www.nasponline.org/resources/crisis_safety/

National Center for Child Traumatic Stress
http://www.nctsn.org/about-us/national-center

National Center for School Crisis and Bereavement
http://www.schoolcrisiscenter.org/

Trauma Center at Justice Resource Institute
http://www.traumacenter.org/training/training_landing.php

Supplemental Activities

Discussion Questions Around School Crisis for Counselors in Training

- What is the foremost issue that you must tackle when dealing with a school crisis?
- In what ways can you involve the community during and after a school crisis or community incident?
- What do you believe is the role of the counselor before, during, and after a crisis occurs?
- How does racism affect the work that you will do as a school counselor?
- What is your role in combating racism in schools and communities?

In small work groups (perhaps by level: elementary, middle school, and high school), have students work collaboratively to design a school crisis management plan. Check your state's Department of Education website for examples.

Learning Activities

- Create an outline of a school crisis plan. Include responsibilities for all stake-holders, including administrators, teachers, parents, and students. Interview a current school counselor about crisis. Ask the counselor if he or she has ever encountered a crisis at the school and what his or her role was in the action plan. Please also include a copy of the school's crisis management plan.

- Create a small-group curriculum based on grief counseling. Incorporate art therapy techniques to help students self-soothe during the small-group time. Teachers should identify students who need small-group therapy, on the basis of conversations and behavioral observations. The counselor can plan for activities such as creating art pieces that help self-soothing and writing letters to the person for whom they are grieving.

- Create a list of questions that you would use to help elementary school students process this trauma as a whole group. Some examples might include: What memories do you have of the coach? What would you want other people to remember about the coach? If you were to tell other students about how to heal after someone in their school dies, what would you say?

- Create a list of resources for new school counselors that aims to address racism in schools.

Reflection and Discussion Questions

- What might a student's experience be like if he or she were attending a school where students were predominantly of a different ethnicity from his or her own?

- What might it be like for you, as an educator, working in a school where students were predominantly of a different ethnicity from your own? What are the advantages/disadvantages?

- If you lived in the same community as the school where you worked, how might this influence community members' expectations of your role as school counselor?

Chapter 8

Suicide:
Who Are You Going to Call?

Judith A. Harrington

The school counselor has been working with 17-year-old male, Derrick, because of suicide risk. Derrick has written a suicide note detailing his intentions. He shared these intentions with the school counselor. However, because of the tenuous nature of his parents' relationship, he does not want his father informed of his suicidal intentions. The school counselor knows that she should notify one or both parents about Derrick's suicide risk, but she is unsure whether she should notify Derrick's mom, dad, or both parents.

Background

Derrick has a girlfriend, Rachel, with whom he spends a great deal of time. Derrick's parents divorced about 1 year ago, and his father has primary custody of Derrick. Derrick lives with his father and spends 4 to 6 days per month with his mother. Rachel's mother stumbled upon a note written by Derrick on Rachel's bookshelf. The note detailed his plan to attempt suicide before the school year is over, so he will not have to contend with living at his father's house throughout the summer months. He wrote with specificity of his love for Rachel, stating his goodbyes to her and their friends. In the note, he detailed his suicide plans: going to the lake where they had experienced their first kiss and hanging himself from a specific tree on the day after the senior field trip. Rachel and her mother are familiar with Derrick's previous suicide attempt a year ago, shortly after his parent's divorce. He crashed his father's car and woke up in the hospital, angry that he had survived. Rachel's mother shared the suicide note with the school counselor, Ms. Gray.

Incident

Ms. Gray became familiar with Derrick's situation when his parents divorced. The principal has documentation that Derrick's father is the custodial parent and handles all matters related to his education. Ms. Gray spoke with Derrick privately in her office, explained how she learned about the suicide note, and began a preliminary suicide risk assessment. Derrick confirmed his suicidal intent, presented with several risk factors and warning signs, and explained how hopeless he has felt since his parent's divorce. He reported feeling guilty for not living with his mother, even though her alcohol dependence contributed to her losing primary or joint custody. He wants to do the right thing according to his father's expectations. He believes that he is a burden to his father and feels trapped in his perception of being disloyal to his mother.

At the start of their session, Ms. Gray provided informed consent information about the potential need for her to contact his parents if she learned that Derrick may be a danger to himself. On confirming his suicidal thoughts and a plan, method, and timetable, Derrick knew that Ms. Gray would have to call his parents and begged Ms. Gray not to call his father. He requested that, if she must call, she call his mother, who has now been sober for about 11 months.

Ms. Gray decided to consult with her counseling supervisor about whom to notify regarding Derrick's level of suicide risk. Her supervisor checked with the administrative office about the legal custody situation. Additionally, Ms. Gray called the ethical and legal helpline of her professional association, as well as the National Suicide Prevention Lifeline as a concerned third party. All three consultants responded to Ms. Gray's questions with three different recommendations.

Discussion

This incident invites respondents to consider the school counselor's dilemma related to the duty to warn and duty to protect, privileged communication, confidentiality, a minor's consent and preference, therapeutic alliance, divorced parents and custody tensions, legal accountability to the appropriate parent, safety planning, the client's fitness to "direct" the counseling practices while having thoughts of suicide, etc.

Questions

1. How should Ms. Gray serve the needs of the stakeholders: Derrick, his father, his mother, the legal custody arrangement, the school system, and standards and best practices related to suicide prevention?
2. What are the advantages and disadvantages of contacting only one parent and, similarly, the advantages and disadvantages of contacting both parents?

3. Should Ms. Gray consider notifying one parent, or should she notify both parents at the expense of his request and trust?
4. Whom should Ms. Gray contact (Derrick's mother and/or father) and why?

Response 1

Christy W. Land

Professional school counselors are in a unique position, because their primary obligation is to the students; however, school counselors must simultaneously consider parental rights and school district's protocol. Derrick has expressed in writing and verbally to the school counselor that he has a plan to kill himself. In this instance, the school counselor has a duty to protect Derrick, because she is legally required to break confidentiality when students state that they plan to kill themselves. Since Derrick is a minor, one or both parents must be notified. The given information indicates that Derrick's father is the custodial parent (designating where the minor child resides) but does not indicate legal custody; additionally, Derrick spends time at his mother's house. Therefore, the school counselor should inform both Derrick's mother and father to ascertain that both of his caregivers have been informed of his potential risk of suicide. The school counselor, as a school employee, must also carefully follow the school district's protocol based on Derrick's level of suicidal risk. The school counselor should have a copy of the suicidal protocol readily available for use. Last, the school counselor, in alignment with the standards and best practices related to suicide prevention (National Suicide Prevention Lifeline, n.d.), should focus on decreasing Derrick's rick factors while increasing his protective factors.

There are advantages and disadvantages of contacting only one parent as well as of informing both parents of Derrick's suicidal ideation. The advantage of contacting only one parent is that the school counselor has warned a parent of Derrick's intent to harm himself and, therefore, fulfilled her legal duty to warn. However, the disadvantage is that the school counselor cannot ensure that open communication will occur between the two parents. Given that Derrick does spend time at both his mother's home and his father's home, it is imperative that both parents be made aware of his potential risk to himself. Although the immediate safety of Derrick is the priority, a disadvantage of contacting both parents would be damaging the therapeutic alliance between Ms. Gray and Derrick. Furthermore, by contacting both parents initially, the school counselor is setting the stage for a collaborative approach to help Derrick remain safe and get the support that he needs. However, given the tumultuous divorce situation according to Derrick, a disadvantage may be the parents' ability to successfully support Derrick as a cohesive unit.

If Ms. Gray chose to notify only one parent, she would not be proceeding with Derrick's best interest in mind yet legally covering the minimum standards. To ensure Derrick's safety, treatment, and recovery, it is imperative that both parents are notified of his potential risk. To protect the therapeutic alliance and work to keep Derrick's trust, Ms. Gray should inform Derrick that she feels it is in his best interest to make both his mother and father aware of the situation.

For the aforementioned reasons, I would contact both parents and inform them of Derrick's suicidal intentions and risk. As an advocate for students, while following district protocol, I would suggest that Derrick be taken for an immediate evaluation by a mental health or medical professional. I would follow up with Derrick's parents to hear the evaluation outcome and collaborate on a plan of action to assist with Derrick's recovery from a holistic (i.e., home, school, and community) perspective.

Often, situations in a school setting bring a myriad of complexities related to legal and ethical issues. Therefore, school counselors when in doubt must consult with appropriate colleagues within their school buildings, districts, communities, and professional associations/organizations with the best interest of the student as a priority (Chen-Heyes et al., 2014). Furthermore, the school counselor should document specifically what occurred in each consultation to include the recommendations offered; this is especially important in any incident involving potential harm to self or others. In this case, Ms. Gray consulted and received three different recommendations, all of which should be documented. In the event that a school counselor does not feel that he or she received clear direction from consulting with various stakeholders, the school counselor should seek additional guidance.

Given that there was a previous interaction between Derrick's father and the school office personnel, the school counselor and administration should have carefully reviewed the legal documents the school had on file. The documentation should include specifics as to the communication allowed with mother and father beyond school and educational decisions. For example, who makes decisions related to medical or religious concerns? This proactive approach could have alleviated some of the ethical and legal challenges that Ms. Gray experienced in relation to the incident.

Ms. Gray also needs to consider Derrick's previous statement regarding being angry that he had survived after he crashed his father's car. It would be important for Ms. Gray to discuss the information with Derrick's parents to ascertain whether they too saw the car crash as a suicide attempt. Furthermore, Ms. Gray may also want to obtain information on services that Derrick did or did not receive after the previous suicide attempt.

Ms. Gray needs to obtain a signed release of information from the appropriate authorizing parent so she can communicate with the outside agencies and providers that may offer treatment to Derrick. Once Derrick is no longer considered a risk to self, it will be important to address his underlying issues related to the relationship with his father and the guilt that he feels toward his mother for him to heal. Ms. Gray should share this information with the outside providers so that a counselor can assist from a family systems theoretical framework.

Response 2
Carolyn Stone

School counselors at every level know the unfortunate reality of student suicide. Must we breach confidentiality when placed on notice that a suicide is possible, and if so, to whom? School counselors are acutely aware and protective of the potential damage to the trusting relationship if they breach confidences. The dilemma of protecting students' willingness to confide in the school counselor and the need to respect parents' rights to guide their child's life is a constant struggle. There are many variables in a child's life that affect school counselors' decisions, and custody issues can complicate our confidentiality. This case involves a possible suicide, so our standard of care is straightforward. In order to meet our legal and ethical obligations toward Derrick, his parents/guardians, and the school district, a parent (or both parents) must be called. Let us examine this from a legal and ethical perspective.

Negligence involves injury or damage to another through a breach of duty owed to that person. Duty owed is a legal responsibility that one person has to another, such as operating your vehicle so as not to injure another person (Alexander & Alexander, 2011). Negligence requires the presence of four elements: (1) a duty is owed; (2) the duty owed was breached; (3) there is a causal connection between breach of duty and injury; and (4) an injury has occurred. For the first time, the *Eisel v. Board of Education of Montgomery County* (1991) court case strengthened school counselors' legal obligation to students by stating that counselors have a duty to try to prevent a student's suicide.

The Maryland Court of Appeals in the *Eisel* case ruled that school counselors had a duty to notify the parents of a 13-year-old student who made suicidal statements to her classmates. Nicole vehemently denied to her school counselors the rumors that she was suicidal, and they did not notify either the parents or the school administrators about these events. Shortly thereafter, Nicole and her friend tragically consummated their murder/suicide pact.

The *Eisel* case hinged largely on the *in loco parentis* doctrine, meaning that educators are legally standing in for parents primarily for safety needs while students are in their care. *In loco parentis* is a hot fire under a school counselor's feet, as school counselors are the primary keepers of the emotional needs of students in schools. When a school counselor is placed on notice that a suicide is possible, this triggers a duty to exercise care to protect the student from harm. The *Eisel* court recognized that school counselors have the complicated task of trying to determine which threats are real, yet the court stated that, "The consequence of the risk is so great that even a relatively remote possibility of a suicide may be enough to establish duty" (*Eisel v. Board of Education of Montgomery County*, 1991, n.p.). In other words, the court implores us to involve parents, as it is too risky to try to determine low risk, moderate risk, or high risk. The *Eisel* case did not deliver the final word, as courts in at least five states have rejected, for school counselors, the concept of duty owed to prevent suicide; however, school counselors continue to be the subject of court cases, many of which could have been avoided if the counselor had notified school authorities and parents that a student is at risk, with recommendations for actions.

Each case involving a suicidal threat should generate the affirmative duty to call parent(s). It was only a year ago that Derrick attempted suicide in a very lethal way, resulting in hospitalization. Risk assessments are controversial practices in school settings. How would we determine from an assessment in the school that Derrick is at low, moderate, or high risk for suicide? From all indicators, he is at high risk: through his own admission and his past attempts, as well as the fact that he is in the gender and age group that chooses the most lethal methods and is the most successful in suicide (Centers for Disease Control and Prevention, 2010). Nicole Eisel, days away from dying, was placed in a no-risk category. School counselors cannot afford to rely on suicide assessments while attending to a caseload of hundreds. School counselors who rely on suicide assessments for definitive answers are risking danger for themselves and their students. Using a suicide assessment to negate the possibility of a suicide is faulty practice at best and dangerous at worst. If used at all, a suicide assessment should be a tool to underscore to parents/guardians the urgency of the need to monitor their children and get them professional help. The school counselor's role is to help parents/guardians find available resources to help suicidal students.

A middle school counselor met with a student who said he wanted to blow his brains out. She determined that he was not at risk and told the parents that she determined he was fine and that they did not have to seek counseling, pick him up from school, or seek an evaluation. Following the student's suicide, the parents argued in court that, by making the determination that their child was fine, the counselor took over custody and control of their child's well-being (*Mikell v. School Administrative Unit No. 33*, 2009). School counselors cannot possibly know whether a child is bent on suicide and should take threats seriously and supply parents/guardians with counseling referrals until placement is secured for that student (Capuzzi, 2002; Stone, 2013a, 2013b).

This school counselor is not expected to do the impossible and prevent Derrick's suicide should he be intent on taking his life. Rather, the court's message is that the consequence of not involving Derrick's parents is just too great a risk. Both of Derrick's parents must be given the chance to intervene on his behalf. Derrick lives with his father and spends only 4 to 6 days per month with his mother. Even though he does not want his father to be notified, the school counselor cannot comply with this request. This life-and-death information cannot be kept from Derrick's father, who has custody day in and day out. His mother should also be notified, as her parental rights have not been severed in a court order. Yes, the father has custodial rights for Derrick's education, but this in no way severs his mother right to support Derrick's emotional and physical well-being.

Parents/guardians have rarely succeeded in establishing liability for student suicide, and none of the known decisions have resulted in an educator being held responsible. There may be unpublished cases or settlements, but precedents to date should reduce any undue fear of school counselor liability. This case is not about a counselor's legal liability as much as it is about being aware of the legal reasoning behind the court decisions and the ethical imperatives that should guide school counselors' behavior in life-saving decisions. A breach of confidentiality pales in comparison to death of a child. Err on the side of caution. Call parents, and when there is a conflict as to who should be called, contact both parents.

Supplemental Readings, Online Resources, and Supplemental Activities

Supplemental Readings

Bodenhorn, N. (2006). Exploratory study of common and challenging ethical dilemmas experienced by professional school counselors. *Professional School Counseling, 10*(2), 195–202.

Capuzzi, D. (2002). Legal and ethical challenges in counseling suicidal students. *Professional School Counseling, 6*(1), 36–46.

Centers for Disease Control and Prevention. (2015). *Suicide: Facts at a glance.* http://www.cdc.gov/violenceprevention/pdf/Suicide-DataSheet-a.pdf

Centers for Disease Control and Prevention, National Center for Injury Prevention and Control. (2014). *Suicide prevention: Youth suicide.* https://www.cdc.gov/healthcommunication/toolstemplates/entertainmented/tips/SuicideYouth.html

Centers for Disease Control and Prevention, National Center for Injury Prevention and Control, Division of Violence Prevention. (2014). *National suicide statistics.* Available at http://www.cdc.gov/Violenceprevention/suicide/statistics/index.html

Gibbons, M., & Studer, J. (2008). Suicide awareness training for faculty and staff: A training model for school counselors and teachers. *Professional School Counseling, 11*(4), 272–276.

King, K. A., Strunk, C. M., & Sorter, M. T. (2011). Preliminary effectiveness of Surviving the Teens® suicide prevention and depression awareness program on adolescents' suicidality and self-efficacy in performing help-seeking behaviors. *Journal of School Health, 81*(9), 581–590.

Lowry, R., Crosby, A. E., Brener, N. D., Kann, L. (2014). Suicidal thoughts and attempts among U.S. high school students: Trends and associated health-risk behaviors, 1991–2011. *Journal of Adolescent Health, 54*(1), 100–108. doi:10.1016/j.jadohealth.2013.07.024

Solnick, S. J., & Hemenway, D. (2014). Soft drinks, aggression, and suicidal behaviour in US high school students. *International Journal of Injury Control & Safety Promotion, 21*(3), 266–273. doi:10.1080/17457300.2013.815631

Strunk, C. M., Sorter, M. T., Ossege, J., King, K. A. (2014). Emotionally troubled teens' help-seeking behaviors: An evaluation of Surviving the Teens® suicide prevention and depression awareness program. *Journal of School Nursing, 30*(5), 366–375. doi:10.1177/1059840513511494

Winsler, A., Deutsch, A., Vorona, R., Payne, P., & Szklo-Coxe, M. (2015). Sleepless in Fairfax: The difference one more hour of sleep can make for teen hopelessness, suicidal ideation, and substance use. *Journal of Youth and Adolescence, 44,* 362–378. doi:10.1007/s10964-014-0170-3

Young, R., Sproeber, N., Groschwitz, R. C., Preiss, M., & Plener, P. L. (2014). Why alternative teenagers self-harm: Exploring the link between non-suicidal self-injury, attempted suicide and adolescent identity. *BMC Psychiatry, 14*(1), 137. doi:10.1186/1471-244X-14-137

Online Resources

American Foundation for Suicide Prevention
   www.afsp.org

Ask for Help Campaign
   www.trvr.org/askforhelp

Centers for Disease Control and Prevention (CDC)
   www.cdc.gov

> The CDC is one of the major operating components of the U.S. Department of Health and Human Services. CDC works 24/7 to protect America from health, safety and security threats, both foreign and in the United States. Whether diseases start at home or abroad, are chronic or acute, curable or preventable, human error or deliberate attack, the CDC fights disease and supports communities and citizens to do the same. The CDC increases the health security of our nation. As the nation's health protection agency, the CDC saves lives and protects people from health threats.

Cry for Help: Teenage Mental Illness and Suicide
   http://www.pbs.org/wnet/cryforhelp/episodes/resources/hotlines-and-web-sites-for-teens/11/

> Cry for Help takes an intimate look at the efforts of two high schools to identify adolescents at risk. Hamilton High School in Ohio and Clarkstown North High School in New York have both been affected by teen suicide and have launched powerful new programs to prevent future tragedies. Cry for Help also examines the often difficult transition from high school to college through a first-person account of a young woman who has battled mental illness. Cry for Help gives out a variety of resources and information for teens battling depression and/or suicidal thoughts. It provides videos, documentaries, and much more about real-life situations of teens battling depression/suicidal thoughts.

Erika's Lighthouse
   http://erikaslighthouse.org/

> Erika's Lighthouse is a not-for-profit teen depression and mental health education organization that provides free and effective programming to schools, teens, parents, young adults, health professionals, and community

organizations. The Erika's Lighthouse philosophy is that, for our programs to be successful, we must be flexible. We provide the guidance, materials, and support required to implement depression and mental health education programs that respect a community's culture.

Kids Helpline
http://www.kidshelp.com.au/teens/get-help/who-else-can-help/helpful-links/depression-mental-health.php

You'll talk directly with a counselor when you call Kids Helpline. Each time you call: You will hear a recorded message that tells you about how Kids Helpline works. After listening to this message, you will be connected with a counselor. When Kids Helpline gets really busy, we may need to put you on hold until a counselor is available. The counselor you speak to will tell you his or her name, so if you call again, you can ask to speak to the same person. Your counselor will ask you what you would like to talk about and ask you some questions to help understand what's going on for you. Our counselors can help find the right service for you.

Mayo Clinic
https://www.mayoclinic.org/diseases-conditions/teen-depression/symptoms-causes/syc-20350985

Mayo Clinic is a nonprofit worldwide leader in medical care, research, and education for people from all walks of life. Their mission is to inspire hope and contribute to health and well-being by providing the best care to every patient through integrated clinical practice, education, and research. Mayo Clinic provides information regarding symptoms surrounding teen depression and how to learn coping skills and receive support.

Model School District Policy for Suicide Prevention
www.trvr.org/modelpolicy

QPR Institute
http://www.qprinstitute.com/

Resource phone numbers: 1-800-273-TALK; 1-800-SUICIDE (784-2433)

Suicide.org suicide prevention, awareness, and support
http://www.suicide.org/teen-suicide-and-youth-suicide.html

Suicide.org has launched a closed, private, and highly confidential online support forum exclusively for suicide survivors (people who have lost loved ones to suicide). Suicide.org has an emergency hotline for teens who are depressed and/or having suicidal thoughts. Suicide.org has information regarding a variety of issues surrounding suicide risks and data.

This website has forums for support groups, poems written by those who have suffered from depression, stories, and much more.

Teen Line
https://teenlineonline.org/

Do you need help working something out? Do you want to talk to someone who understands, like another teen? We're here to help! You can call, text, or email and speak to a trained teen or adult who will provide help and support with the problems you are going through.

Supplemental Activities
Learning Activities

The American School Counselor Association's (ASCA's) Ethical Standards for School Counselors (2016) include a nine-step process for ethical decision making from the Solutions to Ethical Problems in Schools (STEPS; Stone, 2001, available at https://nhsca.wildapricot.org/resources/Documents/Steps%20rev.pdf):

- Define the problem emotionally and intellectually.
- Apply the ASCA Ethical Standards for School Counselors and, the *ACA Code of Ethics,* and the law.
- Consider the students' chronological and developmental levels.
- Consider the setting, parental rights, and minors' rights.
- Apply the ethical principles of beneficence, autonomy, nonmaleficence, loyalty, and justice.
- Determine potential courses of action and their consequences.
- Evaluate the selected course of action.
- Consult.
- Implement the course of action.

Chapter 9

What Do I Do When My Supervisor Lacks Supervision?

Claire Merlin-Knoblich

This critical incident is about supervision, an intervention in which a superior member of the counseling profession provides guidance to a more junior member of the counseling profession. In school counseling, supervision often occurs between school counseling interns, or supervisees, and their school counseling site supervisors.

Background

I am in my second year as a professional school counselor at an urban middle school that serves approximately 1,200 students. This is my first school counseling position, and I work along with two other school counselors who have many years of experience. One of those school counselors is our department chair and makes all major decisions for the department, though he often consults with the rest of us. This year, we have been assigned a school counseling intern from a nearby university. Previously, there was a lack of interest in hosting an intern. This is the first school counseling intern at our school in 15 years.

Incident

Kevin, the school counseling intern, is enthusiastic and eager to learn. However, he is just beginning to learn about building relationships with students, refining counseling skills, and understanding how a school counseling department operates. Kevin is assigned to work with Jenny, one of the school counselors in our department. Jenny has approximately 10 years of experience. She has never been a clinical supervisor but is happy to supervise the intern, particularly because the department chair is too busy to serve as his supervisor.

Kevin's internship is scheduled to last the entire school year. His master's program is not yet accredited by the Council for Accreditation of Counseling & Related Educational Programs (CACREP), and Kevin's faculty supervisor has little contact with our school. The university requires Jenny to complete a final evaluation of Kevin at the end of his internship. There are no additional specified requirements for Kevin to fulfill throughout his internship. Despite this, Kevin frequently seeks opportunities to learn and practice his counseling skills. He has asked each of us for student referrals. Last, he helps organize department projects, such as the career fair, and leads several small counseling groups.

Although Jenny appreciates Kevin's extra help in the department, she often becomes frustrated with him. She is annoyed when he arrives late (which has happened several mornings in a row), and she is concerned about him growing too close to students, beyond a professional manner. Jenny and Kevin see each other most days, but they never engage in formal supervision sessions, and Kevin mostly reaches out for help when he is in a crisis situation. He will often seek out my guidance on students' needs.

With 1 month left in his internship, Jenny meets with Kevin and informs him that his internship is over. When Kevin asks why this is the case, Jenny gives Kevin his final evaluation, including concerns she has had over the course of the academic year. The list includes a lack of responsibility, professionalism, and appropriate counseling behaviors.

Kevin is feeling devastated and approaches me for guidance. He does not understand why he was not provided feedback throughout the academic year. He is concerned that because his internship is being cut short, this does not provide sufficient time to terminate with his students.

Discussion

When Kevin meets with me, I try to console him and provide supportive listening. However, I am unsure how to help him or even future interns at our school. I am bothered that Jenny did not provide appropriate formative feedback throughout the year, and I find it unprofessional that she is not allowing him to terminate with students. On the other hand, I do not want to speak poorly to an intern about another school counselor.

Questions

1. How can I support Kevin and his professional development without betraying Jenny?
2. Should I be concerned about Jenny's opinion of me? Should I be concerned about the welfare of Kevin, even if he is not my supervisee?

3. How should I involve the third counselor, our department chair, in this situation, if at all? I would like for him to be aware of what Jenny has done and how Kevin feels, but I wonder how I would be perceived if I did so.
4. What kind of policies could our school implement regarding future supervisees to prevent a situation like this from happening again?
5. Is it unethical if my colleagues refuse to accept another intern in future years? I think that giving back to the profession in this way is an obligation, but they disagree.

Response 1

Sarah I. Springer and Christine Hennigan Paone

There is an ongoing dialogue concerning school counselors' preparedness for supervisory responsibilities (e.g., Dollarhide & Miller, 2006; Studer, 2005; Wood & Rayle, 2006). Practicing school counselors do not often receive adequate clinical supervision (e.g., Borders & Usher, 1992; Dollarhide & Miller, 2006). Among other consequences, this has led some school counselors to undervalue supervision in professional practice. Because many school counselors assume the role of site supervisor for practicum and internship students, it is especially important to address these attitudes towards supervision (Herlihy, Gray, & McCollum, 2002).

Counselors and counselors-in-training must adhere to the American Counseling Association (ACA) *Code of Ethics* (2014). Likewise, the American School Counselor Association (ASCA, 2016) has defined similar ethical standards that are specific to the practice of school counselors and supervisors. These sets of ethical standards are expected to inform both clinical decision-making and training practices. Subsequently, both documents outline ethical practices surrounding the development and supervision of preservice counselors. The following discussion examines the decision-making and ethical implications associated with the case: When the Supervisor Needs Supervising.

Various ethical considerations deserve attention in the case at hand. According to both the *ACA Code of Ethics* (2014) and the ASCA Ethical Standards for School Counselors (2016), when possible, school counselors should directly approach colleagues with any concerns regarding their practice (ACA, 2014, Standard D.1.d.; ASCA, 2016, Standard E.b.). Speaking to Jenny becomes a colleague's ethical responsibility if certain behaviors are in question. At this point, the incident author has determined a number of areas worth discussing with Jenny.

As referenced in ASCA's ethical standards (2016), site supervisors should be aware of supervisees' limitations and, in turn, aid them in finding appropriate forms of remediation (Standards D.l. and D.m.). Kevin's account of his experience suggested that he was not apprised of his shortcomings until he was terminated. This lack of communication could have had numerous consequences. First, Jenny's failure to correct and redirect Kevin's approach may have endangered students, particularly if boundaries were an issue. Second, she may have done Kevin a disservice by not guiding him toward best practices. As his supervisor, she was implicitly tasked with furthering his development as an emerging professional (Association for Counselor Education and Supervision [ACES], 2011). Finally, Jenny may have put her own career and credibility in jeopardy, since she was ultimately responsible for Kevin's services (ACA, 2014, Standard F.1.a). Seeing that the supervision of Kevin involves many stakeholders, the incident author has an ethical responsibility to approach Jenny about intervening and facilitating remediation for supervisees.

The *ACA Code of Ethics* (2014) states that supervisors must document consultation efforts in decisions that lead to dismissal or referral of supervisees (Standard F.6.b.). Furthermore, the supervisor must provide adequate notice and appropriate referrals to alternative supervisors (Standard F.4.d.). This is particularly important in this situation, as Kevin had not completed his internship hours, and an alternative supervisor was not identified. Approaching these specific concerns with Jenny as an offering of collegial support may be a beneficial step toward maintaining a positive and professional relationship.

It may be helpful to have Jenny review the *ACA Code of Ethics* (2014). This may help Jenny understand her role in which site supervisory practices should be consistently monitored through a collaborative partnership between the university and onsite supervisor (Standard F.7.g.). Kevin's status as a university student and site supervisee should, therefore, fall under the responsibility of both his university graduate program and his site supervisor. According to ASCA's ethical standards (2016), the supervisor, together with building administrators, must communicate concerns directly with the university/college supervisors (Standard D.n.) in the event that the supervisee does not demonstrate school counselor competence. Assisting Jenny and Kevin in connecting with the university supervisor may be another avenue through which the incident author can support this situation.

Both Jenny's and Kevin's openness to this dialogue may influence how and when the incident author involves the department chair. As noted previously, Kevin's development affects the welfare of his students; ultimately, this becomes the responsibility of the entire counseling department. Just as Jenny is required as a site supervisor to meet regularly with Kevin and review his cases (ACA, 2014, Standard F.6.a; ASCA 2016, Standard D.c.), so too should the counseling department chair ascertain whether his or her team members are fulfilling the duties of supervision. Arguably, the incident author has an ethical responsibility to broach these topics with the department chair on behalf of Kevin and his students, either independently or together with Jenny. By speaking with the chair, the incident author would promote the monitoring of client welfare and supervisee performance, a guideline promoted by the *ACA Code of Ethics* (2014, Standard F.1.a).

The incident author can use this situation as an opportunity to recommend policies for future supervisees. She may propose that intern placement be a departmental decision rather than an assignment by the district support staff. Although giving back to the profession is an important responsibility, hosting an intern requires relevant supervisory training (ACES, 2011).

Supervisors should have a theoretical grounding for their work as well as training in methods, techniques, and supervision models (ACA, 2014, Standard F.2.a). This includes orienting supervisees toward professional and ethical standards through supervision disclosure statements and ongoing formative feedback. Had this structure been in place when Jenny began supervising Kevin, the supervisory experience may have looked very different. Supervision training for all department members is an essential recommendation before any additional intern is accepted. Additionally, ASCA (2016) indicates that site supervisors should engage in continuing education related to supervision (Standard D.b.). In a sense, school counselor administrators share in this responsibility, as they are tasked with ensuring the availability of relevant training resources and professional development opportunities (ASCA, 2016, Standards D.b. and C.c.). Without support for these resources, Jenny and others in the department may not be adequately or ethically prepared to supervise future students.

This case clearly involves many ethical considerations. School counseling supervisors must adhere to both the *ACA Code of Ethics* (2014) and the ASCA Ethical Standards for School Counselors (2016) when making decisions that affect supervisees and their respective clients. As suggested, the training of supervisees does not exclusively fall on the site supervisor; rather, supervisee and client welfare are the responsibility of the many stakeholders involved with the development of preservice students. Collaboration, consultation, and clear communication between university programs, supervisors, and, at times, other department and school staff are all necessary to ensure that school counseling trainees are prepared to enter the workforce with the appropriate knowledge, skills, and demeanor to be productive school counselors.

Response 2

Melinda M. Gibbons

Supervision is a critical component of the school counseling training process. During supervision, counseling students learn about school counselor roles and can process the many activities they experience as interns. Effective supervision involves open discussion, positive interpersonal qualities, consistent and constructive feedback, and engagement from both the supervisor and supervisee (Ladany, Mori, & Mehr, 2013). Ladany et al. (2013) included signs of ineffective supervision, including poor interpersonal qualities, insufficient feedback, emphasis on evaluation, and lack of supervisor involvement. This case demonstrates several signs of ineffective, and possibly harmful, supervision.

My initial reaction to the case includes a need to review both ethical and developmental considerations. Developmentally, Kevin is at Level 1, according to the Integrated Developmental Model of Supervision (Stoltenberg & McNeil, 1997). Level 1 supervisees are at the beginning of their counseling career; they have limited exposure to counseling, are typically anxious and reliant on others for guidance, have high motivation to succeed, and demonstrate a strong dependency on their supervisors. These supervisees need structure, positive and constructive feedback, and minimal confrontation. On the basis of the incident description, it appears that Kevin's developmental level was not accounted for during his internship. He was primarily left on his own with limited structure, he did not receive ongoing supervision, and his negative behaviors were not remediated in an empathetic and gentle manner.

I noticed several potential ethical issues in the case. By taking on the role of site supervisor, Jenny agreed to abide by ethical standards. ACES's Best Practices in Clinical Supervision (ACES, 2011) suggests that supervisors provide due process rights, work to minimize power issues in the supervisory relationship, and provide ongoing assessment and evaluation. Kevin was not provided ongoing evaluation of his work as an intern, so he may not have known about Jenny's negative views about his work behaviors. Because Kevin received a negative final evaluation and was immediately dismissed from the site, he did not have the opportunity to improve or alter his performance; thus, this action prevented his due process rights (Bernard & Goodyear, 1998). Jenny used her position of power to dramatically affect Kevin's future career path, suggesting a strong and negative power differential in their supervisory relationship. Ideally, policies and procedures would be created and implemented by the university, but supervisors must attend to these issues, regardless of whether they are required by the university making the placement. Therefore, Kevin has the right to have time to address Jenny's concerns about his performance and then to be re-evaluated.

The incident author's role in this situation is a tenuous one. Jenny is Kevin's site supervisor, and there is additionally a department chair. My initial thought is to request a school counseling departmental meeting between Jenny, the department chair, and the incident author, without Kevin present. The meeting goal could be to discuss the situation and concerns. Perhaps Jenny is not aware of how to be a site supervisor, or perhaps she has voiced her issues to Kevin before his receiving the negative final evaluation. It is important to discuss this with colleagues before jumping to any conclusions. During this meeting, the three of you might also discuss the repercussions of having Kevin leave before the semester's end: What about his student–clients, his ongoing projects, and the school's relationship with the local university?

As to whether the school should accept future interns, I believe it is unethical to host interns without following supervision best practices. It is better to decline an intern than to engage in questionable ethical practices. I agree that giving back to the school counseling profession is important, but demonstrating a positive and healthy work environment for interns is also important. If your school were to host future school counseling interns, it would be essential to create policies on addressing these best practices before the intern begins work. For example, the counseling office might create an informed consent document that includes: the name and contact information of the supervisor, supervision strategies, evaluation strategies, the time and place where supervision will be conducted, responsibilities of supervisor, responsibilities of supervisee, and due process information. This document could serve as a contractual agreement between the intern and the site.

Supplemental Readings, Online Resources, and Supplemental Activities

Supplemental Readings

American Counseling Association. (2014) *ACA code of ethics*. Retrieved from: http://www.counseling.org/resources/aca-code-of-ethics.pdf

American School Counselor Association. (2016). *Ethical standards for school counselors*. Retrieved from: https://www.schoolcounselor.org/asca/media/asca/Ethics/EthicalStandards2016.pdf

Association for Counselor Education and Supervision. (2011). *Best practices in clinical supervision*. Retrieved from: http://www.acesonline.net/wp-content/uploads/2011/10/ACES-Best-Practices-in-clinical-supervision-document-FINAL.pdf

Bernard, J. M., & Goodyear, R. K. (2019). *Fundamentals of clinical supervision* (6th ed.). Upper Saddle River, NJ: Pearson.

Council for Accreditation of Counseling & Related Educational Programs. (2015). *CACREP 2016 standards*. Alexandria, VA: Author. Retrieved from www.cacrep.org/wp-content/uploads/2012/10/2016-CACREP-Standards.pdf

Caldwell, M. (2012). *Six steps to intern supervision*. Retrieved from http://soe.unc.edu/academics/med_sch_counseling/docs/asca_supervision_article.pdf

Campbell, J. M. (2006). *Essentials of clinical supervision*. Hoboken, NJ: Wiley.

Counseling Today: A Publication of the American Counseling Association. Retrieved from http://ct.counseling.org/

DeKruyf, L., & Pehrsson, D. (2011). School counseling site supervisor training: An exploratory study. *Counselor Education & Supervision, 50*, 314–327.

Luke, M., & Bernard, J. M. (2006). The school counseling supervision model: An extension of the discrimination model. *Counselor Education and Supervision, 45*, 282– 295.

Murphy, S., & Kaffenberger, C. (2007). ASCA National Model: The foundation for supervision of practicum and internship students. *Professional School Counseling, 10,* 289–296.

Springer, S. (2013). Confidentiality with children. In D. Heller Levitt & H. J. Hartwig Moorhead (Eds.), *Values and ethics in counseling: Real-life ethical decision-making* (pp. 77–84). New York, NY: Routledge.

Springer, S. I. (2016). When values blur the lines: Navigating an ethical dilemma in school counseling. *The Journal of Counselor Preparation and Supervision, 8*(2), Article 5. doi:10.7729/82.1082

Swank, J. M., & Tyson, L. (2012). School counseling site supervisor training: A web-based approach. *Professional School Counseling, 16*(1), 40–48.

Wood, C., & Rayle, A. D. (2006). A model of school counseling supervision: The goals, functions, roles, and systems model. *Counselor Education and Supervision, 45,* 253–266. doi:10.1002/j.1556-6978.2006.tb00002.x

Online Resources

Association for Counselor Education and Supervision (ACES)
http://www.acesonline.net/

American School Counselor Association (ASCA)
http://www.schoolcounselor.org/

The Professional Counselor Journal
http://tpcjournal.nbcc.org/

Supplemental Activities

Further Questions for Reflection and Discussion

- What is your internal reaction to Kevin's situation? How might you address your feelings and thoughts before moving forward in this situation? Think about your own experience as an intern. What was most and least helpful for your development as a school counselor?

- How might this scenario have been different if the university were CACREP accredited? What might supervision training look like for practicing school counseling site supervisors? How might you collaborate with Kevin's university supervisor to support the duration of his training?

- If Jenny were to have responded in a dismissive manner, how might you approach your next steps? If the department chair were to have responded in a dismissive manner, what might be your next ethical steps?

- In Class Role-Play: Practice role-playing discussions with Jenny and the department chair regarding your concerns.

- Presentation Activity: Write a proposal/devise a presentation to the board of education of district "x" proposing supervision training for all practicing school counselors in district. Provide a rationale for supervision training, relevant professional development opportunities for such training, and benefits to the school district.

Chapter 10

We're Counseling as Fast as We Can! Trapped in the Cracks of the System

Kenya Bledsoe

I am fortunate to work in a high school that is ranked by *U.S. News and World Report* as a "Best High School." Our school has approximately 1,000 students and is diverse in socioeconomic status, ethnicity, and religion. We have students enrolled from all over the world. Fortunately, we are staffed with a strong administrative team and teachers, and we have grade-level school counselors, one of which is a college counselor, and a system-level social worker. Each school counselor services approximately 250–275 students and has additional responsibilities, including master scheduling, director, peer helper sponsor, building test coordinator, and other roles as assigned.

Background

Each year, our department identifies goals that will enhance our program in an effort to implement a successful comprehensive school counseling program. These goals include identifying and addressing the needs of students in our school. One year, the school counseling department decided to submit to the state school counselor association award, Recognition, Accountability, Verification, and Excellence (RAVE). In an attempt to support our efforts, two of our counselors attended the RAVE training at the annual state conference, along with a summer training sponsored by a neighboring school district. Coincidentally, our local school decided to require group versus individual professional plans, so working on a RAVE submission appeared to be a natural fit for the school counseling department.

Early on, our group professional plan strategy meetings were centered around the RAVE document: re-reading submission criteria, reviewing sample RAVE documents presented by other schools, and identifying sources of data that were collected or needed to be collected to support our RAVE document. We brainstormed sources of data that were already being collected by our high school and/or district including: school climate data, annual yearly progress data (reading/language/math intervention), discipline referrals, attendance, American College Testing (ACT) data, and Preliminary Scholastic Aptitude Test (PSAT) data. Quarterly meetings were scheduled in an effort to assign tasks, provide updates on previously assigned tasks, data collection, etc. Additionally, scheduled meeting times were created to update our RAVE document and continue discussions among group members.

Incident

In April, our RAVE document was completed and submitted to the administration for review. By submitting our document, we satisfied our school/district group professional development requirements. We knew that it was not "RAVE" ready but felt that it satisfied the professional plan requirements. During the months of May and June, school counselors (depending on whether they worked a 10-month or 12-month contract) were busy mailing home report cards, failure letters, and summer school and ineligibility letters. At that time, school counselors filtered calls about online credit recovery options and options outside of our school. The 10-month counselors were scheduled to leave; summer school had started, and school counselors began the master schedule.

By mid-July, all of the counselors were back on campus and working. The 10-month counselors, along with the 12-month counselors, were busy enrolling new students, verifying summer school credits, and reviewing student schedules for each student in their grade level. Additionally, counselors were consumed with registration, back-to-school meetings/trainings, filtering teacher questions, student enrollments, and additional duties. The deadline for submitting our RAVE document was mid-August and quickly approaching. Revised RAVE requirements were sent to the lead school counselor from the state school counselor association. The lead school counselor forwarded the revisions to the department. She inquired whether the department should proceed with officially submitting to RAVE, since the bulk of the document was completed. After a few discussions, it was determined there was not enough time to identify changes, if any, related to the revised RAVE submission requirements. Additionally, we identified that our school climate data highlighted increased drug and alcohol abuse within the school.

Because our version of the RAVE document was formulated on "dated" guidelines, the school counselors needed to determine whether updates were needed for the document completed last April. The group disagreed about how to proceed. On one hand, some believed that the majority of the work had been completed and that the department should submit. On the other hand, others were not sure how much work would be required in less than a week to have it ready to submit.

Questions

1. Should counselors have "forced" the issue and taken the time to compare the incomplete RAVE document with revised standards and submitted?
2. Should the lead school counselor have made an executive decision to submit to RAVE, since the work was almost finished?
3. If counselors don't look into the data closely and use the data to enhance the current program, how do they expect changes to occur within the school?
4. Why is the RAVE submission due in late August/early September—the busiest time of the year for school counselors?
5. Why is it so difficult to pull away from the day-to-day tasks to fully commit to data review, discussions, and working toward solutions?

Response 1

Jolie Daigle

This incident is complex because of several factors, including multiple counselors being involved in the department, the RAVE process being used as both evaluation and recognition, and the importance of time management in comprehensive school counseling programs. I would disagree that the counselors would have "forced" the issue if they were to complete the RAVE document with the updated standards, because all members initially agreed upon the RAVE application. The more likely scenario seems to be that the counselors were following through with what had been decided by the group, including sending two school counselor to the RAVE training.

When working as a group, it is important to review group agreements. The group let the chaos of the school year ending and the next one beginning interfere with their program goals. After having a conversation with his or her coworkers, it would have been appropriate for the lead counselor to submit the RAVE document on behalf of the department. At times, chairs of counseling departments need to make executive decisions for the sake of the program and group members.

The RAVE reviewers would have provided both positive and constructive feedback. I would assume that details of the RAVE document would include describing the school counseling program vision and mission statement, goals, programs offered, and a sampling of interventions, assessments, and outcomes. When school counselors proactively create an assessment plan with these goals and outcomes in mind, that work indirectly provides services to students. At this level, school counselors are "examining the relations between, and expectations of, larger systems that impact the individual, such as school, family, community, and society" (Lee & Goodnough, 2007, p. 122). This examination of the subsystems also highlights the interconnectedness and interdependence of all subsystems within schools that are more likely to address policy and procedural barriers to access, achievement, and attainment. Attending to data and reporting to stakeholders are important functions of the school counseling program and necessary to keep programs relevant.

The RAVE document is most likely an assessment of the comprehensive school counseling program. However, the school counseling department used the RAVE document for evaluation purposes. Therefore, it would be appropriate for the lead counselor to submit the RAVE document on behalf of the school counseling department. As Erford (2007) discussed, assessment provides answers to program questions, involves stakeholders, and is ongoing. The assessment is not focused on evaluating the individual school counselors' performances.

The RAVE document is most likely due in early fall for a few reasons. First, the state organization will review and list finalists before the state conference or meeting. Second, the state organization allows the counseling department to meet, review previous school year data, and complete the RAVE document in the summer, before the new school year begins. It is challenging for school counselors to pull themselves away from their daily duties and set aside time to discuss school-level data, make progress on program goals, and write reports. However, school counselors must include data collection and analysis as priorities in their practices, just as they would consider working with a student in crisis. Arrangements can be made in advance regarding a master calendar, and stakeholders (e.g., school social workers, administrators, or peer leaders) can be identified who could occasionally cover in the event of a crisis. This would allow school counselors time to include ongoing data collection, evaluation, and report writing in their practices.

Hatch (2014) discussed using a counselor of the day as a time management strategy for all members of the school counseling program. This strategy would work for school counselors in large schools where one school counselor can rotate and respond to student crisis, parent visits, and immediate needs while others continue with scheduled events, guidance programming, school-level or district-level meetings, and data collection and analysis. Another strategy or program philosophy that Hatch (2014) presented is collegial talk time, which could consist of information or announcements, student reviews, program management, and school counselor concerns. The school counselors in this case study would have benefited from scheduled collegial talk time or peer supervision leading up to the end of the spring semester, at certain points during the summer, and during designated professional learning days. This scheduled time could have been spent reviewing the changes in the RAVE guidelines and working on the preparation of the RAVE document. This time seems to have been designated by the program to review data and complete reports; however, attending to the RAVE application during this time did not occur. Furthermore, the school counselors could have considered splitting up duties and giving the department chair or another counselor dedicated time to work on the document during the week before the RAVE application submission deadline.

Response 2
LaWanda Edwards

The department engaged in a discussion about whether the department should proceed with submitting to RAVE. After the discussion, it was decided that there was not enough time to identify changes related to the revised RAVE submission requirements. Although the school administration did not require the RAVE submission, the school counseling department did identify the RAVE submission as a goal for the current school year. Therefore, the school counselors should have followed through with revising and submitting the RAVE document. There is another option they did not consider: The school counselors could have decided to ask a few colleagues to review and report the revised requirements. This step would have informed the school counseling department on whether there were multiple changes required for submission before they decided not to submit the RAVE document.

The lead school counselor should not have made an executive decision to submit to RAVE since the work was almost finished. In her role as the lead school counselor, it is her responsibility to ensure that the school counselors assess the effectiveness of the school counseling program, but the department does not have to submit an application to RAVE to assess their effectiveness. According to the ASCA Ethical Standards for School Counselors (2016), professional school counselors should assess how school counseling programs affect students' academic, career, and social–emotional development. The school counselors may not have the new data requested in the state school counselor association's revised RAVE requirements, but they did complete the RAVE documents requested by the administration for review. The lead school counselor is also only one of the school counselors at the school, and she should consider the suggestions of the other school counselors when making decisions about completing tasks that are outside of the required school counselor responsibilities.

Some studies have reported that school counselors do not collect, analyze, and report data because they perceive it as unnecessary (Whiston,

1996), because they have not given it much thought (Topdemir, 2010), and because of the negative consequences if the data report unfavorable results (Lusky & Hayes, 2001; Topdemir, 2010). This may be true for this school counseling department, especially with the school counselors being concerned about the unfavorable climate data. Not only is it ethical that school counselors look at the data closely and use them to enhance the current program, but it would also help to eliminate many of the barriers that school counselors experience in schools. Administrators would see the connection between school counselor interventions and student achievement if school counselors collected data to show the impact on student achievement and make data-driven decisions.

RAVE submission is in late August/early September for a couple of reasons. First, the data collected for RAVE submission include annual yearly progress data, discipline referrals, attendance, ACT and PLAN data, and PSAT data. Most of these data are not available until the end of the school year, and some of the data are not available until the beginning of the following school year. Because the data are not available until after the end of the current school year, the school counselors are not able to collect, analyze, and report the data until the beginning of the next school year. Some school counselors are also on a 9- or 10-month contract, so they are not working during the summer. With the submission being due in late August/early September, the school counselors have enough time to analyze and report the data collected from the previous school year.

It is difficult for school counselors to pull away from the day-to-day tasks to fully commit to data review, discussions, and working toward solutions for multiple reasons. First, school counselors are asked to engage in nonguidance duties. These nonguidance duties include serving as testing coordinator, developing master schedules, serving as RTI coordinator, covering classes for teachers, data entry, and serving as an assistant principal. School counselors are also faced with high ratios of school counselors to students. ASCA recommends a 1:250 ratio, but most schools across the nation have ratios higher than this recommendation. High ratios prevent the counselor from reviewing data and developing proactive programs. School counselors are then forced to engage in responsive services. Another reason why it is difficult for school counselors to pull away from day-to-day tasks is the lack of administrative support. The lack of support comes in the form of not hiring enough school counselors, hiring individuals who are not certified school counselors, and not understanding the comprehensive guidance and counseling program requirements. When administrators are not informed about the appropriate roles and responsibilities of the school counselor, the school counselor is assigned nonguidance duties; as a result, there is limited time to conduct data reviews and discussions and to work toward proactive and preventative comprehensive school counseling program solutions.

Supplemental Readings, Online Resources, and Supplemental Activities

Supplemental Readings

American School Counselor Association. (2012). *The ASCA National Model: A framework for school counseling programs.* (3rd ed.). Alexandria, VA: Author.

Campbell, C. A., & Dahir, C. A. (1997). *Sharing the vision: The ASCA national standards for school counseling programs.* Alexandria, VA: American School Counselor Association.

Chen-Hayes, S. F., Ockerman, M. S., & Mason, E. C. M. (2014). *101 solutions for school counselors and leaders in challenging times.* Thousand Oaks, CA: Corwin Press.

Dimmitt, C., Carey, J. C., & Hatch, T. (2007). *Evidence-based school counseling.* Thousand Oaks, CA: Corwin Press.

Hartline, J., & Cobia, D. (2012). School counselors: Closing achievement gaps and writing results reports. *Professional School Counseling, 16*(1), 71–79.

Hatch, T. (2014). *The use of data in school counseling: Hatching results for students, programs, and the profession.* Thousand Oaks, CA: Corwin Press.

Kaffenberger C., & Young, A. (2013). *Making DATA work* (3rd ed.). Alexandria, VA: American School Counselor Association.

Myrick, R. D. (2003). Accountability: Counselors count. *Professional School Counseling, 6*(3), 174–179.

Sabella, R. A. (2006). The ASCA national school counseling research center: A brief history and agenda. *Professional School Counseling, 9*(5), 412–415.

Stone, C., & Dahir, C. (2011). *School counselor accountability: A measure of student success* (3rd ed). Upper Saddle River, NJ: Pearson Education.

Online Resources

American Counseling Association
www.counseling.org

American School Counselor Association
www.schoolcounselor.org

ASCA National Model
http://www.ascanationalmodel.org/

Center for Excellence in School Counseling and Leadership
http://www.cescal.org/index.cfm

EZAnalyze
http://www.ezanalyze.com/

Hatching Results
http://hatchingresults.com/

The Ronald H. Frederickson Center for School Counseling Outcome Research and Evaluation
http://www.umass.edu/schoolcounseling/past-projects.php

UMass Amherst College of Education
http://www.umass.edu/schoolcounseling/

Supplemental Activities

Learning Activities

- Do a survey of the school counselors in your local school system to see how many school counselors are assessing the effectiveness of their program in having an impact on students' academic, personal/social, and career development. Ask them what data they are collecting and analyzing to assess their effectiveness.

- Have a panel of practicing school counselors to answer questions about collecting and analyzing data, reporting results, and barriers that they experience as a school counselor.

- Go to the American School Counselor Association (ASCA) website (www. schoolcounselor.org) and look at the requirements for Recognized ASCA Model Program (RAMP). What documentation do you think would be difficult for you to collection? Why?

Chapter 11

When It Rains, It Pours! Where Do I Begin to Help?

Tiffany Stoner-Harris

This incident addresses the trauma, multicultural, and collaborative counseling needs of an African American, female high school student. The impact of childhood sexual abuse from a trauma-focused perspective, as well as from a multicultural perspective, is incorporated.

Background

Toni Miller is a 16-year-old African American girl who was referred to the school counselor, Ms. Leman-Wong, by her English teacher for achievement concerns. Toni historically has good grades, maintaining an A/B average, but she has recently missed several days of school. Toni has fallen behind in several of her classes because of the absences.

Incident

Ms. Small, the English teacher, took note of another concern of increasing isolation and lack of engagement with other students in the classroom. Ms. Small, a biracial White/African American woman in her mid-30s, approached Toni after class one day to inquire as to whether there were any concerns troubling Toni. Toni immediately started to cry but expressed that she was okay. Ms. Small encouraged Toni to speak to the school counselor. Since Toni had seen the school counselor in the past, she agreed to approach Ms. Leman-Wong. Toni expressed feeling comfortable with the school counselor and felt that she had a good relationship with Ms. Leman-Wong, a White female in her mid-50s.

Toni has a history of self-harm and identifies as a "cutter." The school counselor is aware of Toni's past and has been monitoring the behavior over the past year through weekly counseling sessions with Toni. After her teacher's suggestion, Toni arranged to meet with Ms. Leman-Wong briefly outside of their regular time. During this brief session, Toni disclosed to the school counselor that she was sexually abused by her uncle when she was between the ages of 8 and 12 years old and that she has recently been thinking about it a lot. At the time, this 21-year-old uncle lived in her noncustodial parent's (her father's) home, which she still visits on a biweekly basis. Toni reports that she has not disclosed this past abuse to her father or to her mother. She is fearful that she will not be able to visit her father anymore or that her uncle would face legal trouble. Toni discloses more about her family dynamics and the existing relationships to the school counselor. This story included pointing out that her uncle is no longer living in her father's home, and she has not seen him since she was 13 years old. However, her family is very close, and often, multiple family members will reside at one residence. Upon hearing this information, the school counselor made a referral to the local sexual assault counseling program. The sexual assault counselor agreed to come right away to the school to meet with Toni, in both a counseling and an advocate role.

The sexual assault counselor arrived in a timely manner to complete an assessment to determine whether the counseling services were appropriate for Toni. The school counselor made the appropriate introduction, with the sexual assault counselor greeting Toni from a victims' services counseling role, assuring her that the abuse was not her fault, and approaching the student from a supportive and client-centered perspective. The sexual assault counselor discussed the various services offered to victims of sexual violence through the sexual assault counseling program. The school counselor and the sexual assault counselor also assured Toni that the counseling services she would receive would be confidential. The school counselor exited the room, assuring Toni that she would still be available as needed but indicating that sexual assault counseling may be best at this time.

Toni repeated her recent disclosure of a history of sexual abuse to the sexual assault counselor. In addition, Toni explained that, although her mother and father were never married, she has always had close relationships with both of her parents and their extended family members. Toni reports consistently living in both her mother's and father's homes over the years. She is the only child between her parents but has younger half-siblings on both sides. Toni reports having very close relationships with all of her siblings. Toni is worried that disclosing the past abuse to her parents could cause significant rifts within and between her various family members because of their close-knit relationships.

Discussion

Toni presented as a well-groomed adolescent of average height and weight. She appeared to be very friendly and open to the counseling process. She initially presented with small talk and seemingly avoided talking directly about the reported abuse. As the session progressed, Toni appeared very distraught as she began to talk about the past abuse and the impact it has had on her life. She also talked about the concern that she has not been able to disclose this information to either of her parents. Toni states that she feels loved and very close to her parents yet is uncertain of how they will respond to this information. Toni also disclosed to the counselor in this session that she may be pregnant, as she has missed two menstrual cycles. She also has not disclosed this information to either of her parents. Toni openly acknowledges having had unprotected sex with her current boyfriend, who is also a 16-year-old student.

Questions

1. What are the multicultural competence issues in this critical incident?
2. How do you address the legal/ethical issue of student consent, with no parental consent, with the student who has experienced a sexual assault? How would the parental consent laws play a role concerning the sexual assault and the potential pregnancy?
3. What are the expectations regarding collaboration and consultation between the school counselor and clinical mental health counselor from the sexual assault program?
4. What personal counselor values, beliefs, and attitudes could interfere with the counseling being offered to the student embracing a multicultural perspective? How will you avoid any harm to the student?

Response 1

Sophie Maxis

Professional counselors are ethically bound to be culturally competent (American Counseling Association [ACA] and Council for Accreditation of Counseling & Related Educational Programs [CACREP]) and should be able to problem solve using appropriate multicultural frameworks (Whaley & Davis, 2007) to conceptualize critical incidents. This incident highlights the necessary training of multicultural competencies in school counselor preparation programs, specifically the development of awareness, knowledge, and skills needed to effectively work with clients (students) from ethnically and culturally diverse backgrounds (Holcomb-McCoy, 2005). The school counselor can address the critical incident in such a way to further develop the student's sense of agency while she copes emotionally, academically, socially, and medically with a potential pregnancy.

School counselors are trained to immediately report abuse and make appropriate referral to outside services for victims of abuse. From a multicultural perspective, this incident presents a potential conflict between the culture-bound beliefs and behaviors of the student that may have hindered the student from disclosing abuse and the legally mandated obligations of the counselor to report child abuse. The potential conflict does not mitigate the counselor's duty to report, but it does afford an opportunity for the student to self-evaluate her values, beliefs, and attitudes through discussions with the school counselor. The school counselor should acknowledge Toni's cultural background and the richness of her diverse family. The school counselor can discuss with Toni the implications of Toni's family dynamics, decisions that need to be made legally, and options that will be made available to Toni now that she's disclosed childhood sexual abuse and possible pregnancy.

As Toni continues with sexual assault counseling, she will need a strong support network beyond the counseling center and school resources. Her potential pregnancy may have been among the triggers for the memories of past abuse. If a pregnancy is confirmed and regardless of her decisions beyond that confirmation, positive outcomes are more probable for Toni if she has the support of her parents.

Toni, Ms. Small, and Ms. Leman-Wong have three distinct racial backgrounds yet relate to each other in ways that seem to indicate that the adults engage with Toni, as an African American adolescent, in a collaborative and culturally appropriate manner. Despite the intergenerational and racial distinction between Ms. Leman-Wong and Toni, they seem to share a strong relationship that is likely due to the previous counseling Toni received for self-harming behavior. Overall, Toni responds favorably to suggestions made by both the teacher and school counselor to seek help and has a high chance of acting upon the support that will be offered through the sexual assault counseling services, even if acting independently may counter the collective nature of Toni's family dynamic.

Regardless of family structure, the nature of child abuse is such that victims are sometimes afraid to disclose abuse for fear of disrupting family dynamics (see Rape, Abuse, and Incest National Network [RAINN], in the Supplemental Readings, Online Resources, and Supplemental Activities). The fear of disrupting the family dynamics may be exacerbated for Toni's close-knit family, which seems to assume a more collectivist orientation as described by Toni to the sexual assault counselor. A multicultural competence issue would be to understand the implications of Toni's family structure, particularly the extended family or kinship network that is common among African American families. Toni's concern for the feelings of family if she discloses the history of sexual abuse, and resulting consequences, suggest that her primary collectivist worldview may conflict with a more independent and individualized choice to report the abuse. Even though Toni has demonstrated independence in successfully going through individual counseling for self-harming behavior, she may still experience internal conflict with disclosing the abuse to her family, especially if her father maintains a close relationship with her uncle.

School counselors should be prepared to balance the legal obligations, professional ethics, workplace protocols, cultural considerations, family dynamics, and common sense with ethical decision making on a case-by-case basis (Linde, 2015). Ms. Leman-Wong acted appropriately by reporting Toni's previous sexual assault to the local agency. Although a disclosure of childhood sexual abuse is mandated in Toni's case, federal mandates may protect her privacy, even from her parents, should she seek sexual assault counseling and reproductive health services (42 U.S.C. § 290dd-2; 42 C.F.R. Part 2). The school counselor should encourage Toni to consider disclosing the past sexual assault to her parents to support any progress that Toni experiences through mental health treatment, given that Toni describes her family as "close." Although parental consent may not be mandated for Toni for her to seek mental health and possible prenatal care, Ms. Leman-Wong may want to have a conversation with Toni about her protected rights as well as potential benefits and consequences of disclosing her situation to her parents. Ms. Leman-Wong can offer to sit in with Toni and her parents should she choose to disclose her experiences to them during any part of her treatment for past sexual abuse and a potential prenatal care.

A collaborative relationship between the school counselor and clinical mental health counselor from the sexual assault program is needed so that Toni will be supported and positioned to exercise her agency to address meaningfully the trauma she experienced. The school counselor has student consent by virtue of Toni attending the school, but the mental health counselor would need additional informed consent to provide the sexual assault counseling (Linde, 2015). Ms. Leman-Wong has the capacity to monitor and support Toni within the school environment if outside counseling adversely affects her schooling experiences. The mental health counselor has the capacity to provide treatment that can be implemented and supported by the school counselor, with appropriate consent and permission by Toni.

Regardless of Ms. Leman-Wong's personal beliefs and values, she is expected to support Toni's agency to exercise her rights inasmuch as no harm is done to Toni or others. Self-reflection about the sources of the counselor's beliefs and attitudes, especially if they lead to harm for the student, is critical to being a culturally competent school counselor. The school counselor will need to more deeply examine and monitor biases that exist or present about Toni's choices related to sexual behavior and the options that she exercises with a potential pregnancy. The school counselor may also benefit from self-reflection about her assumptions related to Toni's culture and her culturally driven choice of response to family, given that family is Toni's primary reason for not disclosing the trauma she experienced as a child.

Response 2

Jonique Childs

The *ACA Code of Ethics* (2014), the American Mental Health Counselors Association (AMHCA) Code of Ethics (2010), and the American School Counselor Association (ASCA, 2010b) all address the counseling relationship, confidentiality, professional responsibility, relationships to other professionals, assessment, supervision, and resolution of ethical dilemmas (ACA, 2014; AMHCA, 2010; ASCA, 2010b). The sexual assault counselor and the school counselor should collaboratively review with the student the confidentiality statement, including the exceptions, along with the student's right to seek sexual assault counseling. As the counselor, when assessing the student's needs and rights to sexual assault counseling, there should be familiarity with state laws concerning counseling a minor under exceptional circumstances, such as in response to a sexual assault (ACA, 2014; AMHCA, 2010; ASCA, 2010b; Remley & Herlihy, 2013). This understanding should include recognizing when the school counselor is limited in his or her scope of practice and should refer to a sexual assault counselor (ASCA, 2010b). This also includes an awareness of the age requirements for a minor to consent to counseling services for themselves. For instance, in the state of Illinois, statute 410 ILCS 210/3(b) indicates that a minor who is at least 14 years old and the victim of sexual assault does not need to have parental consent to seek mental health counseling (Illinois Coalition Against Sexual Assault, 2015; Illinois General Assembly, 2015). The sexual assault counselor and the school counselor should both have a clear understanding of what the specific laws and statutes are in the state where they are practicing. While the student has the right to consent to sexual assault counseling services by law in some states, the sexual assault counselor and the school counselor must also consider their role as mandated reporters of the actual abuse and neglect. This is a circumstance in which a decision-making model would be beneficial to use in accordance with the governing bodies of the profession (ACA, 2014; AMHCA, 2010; ASCA, 2010b). The student should clearly understand that, without parental consent, future sessions will terminate after the allowable number of sessions, depending on state law. If the student wants to continue beyond the limited number of sessions, then parental consent must be obtained according to the limitations of consent by a minor depending on the state. This explanation should include informing the students of some of the concerns and limitations with this limited consent to services. Specifically, when the information disclosed falls into the exception to confidentiality, the informed consent form should be thoroughly reviewed with the student, including the completion of the signature pages.

Although, according to the student disclosure, she is not currently at risk for harm for further sexual abuse, the nature of her disclosure of unreported sexual abuse is enough to consider the parents' right to know in order to protect their child from being at risk for any future abuse. Another issue to consider is Toni's medical health if she is, in fact, pregnant. Although there has been no confirmation of pregnancy, the medical disclosure could be a concern if she is indeed pregnant and does not receive any prenatal services, if she gets injured, or if she becomes ill from lack of medical care. Essentially, you will need to make an ethical decision on protecting someone who is at risk for abuse and potentially at risk for neglected medical care, which falls into the exception to confidentiality (ACA, 2014; AMHCA, 2010; ASCA, 2010b). It must also be noted that, as a mandated reporter, the safety of the student must be a priority in cases of reported abuse and medical care. Another consideration, as indicated by the ASCA (2010b) model and the Illinois statute 410 ILCS 210/5, is the school counselor involvement in the encouragement of the student to inform the parent(s) and/or guardian of the concerns with the student (ASCA, 2010b; Illinois General Assembly, 2015).

In essence, as indicated by ASCA (2010b) in section G.3, an ethical decision-making model should be utilized in evaluating the rights, responsibilities, and welfare of all the individuals involved. This includes the clinical decision of confidentiality, student safety, and the student's right to sexual assault counseling, as well as determining at what point the parents should be notified (ACA, 2014; AMHCA, 2010; ASCA, 2010b). Consideration should be taken in determining how to best meet the student's current needs of emotional upheaval while working with the student on self-disclosure to the parent(s) and/or guardian about the presenting issues of sexual abuse and potential pregnancy. This may require that the counselor work with the student to identify alternative decisions of including the parents (Remley & Herlihy, 2013). For instance, some of the supportive counseling may include processing the pros and cons of parental involvement, identifying any issues of safety involved, role play of the disclosure to parents, and even a focus on support and honesty in relationships. The goals are to ensure that the student receives the counseling and is kept safe from future harm.

It may be helpful for both the school counselor and the sexual assault counselor to collaborate, along with the student, to assist with addressing the social–emotional needs that may arise throughout the school day (ACA, 2014; AMHCA, 2010; ASCA, 2010b; Remley & Herlihy, 2013). This may include seeking permission for the student to take alternative actions during moments of emotional upheaval or distress that affect the student's ability to focus in the classroom. For example, if a student is experiencing triggers or flashbacks throughout the school day, it may be helpful to have a plan in place in which the teachers will allow the student to seek out the school counselor. This collaborative relationship between the school counselor and the sexual assault counselor may involve coordinating the student's ability to see the school counselor as needed, in between counseling sessions with the sexual assault counselor, to address any immediate responses to trauma or any indication that the student may participate in self-harm behaviors. It may also be necessary to help coordinate the student's ability to make up any work that was previously missed because of additional time out of the classroom. This collaboration will require some lapse in confidentiality with the student's permission, as you will need to provide some (although minimal) information to fellow professionals in your collaboration process to ensure that the student's needs are fully met (ACA, 2014; AMHCA, 2010; ASCA, 2010b).

It will be important to address the internal conflict that may arise for the counselor who is in the process of helping a student address such challenging issues. Some potential concerns could arise if the counselor has strong values regarding parental rights, premarital sex, and issues of diversity concerning family expectations (Sue & Sue, 2016). If the counselor has strong feelings regarding the parents' right to know, that could be a challenge when meeting with the student initially under the pretense of the student being able to consent to service. If the counselor has values that do not approve of premarital sex, there could also be the potential for counselor biases or values to interfere with the counseling process. This may involve a lack of responsiveness in assisting the student with relevant resources in the community that may be helpful in addressing the pregnancy concerns. Regarding the student's family and roles that the family members play in one another's lives, it is important that the counselor respect and consider the multicultural influences that affect the family dynamics and relationships, as the student's extended family have lived together as an immediate family in one or more residences (ACA, 2014; AMHCA, 2010; ASCA, 2010b; Sue & Sue, 2016). Thus, the counselor must work toward understanding the specific concerns that the student has with disrupting the family structure by disclosing the history of sexual abuse to her parents. Finally, the counselor could also potentially have some beliefs and values about self-harm that may impede the ability to objectively and competently meet the needs of the student. There are many factors to consider to avoid causing any harm to the student throughout the immediate response to her needs and the ensuing counseling process (ACA, 2014; AMHCA, 2010; ASCA, 2010b; Remley & Herlihy, 2013).

Supplemental Readings, Online Resources, and Supplemental Activities

Supplemental Readings

American School Counselor Association. (2010). *ASCA national standards for students*. Alexandria, VA: Author.

Council for Accreditation of Counseling & Related Educational Programs. (2015). *CACREP accreditation standards and procedures manual*. Alexandria, VA: Author.

Holcomb-McCoy, C., & Day-Vines, N. (2004). Exploring school counselor multicultural competence: A multidimensional concept. *Measurement and Evaluation in Counseling and Development, 37,* 154–162.

Online Resources

Rape, Abuse, and Incest National Network (RAINN)
https://www.rainn.org/public-policy/legal-resources/florida

Supplemental Activities

Further Questions for Reflection and Discussion

- What additional conflicts may exist in such cases due to multicultural considerations?
- At age 16, what additional factor(s) or potential scenarios within Toni's situation would outweigh her right to privacy?
- What are the limitations to student consent within and outside of the school setting?
- What roles can consultation and collaboration play among teachers, school counselors, and mental health providers in cases of child abuse?

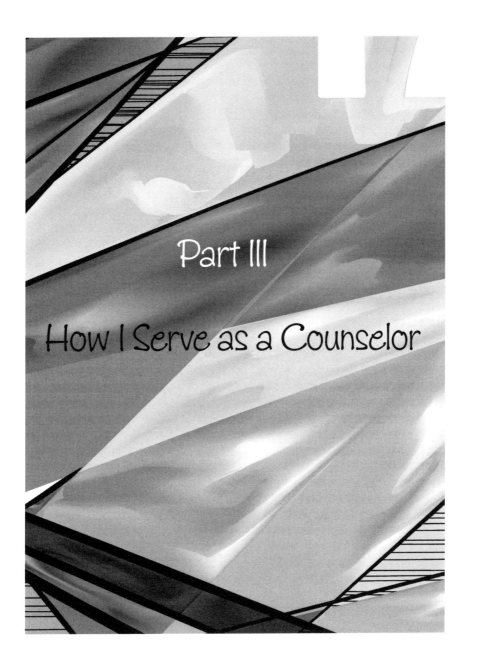

Part III

How I Serve as a Counselor

Chapter 12

Now That I Stand Up, How Do I Survive?

Matthew J. Beck

This incident examines the role of the school counselor as advocate for all students, especially when that advocacy is not popular with the community. Advocacy for every student may place the school counselor in a difficult situation between personal and professional values.

Background

As the professional school counselor in a midwestern rural community, the school counselor's services were enlisted from school officials to address an increasing concern: elementary students using biased language, such as "that's so gay," in negative and discriminatory ways. The school counselor chooses to use the administration-approved method of intervention, which includes a developmentally appropriate and research-driven anti-bullying curriculum from The Gay, Lesbian and Straight Education Network (GLSEN) and a children's book on family diversity. These developmental counseling lessons addressed the documented harassment by teaching children about bullying and bias, family diversity, and gender roles and diversity. However, things changed when a small group of community members pushed back at Alex Lynn's respect-for-all school counseling programming.

Incident

During the first school board meeting, the school counselor walked through a prayer vigil where protestors voiced opposition to one page in the storybook that stated, "Some families have two moms or two dads." Throughout this beginning stage, the school administration supported and worked with the school counselor's change efforts. The superintendent shared with the school counselor that, "These inclusive messages need to happen at school, as it was clear that respectful conversations to inclusive diversity were not happening at home."

Initial advocacy efforts by Alex Lynn, the school counselor, led to explaining the rationale of the challenged materials to the school district's formal curriculum committee, where parents and educators determined that the materials being used were age appropriate and research based and that they included the option for the opposing parents to have their child receive an alternate lesson. Despite this compromise, the opposition became louder and claimed that the school counselor was teaching about homosexual lifestyles and sexuality to students in the classroom. For example, one parent recommended the "use of the Bible as a resource to break down the stereotype barriers" that the school district students were experiencing. The school counselor received verbal harassment from opposing community members and even their children. In addition, this group held meetings at a local church, where strategies were recommended for parents to pull their children out of the school counseling program developmental lessons as a means to mount pressure on school officials to ban these materials.

Discussion

At this point, the school counselor concluded that education was the next step in the advocacy work. The disconnection and interpretation of the anti-bullying materials circling this small community needed to be addressed. First, the counselor individually met with any opposing community member to show that the lessons were age appropriate and did not mention sexuality in any way. One parent exclaimed, "The lessons are fine, but we do not approve, as the lessons originate from an LGBT [lesbian, gay, bisexual, and transgender] organization." Second, Alex worked with board members and advocated by presenting these nationally applauded materials as endorsed by several educational organizations. Third, the school counselor encouraged parents to attend the lessons and preview the materials.

As the number of students unable to participate in the developmental counseling lessons grew, the administration and board of education distanced themselves from the school counselor advocacy efforts and ultimately chose the path of least resistance. The directive followed, stating that "all resources and conversations with students depicting two moms/two dads, gay/lesbian families, same-sex parents, LGBT materials, and sexual orientation were not allowed." The school counselor became torn between the professional ethical obligations to diverse students and families and the fear of losing the job if a social justice stand was held.

After much self-reflection, Alex Lynn realized that there were limited allies who were willing to risk and model the change needed in this school culture and community. After consultation with colleagues, the school counselor removed the resources and worked with advocates outside of the school district. The school counselor's advocacy measures outside of the community were elevated to new levels. Alex sought opportunities for an advocacy role with national LGBT and educational organizations. Partnerships with professional associations and LGBT groups offered a platform for the school counselor's voice for equality to be heard throughout the nation. To combat the community issues, Alex created a family reading night at the town library. This allowed an opportunity for families and children to hear these respectful stories outside of the school ban.

After the media scooped up this story, Alex's advocacy efforts were beyond control, with powerful messages sent about the discriminatory and unethical effects of the sweeping LGBT ban by school officials. Amid the national debate occurring, there was a growing conflict inside the local school building. Teachers expressed their fear, shock, and anger. Some teachers criticized the school counselor's actions in bringing the elementary school into the national spotlight. For several months, there was debate on both sides of this incident. The school board never lifted the ban on the use of LGBT-inclusive materials. After self-reflection, Alex Lynn sent the school district a letter indicating that the affirming materials had been placed back in the school counseling office for the purpose of assisting individual students and families. Alex felt that this was necessary to adhere to the school counseling professional code of ethics when working with multicultural populations. The school counselor felt certain that advocating by reinstating the materials created change, which resulted in positive and respectful results for all of students. The school district or administrators never responded.

Questions

1. What are some potential ethical or legal issues in this case? How might the professional school counselor adhere to the professional code of ethics when the school district does not?
2. How does this professional school counselor conduct advocacy efforts without speaking out against the employer? How does the role of the media factor in change efforts, especially given that counselors' advocacy efforts are considered as more "behind the scenes"?
3. How might this professional school counselor address this harassment and foster respect for LGBT students and families while balancing the non-affirming community culture?

Response 1

Darcie Davis-Gage

The work of professional school counselors can be challenging and difficult at times. Alex Lynn is learning this first hand at this school. In addressing this issue, it is important to clarify the role of the professional school counselor, address the inherent difficulties in handling the incident, and provide a detailed course of action and a plan of implementation. First, it is important for Alex to communicate her role as a professional school counselor. According to CACREP (Council for Accreditation of Counseling & Related Educational Programs) Standards (2016), professional school counselors operate as leaders in the schools, advocate as system change agents, and implement strategies that support and promote equity (Standards G.2.a., G.2.j., and G.3.k.). In addition, Alex is also required to uphold the American Counseling Association's (2014) *Code of Ethics* as a practicing school counselor. The code mandates that counselors advocate for students (A.7.a.), do not discriminate (C.5.), and abide by established professional and ethical standards and obligations (D.1.d.). Furthermore, most states require school districts to have school counselors on staff. For Alex to complete her job as a professional school counselor, she is required to support and address the needs of her LGBT students and families and promote a safe learning environment for all students. Alex upheld these standards by presenting developmentally appropriate material to address the concern brought to her by the administration; explained her approach to students, teachers, the administration, parents, and community members; and advocated and developed programs outside of the school.

Although codes, standards, and policies support Alex's roles, prior actions, and responsibilities, it is not an easy task. Many school counselors struggle with similar issues, and sometimes support during these difficult situations is sparse. It is important for Alex to reach out to other professional school counselors in the district for support and supervision. She could also contact her state or national counseling organization or local counselor education faculty for guidance. Not only could these individuals provide support, but they may also be able to provide additional resources. Ultimately, this situation has the potential to be emotionally and psychologically draining, so gaining support and proper self-care is important during this time.

Once Alex has a support system in place, it is important to use an ethical decision-making model as she decides on a course of action. The *ACA Code of Ethics* (2014) requires counselors to use a model, as it can help them to think thoroughly and develop a step-by-step plan. It is important for Alex to remember that she has the most control over herself and her own actions. If challenged, she must be able to support her choices on a professional level. Alex faces the challenge of continuing to advocate for LGBT students and provide a safe environment within a school and community that is providing a mixture of support and hostility.

Although this is a difficult situation for Alex, many opportunities exist for advocacy, relationship building, and professional growth. Advocacy within a school system can be a tricky balancing act. Alex must serve in her role as a professional school counselor and advocate for all students while also abiding by the policies of her district. A possible course of action could be to meet again with administrators to review her roles and responsibilities as outlined earlier, present a written plan to address concerns regarding LGBT students and families, and discuss how the district could support in the implementation of the plan.

Alex has appropriately advocated in many helpful ways to address the concerns and develop a plan. As a professional school counselor, communication with students, families, and administration is key. First, she can remind people that her duties as a school counselor include advocating for equal opportunities and protection for all students. It is not a choice to advocate but a responsibility. She cannot simply pick and choose which students to support. Since school officials notified her of their "increasing concerns of elementary students using biased language in negative and discriminating ways," she had to address the concerns, as it is her duty as a professional school counselor. Second, she can provide a variety of services for all students. She can continue to provide resource material for LGBT students, conduct individual counseling, create support groups, and create classroom guidance programs on respect for differences. Also, it is important to identify which teachers or staff members might be supportive of these efforts, and they can provide support to students and family members and help advocate at faculty or board meetings. In addition, it would be important to review antidiscrimination policies and bully prevention programming to make sure they include language addressing gender identification and sexual orientation as protected classes. If such language is not included, Alex and other concerned faculty and staff could advocate for its inclusion.

Alex can also continue her advocacy outside of the school. By providing community resources and participating in such activities, Alex models inclusivity for students. Alex also must remember that many of her students are learning about her as an advocate by her actions, not necessarily the results of her actions. She is demonstrating how to advocate respectfully and how to be a leader in the school and community, which are behaviors that most parents want their children to learn.

Advocacy is an important component of a school counselor's duties. Alex has already taken steps toward building a safe, welcoming environment for students. In summary, Alex needs to explain her role and specific duties to students, teachers, and administrators. She may want to meet separately with the principal to gain his or her support. It may be helpful to carefully present an attitude of "*when* supportive programming is implemented" instead of "*if* programming is implemented." Alex would also benefit from building a solid support system of allies within her building as well as other school counseling professionals. It is recommended that Alex continue to engage in programming that supports LGBT students within the school systems and the community.

Response 2
S. Kent Butler

After comprehensively processing the case outlined here, a few ethical and legal issues seem readily apparent. Foremost, the ban posed by school officials on use of educational materials opens the door immediately to action that is both discriminatory and unethical. It also seems that the administration and board of education distancing of themselves from the professional school counselor's (PSC's) advocacy efforts should be a cause for great concern. Besides not being supportive of your employees and members of the student body, it is quite possible that their actions could produce a very unsafe or hostile work and educational environment that may place students and others into harmful situations. In a particularly litigious society, it also seems plausible that their stubbornness to deal with the issue at hand could lead to legal action, which would possibly bring even further scrutiny to the case.

On the advocating side of the equation, reinstating the materials might also be problematic. While it is purposed to create change that is positive and respectful for all of students, it may also have the potential to cause harm because of the serious nature of the issue. Although it is within the PSC's ethical right to do so, the placing of the affirming materials back in the school counseling office may lead to a myriad of disruptive actions that could undermine the purpose for putting them there in the first place. These disruptive actions, hypothetically, might also lead to legal issues for students, teachers, counselors, and administrators.

According to the American School Counselor Association (ASCA) Ethical Standards for School Counselors E.1.a. and E.1.c., PSCs must act within the boundaries of individual professional competence while providing a high level of care and accepting responsibility for their actions. Additionally, Standard G.2. suggests that when PSCs are obligated to work under conditions or accept policies that do not reflect the ethics of the profession, they must make an effort to remedy the circumstance through the correct sources. To this end, the best way for a PSC to adhere to the ASCA Ethical Standards for School Counselors and balance their advocacy efforts within the school environment is to remain completely transparent. Through transparency, the PSC is openly and honestly ensuring that he or she is making a concerted effort to keep the lines of communication open with the school administration as it pertains to safeguarding the rights of each student. This is especially important to abide by in the case outlined here. By remaining transparent with school officials and not openly speaking out against the school's policies within the media, the PSC stays above the fray and, it is hoped, continues to protect his or her employment status as well. In any event, following this game plan should put the PSC in a great position to be protected under the law should any legalities arise.

The role of the media is essential in cases such as this. The story now takes center stage and is taken out of the hands of the PSC, who, in turn, does not have to make official statements concerning matters being promulgated. In the ASCA Ethical Standards for School Counselors, Standard F.1.f. states that a counselor should visibly make a distinction between his or her statements and actions as a global citizen and those made as a school counseling representative. As the media attention and momentum build surrounding the rights of all students, it is likely that advocates from outside circles, inclusive of parents and other stakeholders, will begin to be the spokespersons and express sentiments against the wrongdoings. In addition, the media also provide a great resource for dispelling myths and falsehoods to the public, hopefully enabling those in resistance with opportunities to be educated on the facts pertaining to the issue at hand. Once given legs, the school administration's hands will be tied, forcing them to give voice to their positionality.

The ASCA Ethical Standards for School Counselors E.2.a. through E.2.g. brilliantly provide standards related to multicultural and social justice advocacy and leadership that are beneficial for PSCs to address the harassment and foster respect for LGBT students and families. Each standard also provides excellent opportunities for the counselor to balance the nonaffirming community culture in proactive ways.

To work seamlessly between the two entities, it is essential that PSCs enhance their multicultural and social justice advocacy awareness, knowledge, skills, and ability to take action to support their capacity to be nonjudgmental, fair, and equitable to all involved (Ratts, Singh, Nassar-McMillan, Butler, & McCullough, 2016). PSCs must understand how all forms of prejudice and oppression affect the school community, which could easily be accomplished through acquiring culturally specific and relevant professional development opportunities, making strides to affirm multiple cultural and linguistic identities and to advocate for equitable school and school counseling program policies and practices; and utilizing inclusive and culturally responsible language, providing culturally relevant workshops, and partaking in ways to disseminate information to families to increase understanding in an effort to create a positive school environment that promotes student success. As advocates and leaders within the school, PSCs can foster the concept of an equity-based school counseling program that is designed to support high student achievement.

Enlisting the newly adopted Association for Multicultural Counseling and Development Multicultural Social Justice Counseling Competencies (Ratts et al., 2016), along with the Multicultural and Social Justice Advocacy and Leadership standards within the ASCA Ethical Standards for

School Counselors seems a very practical way to ensure that all students are well served within the school community. PSCs have a very unique and powerful position within the school infrastructure to provide the sound guidance needed to create a positive school environment. Along with the administration and other stakeholders, PSCs can confidently accomplish this daunting but equally rewarding task. Although it takes great effort, a strong commitment to a multiculturally inspired respect for ALL human beings is vital, and EVERY student deserves to have this kind of principled determination working on their behalf.

Supplemental Readings, Online Resources, and Supplemental Activities

Supplemental Readings

Bidell, M. P. (2011). School counselors and social justice advocacy for lesbian, gay, bisexual, transgender, and questioning students. *Journal of School Counseling, 9*(10) 1–22. Retrieved from http://jsc.montana.edu/articles/v9n10.pdf (Note: This article has a comprehensive list of internet resources [p. 21] for school counselors working with LGBTQ youth.)

Black, J., & Underwood, J. (1998). Young, female, and gay: Lesbian students and the school environment. *Professional School Counseling, 1,* 15–20.

Diaz, E. M., Kosciw, J. G., & Greytak, E. A. (2010). School connectedness for lesbian, gay, bisexual, and transgender youth: In-school victimization and institutional supports. *The Prevention Researcher, 17,* 15–17.

King, S. (2008). Exploring the role of counseling support: Gay, lesbian, bisexual, and questioning adolescents struggling with acceptance and disclosure. *Journal of GLBT Family Studies, 4,* 361–384.

Munoz-Plaza, C., Quinn, S. C., & Rounds, K. A. (2002). Lesbian, gay, bisexual and transgender students: Perceived social support in the high school environment. *The High School Journal, 85,* 52–63.

Palma, T. V., & Stanley, J. L. (2002). Effective counseling with lesbian, gay, and bisexual clients. *Journal of College Counseling, 5,* 74–89.

Singh, A. A., & Kosciw, J. G. (Eds). (2017). School counselors transforming schools for LGBTQ students [Special issue]. *Professional School Counseling, 20*(1a).

Online Resources

Advocates for Youth. Resources for Gay, Lesbian, Bisexual and Transgender Youth: Select Organizations, Web Sites, Videos
http://www.advocatesforyouth.org/component/content/article/727-resources-for-gay-lesbian-bisexual-and-transgender-youth-select-organizations-web-sites-videos

American Civil Liberties Union. Library: LGBT Youth & School Resources
https://www.aclu.org/library-lgbt-youth-schools-resources-and-links?redirect=lgbt-rights_hiv-aids/library

Amplify
amplifyyourvoice.org/youthcampaignsandprograms

American School Counselor Association (ASCA) Position Statement on LGBT Youth
https://www.schoolcounselor.org/asca/media/asca/PositionStatements/PS_LGBTQ.pdf

Centers for Disease Control and Prevention. LGBT *Youth Resources*
http://www.cdc.gov/lgbthealth/youth-resources.htm

DoSomething.org
www.dosomething.org

GLBT National Help Center Hotline: 1-888-THE-GLNH (843-4564), Youth Talkline: 1-800-246-PRIDE (246-7743)

Human Rights Campaign
www.hrc.org

IMPACT: The LGBT Health and Development Program
www.impactprogram.org

It Gets Better Project
www.itgetsbetter.org

LGBT Youth Allies
www.youthallies.com

Live Out Loud
www.liveoutloud.info/

Point Foundation
www.pointfoundation.org

Stop Bullying (government campaign)
http://www.stopbullying.gov/at-risk/groups/lgbt/

Thinkb4youspeak
https://www.glsen.org/participate/programs/thinkb4youspeak

Supplemental Activities

Learning Activities

- After reviewing the supplemental materials, what steps may you take to enact school district guidelines or to improve school policies on equal rights for all students?

Chapter 13

Prepared and Not Prepared: Which Culture Decides?

Na Mi Bang

Background

The school counseling intern, Amber (American name given by advisor), is a 30-year-old Asian woman. Amber was trained in a reputable Asian teacher counselor program at the undergraduate level. She worked in an Asian elementary school for 3 years as a teacher counselor before coming to the United States for a master's degree in school counseling.

Amber's school counseling course work was initially a struggle because of some language barriers and the rigor of the courses at her CACREP (Council for Accreditation of Counseling & Related Educational Programs)-accredited counselor preparation program. In her second year of the school counseling program, she excelled in all her classes, with some difficulties with Western acculturation in case conceptualizations. The faculty unanimously agreed: Amber was ready for her clinical practicum experiences.

Incident

Currently, Amber is completing her school counseling K–6 practicum at an elementary school under the guidance of her site supervisor, Mr. Dounuf, who is a Caucasian school counselor. The school counselor intern has been trained in the area of career, academic, mental health, and family-related issues but has limited training in LGBT (lesbian, gay, bisexual, and transgender)-related topics in school counseling.

113

Amber entered the internship and immediately was assigned an individual counseling session with a third-grade elementary female student named Kylie. During the first and second sessions, the focus of intervention was on Kylie's struggles with academic performance. Because Amber had learned skills for working with various academic-related topics in a school counseling setting, the student counseling intern felt confident in identifying the academic-related topics and supporting Kylie. However, during the fifth session, as Amber and Kylie developed rapport, the third grader started to disclose sexual identity issues. Kylie expressed that she identified herself as a lesbian and was still confused about her sexual identity.

After hearing the disclosure from Kylie, the school counseling intern felt unprepared and uncomfortable helping with the LGBT identity issues due to Amber's limited training and exposure to LGBT-related topics during her counselor preparation. Amber disclosed her lack of confidence in working with the student's struggling sexual identity issues to her site supervisor and her university supervisor. Amber feels confident that her ethical responsibility is to quickly refer Kylie to her site supervisor, Mr. Dounuf.

Questions

1. How are Asian and Western cultures different in training school counselors in dealing with sexual identity and LGBT-related issues?
2. What are some potential obstacles in the supervision between the Asian supervisee and the Caucasian supervisor in a school counseling practicum or internship?
3. What are the CACREP requirements for training school counselors to work with LGBT issues in school settings?
4. What educational supports are needed to support the growth of school counseling interns with different cultural backgrounds?

Response 1

Joel M. Filmore

This incident presents with a multitude of issues and concerns that need to be addressed both individually and simultaneously as multicultural counseling supervision is complex and multifaceted (Colistra & Brown-Rice, 2011). For the purposes of our discussion, it is important to first understand and establish that within traditional Asian cultures, sex and sexual orientation are not discussed openly, as these are considered "taboo" topics (Nakamura, Chan, & Fischer, 2013). Because of this unwillingness to discuss topics that are considered taboo, school counselors within Asian cultures can be woefully underinformed on issues specific to sexual minorities and can even be misinformed about this population because of misguided stereotypes (e.g., being LGBT identified equates to having AIDS).

Therefore, it is extremely uncommon that school counselors who received their training in an Eastern cultural setting would receive LGBT-specific training within their counseling programs. Although Amber was trained in a CACREP-accredited counseling program within the United States, research shows that counselors-in-training receive limited training and experience related to LGBT issues (Biaggio, Orchard, Larson, Petrino, & Mihara, 2003; Phillips, 2000). Amber's desire to refer her student to Mr. Dounuf may be related to her self-identified level of competence (or lack thereof) and/or her lack of confidence in working with this student simply due to her own cultural embarrassment or discomfort as well as lack of understanding.

Because of cultural issues, therein lie some of the central issues of supervision between Amber and her supervisor: how to address her cultural norms, her professional responsibilities, and the client's needs. Initially, there would need to be an intentional conversation between Amber and her supervisor to help her understand the process of supervision and what is expected of her. As Bernard and Goodyear (2004) stated:

> Supervision is an intervention provided by a more senior member of a profession to a more junior member or members of that same profession. This relationship is evaluative, extends over time, and has the simultaneous purposes of enhancing the professional functioning of the more junior person(s), monitoring the quality of professional services offered to the clients that she, he, or they see, and serving as a gatekeeper for those who are to enter the particular profession. (p. 8)

The CACREP Standards are very clear on the requirements of counseling professionals to be multiculturally competent (CACREP, 2009) and state that counselors do not discriminate based on, among other things, sexual orientation. For her supervisor to do his due diligence, and for Amber to gain the most out of her supervision experience, the supervisor must use this opportunity as a "teachable moment" to help move Amber along the spectrum of multiculturalism toward competency and confidence.

It would be imperative for the supervisor to address the topic of how to discuss sex and sexual orientation within the counseling relationship with Amber. This intentional act must ensure limited interpersonal discomfort and negative communication (Toporek, Ortega-Villalobos, & Pope-Davis, 2004) with Amber. Although this may be an uncomfortable conversation for Amber to have, for her to become a practicing clinician in the United States, the importance of this competency transition would need to be impressed upon her. Although the supervisor must do everything in his power to be culturally sensitive to Amber, the priority must be the protection of the client and the client's rights (Constantine & Sue, 2007).

There is limited research on LGBT counselor competency; however, a recent study by Filmore (2014) found three factors that contributed to counselor-in-training competency: sexual–minority–specific education within the counseling program, clinical experience with sexual minorities during practicum and internship, and personal relationships with sexual minorities over the lifetime. This supports the findings of previous studies on the topic of counselor competency with sexual minorities (Bidell, 2005; Farmer, 2011; Graham, Carney, & Kluck, 2012). Amber's supervisor cannot make her develop friendships with sexual minorities, but it is clear from the research that clinical experiences, as well as intentional sexual minority education, do improve counselor-in-training perception of confidence and competence in working with this population. It would, therefore, be inadvisable for her supervisor to allow her to refer the client out, as that would be counterproductive to her development of the very awareness, knowledge, and skills necessary to be a competent and confident school counseling professional.

Response 2

Erin Lane

On review of the incident, there are several things that stand out in this case. First, using a strengths-based lens, it is important to note that, despite any concerns that may have arisen about her course work, Amber has strong relationship-building skills. Kylie began trusting Amber with a serious personal struggle after working with her in only four short sessions, ones that revolved mainly around academic concerns. Amber's training and practice in her home country may account for the better preparation in this area, but it is impressive nonetheless. Second, Amber has done well enough in her course work to understand and appreciate the ethical code that counselors must follow. Though she likely needs to participate in some consultation in addition to going through her own personal reflection, her thoughtful consideration of the ethical code should be acknowledged as a positive step for someone in the beginning stages of the profession. Third, by using an ethical decision-making model that includes an element of consultation, Amber's supervisor, Mr. Dounuf, would have been able to assist Amber in making a more informed ethical decision. He should use this opportunity to teach her the finer points of bracketing and increasing one's knowledge and awareness. It is important to remember, however, the power and cultural dynamics that come into play within this relationship, given each person's position. Finally, Amber's supervisor and her professors need to be more aware of the specific concerns that Amber and other international students face in a school counseling master's program.

School counselor preparation programs vary greatly from country to country (Hohenshil, Amundson, & Niles, 2013). Because we do not know Amber's country of origin, we will need to generalize from basic knowledge about multiple Asian countries to consider what Amber's former preparation was like in her home country. For example, in many Asian countries, school counselors are primarily teachers who are also training in the basics of counseling and development. They may handle discipline issues (e.g., truancy), academic concerns, and mental health or social–emotional development and education. Although school counselors are seen as holding valuable positions in most Asian countries, there remains a shortage of full-time counselors for students (Grabosky, Ishii, & Mase, 2013; Guo, Wang, & Combs, 2013; Lee & Yang, 2013; Lim & Lim, 2013; Tuason & Arellano-Carandang, 2013; Yeo, Tan, & Neihart, 2013). School counselors are taught to implement basic counseling and deliver guidance lessons for students. Although some Asian school counselor training programs have diversity and antidiscrimination policies and courses in place to help train school counselors, sexual orientation is usually not included among them (Kwok, Winter, & Yuen, 2012). When it comes to dealing with issues of sexual identity and orientation, many Asian cultures follow traditional Confucian or Christian values that tend to be interpreted to imply that, because homosexuality runs counter to procreation, it is immoral and unacceptable (Kwok et al., 2012; Lim & Lim, 2013). Additionally, since many Asian cultures are collectivistic in nature, homosexual individuals bring shame not just to themselves but to their families as well. Therefore, it is often a taboo subject, and many school counseling training programs in Asian countries do not address how to assist with concerns faced by homosexual (*comrade* or *tongzhi* in China and Hong Kong) students (Kwok et al., 2012; Lim & Lim, 2013). Given all this background, we know that Amber's previous training in her home country likely included understanding the basics of counseling, such as rapport building, as well as a general understanding of child development and academic concerns; however, she most likely never received training in how to work with a student struggling with his or her sexual identity.

With that in mind, I can appreciate that Amber felt her ethical obligation was to refer the student because of her lack of training in LGBT issues. When considering this scenario, Amber likely referenced the American Counseling Association (ACA) *Code of Ethics* (2014) Section A, which refers to terminating or referring a client when the counselor lacks competence to assist the client; however, it is important for all students to understand that they will continually be in a period of new situations and scenarios for which they do not feel fully prepared. The practicum and internship experiences required by preparation programs are integral to gain the firsthand knowledge, skills, and awareness that will form the building blocks of your understanding and advocacy for your students. CACREP (2009) Standards specifically refer to the requirement that school counseling students be trained in multicultural counseling issues, including sexual identity, and how they may affect student achievement. Additionally, students who do not feel that they have fully acquired this understanding should be prepared to demonstrate the ability to seek consultation or refer, if necessary (CACREP, 2009). Although the 2016 CACREP Standards are not as explicit, they do refer to the requirement that counseling students be aware of and address multicultural counseling competencies and identity development (CACREP, 2016), which would refer directly to the competencies required for this case.

Given the specifics of the scenario in the context of the CACREP Standards (2009, 2016), it would be prudent to re-examine Amber's ethical decision. In this case, it appears that, as a student in a CACREP program, Amber is expected to be addressing issues of identity development and implementing multicultural counseling techniques as part of her practicum experience. Additionally, it is important to recognize that the *ACA Code of Ethics* (2014) state that one of the fundamental principles of counseling ethics is *nonmaleficence*—that the counselor should do no harm to the client. Amber must consider the ramifications of severing the relationship at this point as paramount to any discomfort she may feel because of lack of training or values (Section A of the *ACA Code of Ethics*). In this case, both Amber and Kylie would be best served by continuing their professional relationship. Kylie has obviously formed a connection to Amber, as she was able to reveal a major concern in a short amount of time and would likely benefit from continuing to talk about these issues. By breaking off their counseling relationship suddenly after Kylie has revealed something deeply personal, Amber may be causing unintended harm to Kylie and inadvertently be telling Kylie that the confusion or uncertainty she is feeling is not acceptable. Additionally, Amber should seek consultation with her practicum and program supervisors. It may be difficult, but Amber will likely learn a great deal about sexual identity issues; be better prepared to bracket her own values in this and other value-laden counseling situations; and ultimately, with guidance from her supervisors, help Kylie sort out some of her questions.

It is important, however, to consider the dynamics in the practicum supervisory relationship when exploring this case. Mr. Dounuf is a Caucasian man from the United States, and Amber is an Asian woman. These individuals likely come from two vastly different cultural norms and values based on their sex and country of origin. For Mr. Dounuf to effectively supervise Amber, especially when it comes to Kylie's case, it is first imperative that he make a conscious and concerted effort to build a trusting and respectful relationship with Amber. As part of that, it is vital that they understand and acknowledge the cultural assumptions and values they hold about each other. It is also important for both individuals to understand Amber's level of acculturation with Western society, as this will affect how she perceives certain situations. We know from the scenario that Amber is still struggling with Western case conceptualization, so we can assume that her acculturation is not very advanced. We also know from research that it is likely that Amber will not be very forthcoming with her supervisor during supervision sessions and will only share what is expressly asked (Reid & Dixon, 2012). It will be important for her supervisor to be cognizant of these multiple factors that may affect Amber's experiences with this case. Issues such as case conceptualization, personal values and cultural norms, and language barriers may be causing concern for Amber in this situation and need to be broached openly by Mr. Dounuf and with respect so that Amber can feel comfortable discussing such matters. Finally, it is important in this supervisory relationship that Mr. Dounuf have clear and explicit expectations of Amber and ensure that she understands her role as a practicum student under his supervision.

Additionally, other supports will be needed at the university level. First and foremost, it is important for professors to understand that Amber is not just an ethnic minority student; she is, more specifically, an international student. Her needs will be different from those of ethnic minority students who have grown up in the United States, and professors and supervisors need to be continually cognizant of this fact. Not only will she encounter more language barriers (especially when it comes to the use of slang or colloquial phrases), but she will also need focused training in conceptualizing cases from a U.S. perspective. International students are not only coping with the transition to a more rigorous course of study, but they are also moving through stages of acculturation. Individuals from collectivistic cultures may have an even more challenging time acclimating to U.S. culture, given the individualistic nature of the schools and classrooms, as well as their lack of immediate support systems (Reid & Dixon, 2012). Finally, it is important that professors and supervisors understand that international students will have vastly different experiences acclimating to schooling in the United States based on their country of origin and personal characteristics. Above all else, the formation of a trusting and respectful relationship is paramount to the success of international students in school counseling training programs. Through this professional relationship, issues of misunderstanding and value clarification can be discussed openly and without fear of reprisal.

Supplemental Readings and Online Resources

Supplemental Readings

Byrd, R., & Hays, D. G. (2012). School counselor competency and lesbian, gay, bisexual, transgender, and questioning (LGBTQ) youth. *Journal of School Counseling, 10*(3), 1–28. Retrieved from http://jsc.montana.edu/articles/v10n3.pdf

Hall, W. J., McDougald, A. M., & Kresica, A. M. (2013). School counselors' education and training, competency, and supportive behaviors concerning gay, lesbian, and bisexual students. *Professional School Counseling, 17*(1), 130–141.

Rainey, S. (2007). *Affirmative school counseling: Working with gay, lesbian, and questioning students.* Retrieved from http://www.shsu.edu/~piic/summer2007/rainey.htm

Rudrow, H. (2013, January). *Resolution of EMU case confirms* ACA Code of Ethics, *counseling profession's stance against client discrimination.* Retrieved from http://ct.counseling.org/2013/01/resolution-of-emu-case-confirms-aca-code-of-ethics-counseling-professions-stance-against-client-discrimination/

Online Resources

Teaching Tolerance (includes classroom and professional resources, understanding biases) https://www.tolerance.org/classroom-resources/tolerance-lessons/analyzing-how-words-communicate-bias

Chapter 14

Not Enough Books and Too Many Students

Maiko Xiong

Background

The Lincoln Junior High School has served as the only junior high school in the Lincoln/Douglas school district for the past 30 years. Recently, several million-dollar houses were built behind fences next to the junior high school. Because of recent growth, the district built another junior high school across town, where most of the money and resources are being directed. The budget for Lincoln Junior High School was heavily cut, and as a result, there were fewer teachers and less class offerings.

Incident

As the only school counselor serving 800 students, Steph Conner was responsible for creating the master schedule and placing students in classes. Because of limitations in course offerings, there was very little flexibility in the master schedule. Teachers became frustrated with the number of students in their classrooms. Many teachers had the maximum number of students per union contract, and some had a couple more beyond the maximum number. As the district continued to cut budgets, discussions of closing Lincoln Junior High School emerged. The closure was supposed to create a new school. Lincoln teachers submitted grievances and requested extra pay for student overloads. This created a pressure on the district administrators to discontinue placing students into classes containing the maximum number of students per union contract.

In October, an 8th grade student, Mai, and her mother, Mrs. Thao, came to meet with the school counselor to discuss Mai's class schedule. The school counselor, Ms. Lin had a strong relationship with Mai. Ms. Lin first met Mai during the previous year, when she joined the Southeast Asian Culture Club that Ms. Lin advised.

Mai was retained in third grade and continued to struggle with school. In seventh grade, Mai realized that she was older than most of her classmates, which prompted her to focus more on her academics, so she could hopefully graduate from high school early. There was a stark improvement in her test scores, grades, and behavior. Mai's English teacher commented that, "Since Mai joined the Southeast Asian Culture Club, she's been much more focused in school and a leader in the classroom." Mai was currently enrolled in Mr. Liner's eighth-grade science class. Unfortunately, Mr. Liner is not known as an effective teacher; however, because he has worked for over 20 years in the district, he holds seniority. Mai and her mother were concerned that Mr. Liner's teaching was not effective in helping Mai learn. Mai reported, "There aren't enough books, so I can't do the homework, and he won't answer our questions. He just yells at us and tells us to read." Mai also reported that Mr. Liner called her "stupid" during class when she asked for help on an assignment. Both Mai and her mother requested to change her class schedule.

Discussion

The school counselor empathized with Mai and Mrs. Thao and told them that she needed to discuss the schedule change with the principal. Before meeting with the principal, Ms. Lin addressed the situation with Mr. Liner. Mr. Liner responded, "I don't remember that happening. There are too many students in my classes, and I don't have enough books." Ms. Lin proceeded to discuss the situation with the principal. The school counselor was given approval to make the change in Mai's schedule, but this caused another student's schedule to be changed to adhere to the teacher union maximum enrollments.

Questions

1. What needs to be considered when making this kind of change that affects not just one student but another?
2. How does a school counselor work with a teacher or teachers who are high on the union seniority list but ineffective in the classroom?
3. What can be done by the school counselor regarding a school not having enough books for students?
4. How does one work creatively with such limited resources?
5. How else could I have handled environmental issues in this situation?

Response 1

Norma Day-Vines

This critical incident provides an illustrative example of the troubling injustices that are far too commonplace in the United States. For instance, the local school district has experienced gentrification that has negatively affected less materially privileged students such as Mai. In fact, Anyon's

(1981) research provides compelling evidence that children from poor communities and ethnic minority children are far more likely to be affected by educational inequality. Perhaps the most obvious consequence of gentrification for school counselors involves the counselor/student ratios that exceed recommendations prescribed by the American School Counselor Association (ASCA, 2013). Essentially, ASCA recommends an optimal ratio of 1:250. Higher ratios may preclude the school counselor from mobilizing with other school counselors to promote academic, career, and personal social development for all students, regardless of their backgrounds.

Ms. Conner will need to work collaboratively with other school counselors and school counseling leaders in her district and state to generate mobilization efforts that parallel efforts waged by teachers in the school district who have advocated more successfully for reduced teacher/student ratios.

Within the past year, Mai has made a significant amount of academic progress. Additionally, the resources available within the school have helped Mai heighten her confidence levels and her racial identity functioning. However, the progress she has achieved could easily be undermined by the toxic interpersonal style of Mr. Liner, the science teacher. Regrettably, Mr. Liner is deemed ineffective, but to date, his seniority prevents him from being censured by the administration. Although Ms. Conner has advocated on Mai's behalf, she has not addressed Mai's social justice needs. When Ms. Conner lobbied the principal about changing Mai's science class, she neglected to address the toxic classroom climate. Although she did approach Mr. Liner before meeting with the principal, she did not inform the principal about the conditions in Mr. Liner's class. By not sharing this information, she may have missed an opportunity for the administration to provide supervision, evaluation, and remediation.

For school counselors, our students are our primary clients. Disturbingly, Ms. Conner has developed a tacit alliance with Mr. Liner that perpetuates the problematic classroom management practices he relies so heavily upon. Ms. Conner seems to suffer from what Bemak and Chung (2008) refer to as "nice counselor syndrome," or the reluctance to serve as a social justice advocate who lobbies against the systemic barriers that negatively affect Mai's academic preparedness, success, and, by extension, the success of all students. Sadly, Ms. Conner seems more preoccupied with currying favor with her colleagues than working to eliminate systemic barriers for students. Ms. Lin may ignore Mr. Liner's problematic teaching style because of limited levels of multicultural competence, fear of challenging the status quo, concern about being perceived as a troublemaker, ostracism by her colleagues, apathy, anxiety, or concerns about job security (Bemak & Chung, 2008; Griffin & Steen, 2011).

Bemak and Chung (2008) recommend a number of strategies for promoting social justice advocacy that include, but are not limited to,

..ient of the school counseling program with multicultural/
..ustice advocacy and organizational change services, use of data-
..en strategies, not personalizing others' reactions to social justice
.ivocacy and organizational change services, recognizing the perni-
cious impact of nice counselor syndrome, and having the intestinal
fortitude to address injustice.

Finally, Ms. Conner lobbied the principal to change Mai's science class.
As a consequence, Mai was removed from Mr. Liner's class. This change
represented an individually oriented strategy that did not address the
systemic issues that plague the students who have Mr. Liner as a teacher
and whose acquisition of science knowledge may be stunted because of
his ineffective teaching practices. Counselors are expected to be oriented
toward advocacy, social justice, and systemic change. Ms. Conner did
not consider the needs of the student body more broadly. She focused
exclusively on Mai's individually oriented needs.

Ms. Conner needs to address this issue more strategically in ways that
mobilize stakeholders such as teachers, parents, students, community
members, and administrators. Holcomb-McCoy (2007) addressed the
importance of equity audits to track inequitable school-based problems
that warrant identification and subsequent intervention.

Response 2
Tina Anctil

In this scenario, the school counselor is faced with a specific issue of equity
and advocacy for an individual student (Mai Thao), as well as the larger
contextual impact of gentrification intertwined with teacher labor issues
in both the district and the community. From a school-system standpoint,
the individual student's request to change her schedule has a ripple effect that extends to—and involves—the teachers affected, the principal,
and another student whose schedule had to be changed to accommodate
class size restrictions.

The best approach for the school counselor is to consider the effect of the
schedule change from the individual student domain, her relationship with
the teacher, and the relationship with the principal. Within each domain
or relationship, equity and access inform the school counselor's response
due to large class sizes, limited textbooks, and the school counselor's large
caseload. Additionally, this scenario highlights how issues of equity and
access often develop in environments that have limited personnel and
physical resources. Such environments can quickly become politically
charged, and volatile and clear paths for resolutions are not always clear.
Because the school counselor is not a teacher or a school administrator,
she might find herself making decisions in isolation without options that
will satisfy all parties. The Education Trust and the National Center for
Transforming School Counseling (TSC) provide tools for school counselors

that are particularly useful when struggling with equity issues (http://www.edtrust.org).

Mai's improvement in her test scores, grades, and behavior may be attributed to her participation in the Southeast Asian Cultural Club that the school counselor facilitates. The school counselor is to be commended for providing specific opportunities for students to explore their ethnic identity in a school-sponsored environment. Strong ethnic identity is an important protective factor that has been linked to academic achievement (Altschul, Oyserman, & Bybee, 2006), and given Mai's age, this is an important developmental period for her to foster an understanding of her own ethnicity and identity. In fact, it is not surprising that students who participate in this group experience psychological changes that could cause a need for school intervention (e.g., a desire for students to engage with others whom they perceive to be "like them" in many ways).

Mai, with the support of her mother, is sending the message that she believes she can succeed in science if she is in an emotionally safe environment where she can ask questions and have adequate access to materials. The school counselor is appropriately advocating for a student who is standing up for herself against a person who has authority and power over her. This is an important expression of self-efficacy that the school counselor positively reinforces by listening to Mai and her mother and by attempting to address the request for a change to her class schedule and teachers. Regardless of whether the request is granted, the school counselor should be direct and transparent with Mai and her mother about her decision and the constraining factors at play. In this way, the school counselor is modeling for Mai how to enact change within a large system where there are competing priorities and limited resources.

An effective school counselor is able to develop and maintain relationships with teachers, which serves as the foundation for the school counselor's role as a consultant within an educational environment. Without a doubt, there is greater pressure and higher expectations on teachers to raise student achievement, often by doing more with less. Larger class sizes, students coming to school with greater needs, and fewer and fewer resources are but a handful of the enduring challenges that face the average teacher. In empathizing with Mr. Liner (Mai's teacher), the school counselor learns that he has too many students in his classroom and a shortage of books. Armed with this information, the school counselor can now offer her consultation to help the teacher explore creative ways to manage relationships with students and parents. The school counselors can collaborate with critical stakeholders in high-needs schools to improve educational environments and outcomes for students of color and students in poverty (see Griffin & Steen, 2011, for examples).

Germane to this scenario, the principal plays a role in collective bargaining, budgeting, and evaluating issues of equity and access to teaching and learning in the school. The school counselor may be asked to provide evidence related to these issues. In particular, she might be asked to address how specific groups of students (e.g., students of color, underachieving students, students on an individualized education plan, or students receiving free or reduced-price lunch) are performing in school. The school counselor may need to consult with the principal if Mai's complaint about Mr. Liner suggests a pattern of behavior directed at specific groups of students in his classrooms. Although likely an isolated incident, the school counselor's role could be to address this issue when looking to identify a pattern. For example, it is fair to ask whether Mr. Liner requires sensitivity training or support when working with Asian American students or students in minority populations. If so, how might this affect the kinds of students who are in his classes, given the demographic of the student population? Union rules dictate many of these answers, but it is the school counselor's responsibility to help the principal to (a) become aware of equity issues in classrooms and (b) explore strategies and solutions to reduce perceived or real unfairness experienced by students.

Supplemental Readings, Online Resources, and Supplemental Activities

Supplemental Readings

Griffin, D., & Steen, S. (2011). A social justice approach to school counseling. *Journal for Social Action in Counseling and Psychology, 3*(1), 74–85.

Online Resources

The Education Trust
  http://www.edtrust.org

National Education Association
  http://www.nea.org/

Supplemental Activities

Learning Activities

How to respond when the teacher ranks high on the seniority roster and there are not enough books.

- Explore the National Education Association website to become aware of equity issues in classrooms.

- Explore strategies and solutions to reduce perceived or real unfairness experienced by students.

- Classroom activity: In small groups, explore ways to receive funding for additional books. What do publishers have as incentives for schools? What are some innovative ways to address this issue?

Chapter 15

Blowing Up in Science Class or Getting Trapped in the System

Rafe McCullough

Background

I work in a Southwestern state urban middle school. Students experience extreme poverty and multiple ongoing systemic barriers. The community where the school is located has significant substance abuse and crime issues, including violent crime. Often, students do not feel safe walking to and from school. Many students have been affected in some way by these issues. Recently, there have been some shootings involving teenagers in the community, and one student from our school was abducted this year. Students and families have experienced racism, discrimination, and many negative interactions from community police; so, often, crimes go unreported.

There are approximately 800 students attending the middle school. Nearly half of students come from homes where English is not spoken. Almost 20% of the student population qualify for special education services and receive an individualized education program (IEP). Approximately 15% of students meet annual reading and math benchmarks on any given year. Over 95% are students of color, with a staff that is 98% White. There are limited interventions provided to students who struggle with reading and math. Once a student fails the reading and/or math benchmarks for 3 consecutive years, our school qualifies them for special education services. Often, this includes English-language learners (ELLs) who have been in the United States for many years but who have not yet achieved academic language proficiency.

Our team of three school counselors monitors the academic progress of each student on our caseload. We disaggregated the grade and attendance data and found some disturbing trends. One trend was that a significant number of students with IEPs were failing more than half of their classes, including their self-contained special education classes. Attendance of students who received a failing grade decreased significantly immediately after the grading period where they were notified of the failing grade. Also, many students who qualify for special education in both reading and math were also failing science and social studies. We scheduled a meeting with our principal to discuss our concerns. Specifically, we were concerned that students who received special education services for both reading and math were not getting enough support in other classes, such as science and social studies. Students with IEPs are treated the same as their peers who do not need the extra support. Our principal was not aware of this equity issue.

Incident

Later that week, a student, Angel, whom I have known for 3 years, was sent to my office from his science class. This was the third time that week he was sent out for "angry disruptions." Angel was receiving special education services for reading, writing, and math learning disabilities. He exited the district's ELL program in fifth grade but still struggles academically. Although he no longer qualifies for ELL services, our ELL program coordinator checks in with him occasionally, as she suspects that some of his reading difficulties are rooted in his continued struggle to reach an academic level of English fluency. Angel's parents reside in another country; he and his sister live with relatives in our school service area. He came to the United States when he was 7 years old. No one in his immediate family has ever graduated from high school.

Angel entered my office and began yelling about how his teacher, Mr. Swenson, was "stupid" and "unfair." Then his face turned red, and he started to cry, "Nobody understands how hard it is for me. I can't read. I can't do math. I'm so stupid." In a flash of anger, Angel stood up, tore his science assignment into pieces, and threw them on the floor. "I can't do it. I can't do this anymore." He sat down, lowered his head, and with tears welling up, he said, "Sorry about your floor. I know you are just trying to help. I'll pick it up." I consulted with one of my colleagues. I did not know how to help him within the current system.

Angel was in my office twice the next week. He said, "How can I be in this class? I can't even read the book. No one will help me. I won't go back there. I'll drop out. You can't make me go to school." He refused to go back to science class and skipped the next 3 days. We scheduled a meeting with his special education case manager, principal, and intervention team. The case manager was not sure how to support him in science. She was teaching during that period, and no instructional assistants were available. The science teacher had 35 students in his class, with nine receiving special education services.

No one could think of a way to support Angel because of the lack of resources. The team decided that he needed to go back to science class, and the teacher would give him a D if he showed up. I was to use my relationship with him to talk him into going back to science class. When that failed and he still refused to go back, I told him that he was right, this was unjust, and I promised to not send him back until we had a better plan. It occurred to me that we could take him out of science class. Science was not "required" at our school. We had some system work to change, but what about Angel, who is living this reality now?

Discussion

After much discussion with Angel's guardians, I advocated to have Angel removed from science class. I suggested that he work as a teacher's aide with Ms. Stone's sixth-grade science class. She was a kind, gentle teacher. Everyone reluctantly agreed. Angel went to Ms. Stone's class. At first, he was withdrawn, but with her encouragement, he started helping the younger students with their labs. As his confidence increased, he walked around the class during work time and answered questions. At the end of the semester, I encouraged Angel to go back to his eighth-grade science class, but in a new classroom, so he could have a new start. He worked hard and earned a C–, but he had missed a semester of eighth-grade science. I still think about this decision and wonder if I made the most just and ethical decision.

He still struggled to comprehend the reading. Not being able to read the directions for the labs made it look like he could not do the math involved in the science formulas. Angel's eighth-grade science teacher noticed that, if someone simply explained the directions to Angel, he could do all the math problems independently. Both the teacher and I suspected that he continued to have difficulties with academic language proficiency, so we called a meeting with his special education case manager and the ELL coordinator. The purpose of the meeting was to determine whether Angel still needed ELL support and whether his continuing struggle with English fluency was making it seem as if he had learning disabilities and compounding his frustration and displays of anger.

Questions

1. What data might have helped the school counselor advocate for Angel?
2. Given the systemic barriers, what other decisions could have been made to mitigate harm to Angel and increase his academic success?
3. What does a professional school counselor do when a system cannot be fixed soon enough to help the current students succeed?

4. How could the evaluation elements of a comprehensive school counseling program systematically identify students like Angel before a class conflict brings their concerns to the attention of the school counselor?

Response 1

Tim Poynton

The school counselor is working under difficult circumstances, serving a population of students in great need of support and attention. Balancing the needs of students with awareness of resources and the need to act is of critical importance.

The data collected by these school counselors foreshadowed, and perhaps foresaw, Angel's incident. These data indicate that more students like Angel exist in the school, and they are likely dealing with their struggles through disengagement, which is hard to notice. Other data that would be helpful to understanding how students like Angel are being served by the school system are reading and math growth scores over time, disaggregated by characteristics such as qualification for special education services and qualification for ELL services (current or past).

Given that Angel was at risk of dropping out of school, keeping him engaged in and attending school to the greatest extent possible is the primary consideration: Students have no chance of progressing academically if they do not attend. The school counselor's choice to keep Angel engaged in school by assigning him to be a teacher's aide in a science classroom for younger students is both creative and academically relevant, as evidenced by Angel's later relative success in eighth-grade science. One must wonder, however, what might have happened if he had been able to go to a new science classroom when the incident initially occurred. Would he have been able to achieve success in science without being a teacher's aide? Although it might be easy to speculate that the student and teacher were simply a "bad match" for each other, we also need to be mindful of the fact that this teacher was working under extraordinarily difficult circumstances himself. Not only did Mr. Swenson have 35 students in his class, but he also had eight students, in addition to Angel, who were in need of special education services.

As was done here, creative solutions can serve as effective temporary bandages until longer term solutions can be implemented. Otherwise, continuing to advocate for attention to the problem and solution implementation is what needs to be done to help all students succeed.

Collecting and analyzing data in a proactive manner helps us respond to incidents such as this before they reach a "breaking point." The data collected and analyzed by these school counselors highlighted inequities and a systemic issue that could not be addressed in time to help Angel. In a comprehensive school counseling program, data are collected and analyzed routinely to pinpoint areas in need of attention and evaluate the effectiveness of interventions. With the data the school counselors in this school have already collected, it is possible for school counselors to create a "risk index" for each student in their school. In other words, they can easily identify the students in need of intervention. The next step is to design an intervention (or interventions) to address the issue. The interventions alluded to in this incident are all systemic in nature—I wonder what school counselor–led interventions may be able to address the issue at hand, in addition to the systemic interventions needed? Although a plethora of possible interventions exists, two that come to mind, given the context of this school, are the Second Step violence prevention curriculum (Committee for Children, 2011) and Student Success Skills (Lemberger, Brigman, Webb, & Moore, 2013), both of which have evidence supporting their effectiveness.

The student in this incident, Angel, seems to be experiencing multiple stressors that are affecting his ability to succeed academically. In addition to the academic challenges that gave rise to the incident in science class, the community in which he lives is itself challenged by violence, crime, and substance abuse; the racial composition of the adults in school is not as diverse as the community it serves; and he is separated from his parents. This is a challenging context within which to learn—even without diagnosed learning disabilities. A focus of school counselors operating in contexts such as these may find direction in promoting hope as part of their comprehensive school counseling program. As noted by Pedrotti, Edwards, and Lopez (2008), the concept of hope can be integrated into individual counseling, group, and curriculum-based interventions, and the research they reviewed has positively linked hope to personal/social, academic, and career-related outcomes.

Response 2
Anita Young

According to the American School Counselor Association (ASCA) role statement (2018), school counselors play a critical role in maximizing student success. Leadership, advocacy, and collaboration skills are used to promote equity and access to rigorous educational experiences using data and accountability strategies (Chen-Hayes, Ockerman, & Mason, 2014). School counselors are not only responsible for academic advisement and career counseling, they also provide sound social–emotional counseling (ASCA, 2012a). They are grounded in the constructs of counseling theories and specifically trained to work collaboratively in educational settings with K–12 students and their parents/guardians by aligning services with the instructional vision and mission of the school. The school counselors were faced with a myriad of issues that challenged the initiation and day-to-day delivery of school counseling services that promote student success. However, school counselors must be held accountable for equitable and culturally relevant services that meet the needs of all students through a comprehensive school counseling program.

Collecting and analyzing data to remove barriers and increase student opportunities should be the catalyst for designing and implementing comprehensive programs for all students (Hatch, 2013). As in the present case, school counselors were monitoring student academic progress and disaggregating data by grade and attendance. As a result, they were able to identify students with disabilities and ELLs who were struggling academically, perhaps disruptive during class, and often not attending school. The efforts of the school counselors in this study should be noted for the diligence of disaggregating data by grade and attendance and informing the principal. However, additional data elements and processes could have aided in advocating on Angel's behalf.

For example, the commitment to advance student achievement is incumbent on all stakeholders. No longer is the principal expected to be the sole educational leader and problem solver in the school. A distributive leadership approach focused on circumventing and intervening on Angel's behalf could have augmented his academic achievement, improved his attendance, and grounded his self-efficacy (Janson, Stone, & Clark, 2009). This approach provides all stakeholders with the opportunities to define the issues from their perspective, brainstorm solutions, and own the successes of working with all students, especially from diverse and underrepresented populations. More important, engaging in courageous conversation about beliefs, challenging inequitable policies from a systems approach, and addressing societal issues that contribute to volatile behaviors can uncover data elements that may not be identified as problematic to student success.

Therefore, data points such as the school improvement plan (SIP), disciplinary referrals (quantitative), and conversations with teachers (qualitative) could guide school counselors to assume leadership roles such as initiating student support teams (SSTs), school–family–community partnerships, or school-wide interventions such as Positive Behavior Interventions and Supports programs. School counselors should also have access to critical data to review social–emotional gaps that might suggest the need for mentoring or resiliency programs that could have provided an outlet for Angel and circumvented disciplinary outbursts.

The intent of the school counselor was to maximize the academic and social–emotional growth of the student (ASCA, 2010b). Although the school counselor consulted Angel's guardians about removing him from science class, it appears that the IEP meeting convened with minimal content and expert advice from the case manager and ELL department chair. The case manager, ELL teacher, and parents are considered "resources" for mitigating solutions. Removing Angel from science class was a temporary and unacceptable "fix," considering that science is a rigorous core class that increases academic exposure and postsecondary preparation. Given that was the decision, using cognitive–behavioral techniques at school and at home could have been a "resource" to increase the student's self-regulated behaviors and provide coping mechanisms when faced with frustrating and challenging situations.

School counselors have social capital and interact with all entities of the school. Systemic change occurs over time and through partnership efforts of stakeholders with a common vision to eliminate barriers and inequities so that all students can achieve optimal outcomes. When school counselors build relationships and forge linkages with teachers, administrators, parents/guardians, and community members, they are able to exert influence and effect change as educational leaders (Young & Bryan, 2015).

School counselors are in the best position in a school to address systemic barriers, and data can be the catalyst for change. What other individual in the school encounters all students? Although teachers, social workers, and school psychologists work with students, they frequently work with discrete student populations relevant to their content expertise. School counselors serve all students and must be vital players who address issues of equity and access posed in today's schools (Holcomb-McCoy, 2007). Therefore, it is inherent for school counselors to forge ahead (undistracted) as leaders and advocates creating equitable opportunities that lead to college and other postsecondary opportunities. School counselors must persist and challenge the status quo and all inequities.

To be an essential resource to the learning environment, school counselors must link their work to the instructional mission of the school with clear accountable outcomes. Effective program evaluation involves continuous formative and summative assessment via quantitative and qualitative methods to determine how to improve student services. Assessment should occur on multiple dimensions. For example, a program assessment can help school counselors identify the strengths and weaknesses of the program, target short- and long-term goals. Creating closing-the-gap reports can help target appropriate needed services, especially for underrepresented populations. Once gaps are determined, data can also be used to identify professional development needs for school counselors and all staff. Clearly, the staff had exhausted their skills to effectively work with students, especially from culturally diverse backgrounds.

Supplemental Readings, Online Resources, and Supplemental Activities

Supplemental Readings

Galassi, J., & Akos, P. (2007). *Strengths-based school counseling: Promoting student development and achievement*. Mahwah, MJ: Erlbaum.

Lemberger, M. E., Brigman, G., Webb, L., & Moore, M. M. (2013). Student Success Skills: An evidence-based cognitive and social change theory for student achievement. *Journal of Education, 192,* 89–100.

Masten, A. S., Herbers, J. E., Cutuli, J. J., & Lafavor, T. L. (2008). Promoting competence and resilience in the school context. *Professional School Counseling, 12*(2), 76–84.

Pedrotti, J. T., Edwards, L. M., & Lopez, S. J. (2008). Promoting hope: Suggestions for school counselors. *Professional School Counseling, 12*(2), 100–107.

Online Resources

American School Counselor Association
   http://www.schoolcounselor.org

The Education Trust
   http://www.edtrust.org

Intercultural Development Research Association
   http://www.idra.org/

Second Step
   http://www.cfchildren.org/second-step.aspx

Student Success Skills
   http://www.studentsuccessskills.com/

Supplemental Activities

Learning Activities

- Review publicly available data on two local school districts from the state's department of education to identify similarities and differences. Ideally, one school will have relatively higher performance than the other. In reviewing the data, look for differences in academic achievement, attendance, post-secondary plans/outcomes, and funding.

- Have students visit two schools that vary in terms of the population of students served and interview the school counselors.

- Have students compare and contrast the work the counselors do, the challenges they perceive to be most pressing, and how their current graduate training prepares them to work in both contexts.

Chapter 16

What Do I Need to Know, and How Can I Get the Answers? Needs Assessment From a "Not Nosy" School Counselor

Jennifer Sharp

A new school counselor plans to conduct a needs assessment as a basis for designing a school counseling program. The data she gathers through the needs assessment will help drive program development, and she considers how to assess needs while navigating the school culture.

Background

After completing graduate school, I relocated for my first school counseling position. I am a first-year junior high school counselor working in a rural setting. There are approximately 300 students in grades 7 and 8, and I'm working in a combined junior/senior high school (grades 7–12) in a district of approximately 3,200 students. There are two senior high school counselors who have strong connections to the community, and they are engaged primarily in inappropriate (guidance) activities for school counselors (American School Counselor Association [ASCA], 2012a). The district recently added elementary school counselors as a result of securing an elementary and secondary school counseling program grant. District administration did not unanimously support the addition of school counselors; in fact, there are several district personnel who have openly articulated their beliefs that the school should stay out of the private lives of students and their families, and that counselors meddle. Therefore, some parents and school employees are excited by the addition of school counselors, but there are also many folks who are suspicious of school counseling.

As the first counselor hired to work with seventh- and eighth-grade students, I have experienced that ambivalence and tension in the community regarding the presence of school counselors. My building administrator is generally supportive; however, he conceptualizes the role of the school counselor as primarily focusing on social–emotional needs and has consistently de-emphasized my role in affecting career development and academics. An additional tension exists between students who are from families who have been in the community for generations and students (mostly of Mexican origin) who have recently relocated to the community. The community has experienced a large influx of Mexican immigrants in the past 5–10 years, and the district has struggled to adapt to the changes in the school population.

Incident

I am constructing a baseline needs assessment for my school, and believe I must tread lightly as I am still very new in the community. I have identified several model needs assessments through consultation and research. Informal consultation with teachers suggests that anxiety, bullying, stress management, and conflict resolution are key areas in which students tend to experience challenges. I want to prioritize personal–social developmental needs, as those are the priority of my administrator, but I also want to begin establishing the impact of school counselors in career and academic domains. I have developed a four-page survey for students to respond to, and I plan to administer this in classes during a classroom guidance session within the first month of the school year.

Discussion

Given the ambivalence about school counselors in the community, it is crucial to navigate the needs assessment process skillfully and diplomatically. There is a counseling intern at the high school who has expressed interest in getting involved with junior high counseling activities. She coaches one of the high school sports teams and is more of an insider in the community than I am. I am considering how I may collaborate with her in the development and administration of the needs assessment and what methods will be most effective for gathering baseline needs assessment data.

Questions

1. Given the local culture and the perception that school counselors are nosy, how would you approach a needs assessment in the school?
2. Given that approximately 40% of the student population speaks English as a second language, how does that affect the needs assessment content? What will I need to consider in constructing the assessment?

3. What other stakeholders (besides students) should be involved in the needs assessment process?
4. With whom might I collaborate to develop and administer the needs assessment?
5. Are surveys the most appropriate method for gathering data? What other methods may be utilized to assess needs?
6. How might collaboration and consultation support the needs assessment process and program development?

Response 1
Brandie Oliver, Tom Keller, and Nick Abel

We applaud this counselor for her commitment to comprehensive, preventative school counseling and encourage her to view the needs assessment process as an opportunity rather than potential obstacle. A team rather than an individual ideally carries out the creation and administration of a survey, and this might, therefore, be an opportunity to begin forming a school counseling advisory council (ASCA, 2012a) made up of key stakeholders such as teachers, administrator(s), parents, students, employers, and community members. Once an advisory is in place, the counselor could allay fears about "nosiness" by assuring students, staff, and parents that the survey would be voluntary and that individual responses would be anonymous (no names or identifying information) and confidential. That said, it would be critical to widely share disaggregated survey results to demonstrate to stakeholders the usefulness of the endeavor, as well as the ways the counselor plans to address various themes and areas of concern evident in the results.

Given the recent influx of Mexican immigrants in this school community, we recommend including questions about school culture to explore the level of diversity appreciation and multicultural awareness among students and staff. A specific section for the ESL (English as a second language) students is suggested to determine their unique needs and what the issues are that they see as critical to their academic, social–emotional, and college/career success. Although these students share the ESL label, each one brings unique challenges and personal resources that should not be overlooked (Rance-Roney, 2009). Ideally, the needs assessment would be fully translated or adapted into a reading level that is comfortable for a majority of students. Another possibility is allowing ESL students to complete the survey during their ESL class where extra support is available. Because of the developmental age of this population, it is also suggested to edit the needs assessment for all students to a maximum of two pages.

As mentioned earlier, this task is ideally carried out by a team (e.g., an advisory council). In creating a team, the counselor should consider including any parties who could eventually contribute to meeting the student/school needs revealed in assessment results. It is easy to imagine that certain community organizations (i.e., those serving ESL students and families, potential employers, local colleges) might eventually assist in meeting student needs and should therefore be involved in the creation of the survey. It would also be wise to include parents in the process to help them understand the role of the school counselor and the importance of developing a comprehensive school counseling program based on demonstrated need. We also feel that it would be critical for the counselor to partner with her colleagues at the high school and elementary schools to better understand the nature of their programs, as some of the student feedback could inform interventions and programming at other developmental levels.

Ideally, collaboration with a group of stakeholders (such as an advisory council) should occur before finalizing the survey. A number of people could offer insight into survey content, and it would be important for the counselor to reach out to, and incorporate suggestions from, as many as possible before finalizing and distributing the survey. The following are examples of stakeholders with whom we might collaborate: teachers (on content and convenient times to administer the survey); ELL teachers (see question 2); a high school counseling intern (on social and existing relationships); an administrator (administrators must be convinced that a needs assessment is critical for designing a comprehensive, preventative program); and counselor educators (on design or data analysis).

Surveys are a great way to gather large amounts of data from a wide audience in a manner that is quick, efficient, and easy to analyze, but they might not always be the "best," depending on the overall goals of the survey. There are quite a few other possible methods for gathering data. Focus groups can provide rich, narrative data that capture stories and personal experiences. Focus group interviewing is particularly suited for obtaining several perspectives about the topics being explored. Other existing school data (e.g., discipline referrals, attendance, and standardized test scores) are easily accessible to the school counselor and critical to informing program development.

It would be advantageous if all school counselors in the corporation formed a district level team. To help gain buy-in for this needs assessment, the junior high school counselor could collaborate with both the high school and the elementary school counselors to develop two or three questions to be included that would help inform their practice and assist in student transition in grades K–12.

As stated throughout the response section, it is important to start slowly and gain the support of key stakeholders in this process. During the coming year, the school counselor's activities to support her vision could include (a) educating the staff and community about the role of the school counselor (using ASCA's Role of the School Counselor statement, the ASCA National Model, etc.), (b) facilitating a presentation at a staff meeting, (c) providing a parent education night on one of the topics that has been shared with her from teachers thus far, and (d) starting a newsletter to disseminate to parents, school staff, and community to showcase the work of the school counselor.

Because it is her first year, she could utilize the data accessible to her (grades, discipline, attendance, etc.) and consult with the administration to develop a few data-informed goals aligned with the school's yearly plan. By focusing her work on these goals, she can demonstrate impact on student outcomes and use these findings to support the school-wide needs assessment as the next step.

Finally, to gain the trust of the community in general, it is advised that she get involved in as many school-wide committees/projects and community groups as time permits to start building capital and interfacing with staff and community members.

Response 2

Richard E. Cleveland

This scenario presents a school counselor who is passionate about establishing critical elements of the foundation component of a comprehensive school counseling program (CSCP) and recognizes the importance of active collaboration with various stakeholders within the sphere of a comprehensive program (ASCA, 2012a). Much of the literature addressing school counseling in rural settings is arguably dated (e.g., Carter, Spera, & Hall, 1992) or composed of mostly opinion (Sutton & Pearson, 2002). However, as the relatively recent shift toward evidence-based school counseling affects the entire discipline, exemplary pieces of research within rural settings have emerged. For example, in their research of CSCP impact on the rural high school setting, Carey, Harrington, Martin, and Hoffman (2012) highlight associated benefits such as lower suspension and discipline rates, higher attendance rates, and higher math and reading proficiency.

As schools within rural areas may often be considered an emotional center of the community (Sutton & Pearson, 2002), it may come as no surprise that a new school counselor (and his or her desire to implement significant programmatic changes) may be met with a degree of resistance. Espousing an ecological school counseling perspective (McMahon, Mason, Daluga-Guenther, & Ruiz, 2014) can benefit the school counselor as he or she expends the requisite time, energy, and resources toward recognition and acceptance as a member of the community. Such a perspective situates the school counselor as a member in micro-, meso-, and macrosystems, illuminating systemic members and forces relevant to the goal of CSCP implementation.

As articulated in Monteiro-Leitner, Asner-Self, Milde, Leitner, and Skelton (2006), various system members (e.g., stakeholders) may hold significantly different views regarding duties that school counselors "should" do versus "actually" do and the amount of time associated with each. Whether at microlevels (e.g., school) or macrolevels (e.g., community), recognizing members within a system, their systemic influence, and the potential differences in beliefs and/or perceptions will benefit school counselors in rural settings as they actively work toward becoming systemic change agents.

A pertinent concern is this scenario is the identification of stakeholders for collaboration surrounding the creation and administration of a needs assessment. Needs assessments (most commonly in the form of surveys with Likert-type scale and/or open-ended responses) are effective tools for evaluating program reach and interventions, identifying systemic needs, and obtaining feedback from system members (Dimmitt, Carey, & Hatch, 2007). Needs assessment surveys are valuable for distilling salient issues and concerns within a system (e.g., teachers reporting their perceptions) but also serve as a tool to provide voice and agency to populations who normally possess limited systemic influence (students, ESL populations, etc.). Thus, the representation of multiple system groups within the school counselor's collaboration in and of itself can lead to systemic change.

However, although it may be beneficial to invite multiple system members in such collaboration, given the circumstances, it is important to remember that member role and responsibilities can vary. For example, with minimal recruiting, active, regularly recognized members of the school microsystem may readily volunteer (e.g., PTA members, paraprofessionals, teachers). Even with relatively limited responsibilities, such members may still have dramatic impact on the process due to their inherent systemic influence.

Conversely, volunteers from the increasing ESL population, while possessing critical information and experience relevant to successful implementation of the CSCP, may have little to no systemic influence. Such stakeholders may be able to speak to the issue of content and relevance in construction of the needs assessment, as well as provide consultation regarding scope of need and supportive services related to translation of the instrument. The school counselor in this scenario may have to exert significant time and energies seeking such an individual within the rural community system, especially one comfortable with exceeding systemic expectations.

Along this spectrum of system members, the counseling intern serves as a representative example. Likely, the intern shares a similar vision regarding role and scope of CSCP and, as a high school sports coach, is familiar with the systemic nuances of pre-K–12 education in that community. Although it may be common for interns to have limited decision-making power reflective of their emerging status (e.g., not yet certificated, non-FTE [full-time equivalent] role), the intern in this scenario may, indeed, demonstrate greater systemic influence because of their recognition as an "insider" within the community. Collaboration here presents a mutually beneficial opportunity in which the intern's role and responsibilities enhance his or her internship experience (e.g., survey piloting, item refinement, coordinating administration, data entry/analysis) while the school counselor effectively utilizes the systemic "capital" available (e.g., knowledge/awareness of community concerns, access to other system members).

Finally, the school counselor would benefit from exploring ways to align his or her CSCP endeavors with relevant academic data, as regardless of setting, student outcomes continue to exert considerable influence across all pre-K–12 systems. Even within initial foundational components (e.g., needs assessment), alignment with relevant educational initiative standards (the school improvement plan, district standards, Common Core State Standards, etc.) may prove beneficial for further CSCP implementation and expansion. Effective utilization of data in conjunction with school-wide collaboration can result in increased program advocacy and services (Gruman, Marston, & Koon, 2013).

Supplemental Readings, Online Resources, and Supplemental Activities

Supplemental Readings

American School Counselor Association. (2015). *Back-to-school resources.* Retrieved from https://www.schoolcounselor.org/school-counselors/professional-development/learn-more/back-to-school-resources

Hatch, T. (2014). *The use of data in school counseling: Hatching results for students, programs, and the profession.* Thousand Oaks, CA: Sage.

Kaffenberger, C., & Young, A. (2013). *Making DATA work* (3rd ed.). Alexandria, VA: American School Counselor Association.

Morgan Consoli, M., Consoli, A., Orozco, G. L., Gonzales, R., & Vera, E. M. (2012). Barriers experienced by Mexican immigrants: Implications for educational achievement and mental health. *Association of Mexican-American Educators Journal, 6*(2), 37–47.

Seddon, J. (2015). *School counselor support for the academic, career, personal, and social needs of ELL students* [Culminating Projects in Community Psychology, Counseling and Family Therapy, Paper 8]. Retrieved from http://repository.stcloudstate.edu/cgi/viewcontent.cgi?article=1007&context=cpcf_etds

Online Resources

ACA School Counselor Connection
https://www.counseling.org/knowledge-center/school-counselor-connection

American Counseling Association (ACA)
https://www.counseling.org

American School Counselor Association (ASCA)
http://www.schoolcounselor.org

ASCA SCENE
http://scene.schoolcounselor.org/home

Center for School Counseling Outcome Research & Evaluation (CSCORE)
http://www.umass.edu/schoolcounseling

Supplemental Activities

Learning Activities

[AU7]

- In small groups, find and review a school counseling needs assessment. Discuss the format, questions, and overall layout of this template. What questions would you add? What other information needs to be included to help inform the development of a comprehensive school counseling program? What are some potential challenges for English as a second language (ESL) students within a school community? In addition, what are other areas to explore with the recent influx of Mexican immigrants in this school community? How can the school counselor best advocate for these students? Multiple stakeholders can provide critical information to inform the development of the school counseling program. What information would you want to gather from parents/guardians? Teachers? How might this information assist program development?

- "An ESC View of the School": Utilizing a flipped-model approach, students are assigned relevant text and journal article readings articulating an ecological systems perspective. Students are asked to articulate (written assignment, bio statement for the site webpage, etc.) what it means to them to serve as an ecological school counselor (ESC). Students then present this information in class via small-group discussion and whole-class shareout. Assigned a case scenario of a school counselor within a community setting, students are then tasked with analyzing the scenario through an ecological systems perspective: Who are the system members? What are the roles? What influence do various members have? What state is the system in? How might comprehensive school counseling program (CSCP) changes be received by the system? How might the ESC go about enacting systemic change?

- "Needs Asssessment Construction": In entry-level foundational course work (i.e., Introduction to School Counseling) students are tasked with locating survey resources (existing surveys, items, tools, and methods for analysis, etc.) to compile within their own individual "toolbox." Students are then either (a) given a fictional school site scenario or (b) tasked with choosing a local school site. Students must utilize resources and materials found to create a needs assessment tool relevant for the school site. Students present their completed surveys to the whole class. Subsequent processing follows a spiral-curriculum approach reinforcing previously explored themes. For example:

    a. *Evidence-based data-driven practices:* How were survey items determined? How are they relevant? What statistical considerations might be relevant? How might this fit within a research paradigm? How about a program-evaluation paradigm?

    b. *Equity:* How might this needs assessment be used as a diagnostic tool for identifying potential inequities within the CSCP and school site?

    c. *Ecological systems:* Who are the system members relevant for this needs assessment? How might this needs assessment increase or decrease their systemic influence?

d. *Logistics:* What aspects of the school site seem most relevant for successful administration of the needs assessment? Who are the system members most likely to be valuable resources? What might a timeline for administration, analysis, and presentation/reporting look like?

Chapter 17

She's Come Undone!
Alternatives for Amy?

James Gondak

Background

I am a school counselor in a high school located in a suburban neighborhood outside of a major metropolitan city. We are the smallest school in the county's district, with a population of 1,350 students. We have four school counselors on staff, along with a full-time school psychologist. It is a working class community that also includes a middle class and impoverished segment of the local population. About 80% of our students are White, and the other 20% is split between African American and Hispanic students. Over the past 10 years, our free and reduced-price lunch population has climbed to nearly a third of the school. Most educators in the building, including me, feel that the reality is that many more students qualify for reduced-price or free lunch, but families do not apply because they are proud. Even with these environmental factors that tend to impede learning, our school has been able to maintain adequate yearly progress in improving our scores on state assessments. Traditionally, most of our students with attendance, grade, emotional, and discipline problems come from those families who are at or near the poverty line. This context made Amy's situation all the more interesting.

Amy comes from a working-class Caucasian family. Her parents are together. Both parents work and display an appropriate level of concern and care for their children. Amy has a fraternal twin sister, and they seem to get along. Amy progressed through elementary school maintaining above-grade level performance in her studies. Upon a record review, her elementary school teacher's comments reflect a good student who is sweet and caring. Amy does not participate in a variety of school-wide activities largely because of her need to carry a 15-hour/week part-time job. She enjoys reading and is a member of our drama club, which produces plays for school.

In middle school, Amy was one of 30 students in a class of over 300 who began taking high school courses in the seventh grade, specifically Algebra 1. She continued to take two high school–level courses in eighth grade, Geometry and Spanish 1, and earned Bs. As a ninth grader, she rarely surfaced with any concerns, and I only met with her for academic counseling and classroom guidance lessons. After her first year of high school, she had earned a 3.75 grade point average.

Amy's life began to change as a 10th-grade student. Amy, being a little overweight, began to complain to her father that she was being bullied. Her father began speaking to me about the concern he had for her. The major sticking point became the fact that Amy would not tell us who was bullying her. She would not tell her twin, her father, mother, the school administration, or me. Her teacher didn't see it, and none of her friends said they knew who was doing it. Shortly after this, Amy was hospitalized for the first time in a local psychiatric unit for an eating disorder. After about a week away from school, she returned, and things went okay at school for the next couple of months. The same scenario started again in the late spring, and she once again went to the local hospital and then to the adolescent eating disorder unit.

In the summer between her sophomore year and junior year, Amy's father came to my office. He shared that the doctors were treating Amy in the eating disorder unit, mostly for insurance purposes. He stated that they were beginning to feel that she was developing a borderline personality disorder, but they would not give such a diagnosis to an adolescent. Amy's father felt that it would be best for his daughter to graduate early and get away from the people who were bullying her. The strategy was to get her out of the drama of high school, and she would be able to start attending classes at our local community college with more freedom and autonomy.

With Amy's application for early graduation approved, she started the school year fine, but the old difficulties quickly resurfaced. The bullying started about a month into the year. The difference this time was that she told her parents the names of students. Unfortunately, it was her twin who first said that she was "making up the bullying," followed by her father expressing doubt. After consulting with our school psychologist about borderline personality disorder, I realized that this was probably the case. After an investigation, the bullying was determined not to be happening, and Amy did another stint in the hospital. Throughout Amy's ordeal, she maintained good grades. She even scored a 1200 on her math and verbal SAT. When she returned to school, her father and I spoke once again about the need to engage in outside counseling, maintain her medication, and not to go far away for college. There are numerous colleges that are within 45 minutes from home, and Amy needs to have supervision to make sure that she is compliant with her treatment. The last straw came in the spring of her junior year. When things started again, we decided that home and hospital teaching was the best course of action for Amy to finish her high school career and keep her out of the hospital. After receiving a note from her psychologist with diagnoses of major depression, anxiety, and an eating disorder, we placed Amy on home and hospital teaching.

Incident

It wasn't until after graduation when I found out that Amy had requested that her final transcript be sent to a state university, 4 hours away. After 2 hard years and a relationship forged with Amy's father, I felt an obligation to voice my concern. Amy's father was not receptive to my concerns and stated that she will continue therapy at the university and that her twin sister will also be attending the university and be able to look after her. I felt this was unfair to her sister and irresponsible of her parents, but the family had made up their minds. My next thought was to contact our admissions representative at the college using the "duty to warn" statute, but I did not want to violate Amy's rights. Upon updating our student services team at the Board of Education, I was given the following advice/directive. Because the family did not request a secondary school report or a letter of recommendation from me, and because the college never requested any information from me, I was not allowed to make contact to voice my concerns.

Discussion

Afterward, I found it interesting that Amy's parents, who were so supportive, would let their child go so far away with the potential for a lifelong and extremely difficult diagnosis. Were they, perhaps, tired of the constant battle with their child? Either way, as a school counselor with over 10 years' experience, she is one of the students about whom I will always wonder—whether she is well and healthy.

Questions

1. Would you have followed the directive from your supervisor?
2. Because my registrar sent a transcript to the university, can this be construed as the university asking me for a secondary school report?
3. Do you think placing her on home and hospital teaching was the best way to meet her personal and academic needs?
4. To what additional outside resources would you refer her?
5. What additional assessments or data might have been useful?

Response 1

Linda Foster

Just as mental health practitioners face challenges in the treatment of clients, school counselors also face challenges in addressing the mental health needs of students. One of the challenges in addressing the needs of students under the responsive services described in the American School Counselor Association (ASCA) National Model (2012a) may include many aspects of counseling and crisis response. Another challenge for school counselors may be the role confusion that plagues many counseling professionals who work in systems with multiple providers and stakeholders (Osborn, 2004). In the case of Amy, there are multiple stakeholders involved who are all invested in the wellness of this student. The school counselor clearly is passionate and caring about Amy's future, but there must be clarity on the ethical and legal guidelines and assessment questions that dictate the school counselor's response.

First, working within a school system has its own set of regulations and "chain-of-command" guidelines, which requires school counselors to maintain a consultative and collaborative system for indirect student services (ASCA, 2012a). First and foremost, school counselors must take special care to follow the ASCA Ethical Standards for School Counselors (2010b) regarding any referrals, consultation, or collaboration and sharing student information. In Amy's case, the school counselor received a directive to maintain "radio silence" with her concerns. This supervisor directive was in keeping with maintaining the confidentiality of the student (and parents). Moreover, the ASCA ethical standards (2010b) give school counselors clear guidance on the issues of confidentiality. Specifically, Standard A.2.d states that school counselors: "Recognize their primary obligation for confidentiality is to the students but balance that obligation with an understanding of parents'/guardians' legal and inherent rights to be the guiding voice in their children's lives, especially in value-laden issues." In the case of Amy, the parents also gave clear direction to the school counselor about their desires regarding Amy's future. Although the school counselor had strong feelings, thoughts, and ideas about what was best for Amy, it behooves the school counselor to remember the legal parameters regarding minors and the role of parents in any release of information.

I believe that the school counselor would have breached confidentiality by releasing information. The school counselor believed that a "duty to warn" existed; however, again, the ASCA (2010b) ethical standards, Section A.7. Danger to Self or Others, clearly outlines the circumstances when it is acceptable to breach confidentiality: "Professional school counselors: a. Inform parents/guardians and/or appropriate authorities when a student poses a danger to self or others. This is to be done after careful deliberation and consultation with other counseling professionals." In Amy's case, there was not a clear and imminent danger to self or others, and the school counselor failed to follow the standard regarding consultation with other counseling professionals.

One of the points for discussion is whether the decision for home and hospital teaching was appropriate. The school counselor does not work alone, and again, the ASCA National Model (2012a) gives clear guidance to school counselors regarding indirect student services. The National Model outlines how the school counselor can work with the student, parents, teachers, administrators, school staff, and community stakeholders to address the needs and support the academic achievement of all students; in Amy's case, the plan that was created seemed to meet her academic needs and her parents' wishes.

The school counselor had an obligation to Amy and her parents when Amy was a high school student, and outside resources such as support groups for both Amy and her parents could have been offered. Although the school counselor's caring and concern was evident, it appeared that the parent was reluctant to take the advice of the school counselor once Amy graduated. After Amy's graduation, the school counselor no longer had an obligation to offer outside resources or guidance on her college plans.

Additionally, another discussion point was what, if any, other assessments or data could have been helpful. One assessment tool that could have been used is a complete biopsychosocial assessment or intake interview. An interview is an effective tool to gather information about multiple factors possibly affecting Amy's academic, personal, and social performance at school, allowing the school counselor to see the "big picture." An intake interview gathers a myriad of information ranging from family history and demographics to the current living situation, to medical information that could potentially affect Amy. By using a thorough interview, the school counselor could determine whether there were other influencing factors such as possible abuse, violence in the home, eating disorders, depression, anxiety, and the possibility of attention-deficit/hyperactivity disorder (Neukrug & Fawcett, 2015).

Finally, it is important to recognize the limitations of our work as professional counselors. Counseling professionals must safeguard their own well-being and recognize their own limitations with respect to professional expertise. In the case of Amy's school counselor, it is apparent that the counselor was passionate and concerned. Osborn (2004) has reminded counselors that, to be an effective counselor, we must recognize the things that we can and cannot do to help our clients. Furthermore, Osborn created helpful suggestions on how to create meaningful perspectives on our practice and profession. School counselors are often challenged to "do more with less" because of economic constraints on public and private education. Consequently, we are reminded that creating boundaries and recognizing our own limitations helps to promote wellness in ourselves, which, in turn, promotes our ability to be effective counseling professionals.

Response 2
Bradley T. Erford

In this case, the professional school counselor should adhere to the directive from the Board of Education supervisor and not contact the university to which Amy had applied. No indication was given that Amy was a danger to herself or others, so no "duty to warn" statute applies. Thus, confidentiality of the student's information and circumstances should be maintained until legal requests or parent consent is obtained to forward additional information. As serious as multiple mental health diagnoses (e.g., eating disorder, anxiety disorder) and a potential, albeit undiagnosed, borderline personality disorder may be, a large percentage of the U.S. population has been diagnosed with a mental or emotional disorder, and many are able to lead healthy, productive lives with supportive counseling and medication treatment regimens (Assistant Secretary for Planning and Evaluation, U.S. Department of Health and Human Services, 2008).

A request for a transcript is just that; if a university requests additional information, schools may supply the requested additional information while following appropriate legal guidelines. However, if a school sends more unsolicited information than just the requested transcript, federal and state laws (e.g., the Family Educational Rights and Privacy Act, the Health Insurance Portability and Accountability Act), regulations, and even school board policies may be violated. Looking at this from another direction, if the professional school counselor contacts the university admissions representative, shares confidential information without parent or student consent, and Amy is denied admission on the basis of that protected, unsolicited information, the school system (and school counselor) could be legally liable if a court case is brought by Amy or her parents.

Regardless of whether the home and hospital instructional intervention was optimal would depend on Amy's specific educational and emotional needs at the time. Home and hospital teaching is undertaken because it is in the best interest of the individual student, not in acquiescence to parent or student demands. Ordinarily, this alternative educational opportunity provides reduced academic rigor, but Amy has already missed many days from school, views the school environment as hostile (whether her perception is reality based or not), reportedly gets good grades, and achieved a 1200 on the SAT-I, so she may benefit from the more individualized learning experience. Furthermore, this is the natural bridge between the first two questions and how to legally and ethically communicate with the university. Home and hospital curricular modifications raise a red flag at nearly all university admission offices, and it is up to the university employees to exercise due diligence to make sure they understand the circumstances that led to the home and hospital schooling, ongoing treatment, and how those circumstances are likely to influence Amy's undergraduate experience at their university. That is, this curricular modification should be documented on the transcript, and a university admissions officer should inquire (many universities actually investigate and document) why Amy needed to complete her high school experience with home and hospital instruction.

It is essential to know what Amy's role has been in her own treatment and whether she willingly complies. If she is motivated to comply with ongoing treatment and positive support systems are in place at the university, the potential for positive outcomes is enhanced. Many university counseling centers offer counseling and support groups for students with mental health diagnoses, sometimes specifically related to eating disorders or stress/anxiety management, among many others. Community support resources should also be sought to ease Amy's transition into a university experience.

In hindsight, this was a perfect opportunity for the high school and professional school counselor to view Amy's situation from a systemic perspective and engage in consultation using a collaborative-interdependent model (Erford, 2019) in which the school, family, and community resources (e.g., hospital personnel, primary care physician, mental health counselor) are assembled to all understand the problem, identify specific educational and treatment objectives, plan interventions, carry out the interventions through various roles, and monitor and evaluate progress. This collaborative-interdependent consultation model is tailor-made to address issues with multiple causes across multiple contexts in the most cost-effective manner. In this model, school counselors often become coordinators and brokers of interdisciplinary resources, bringing together teams of professionals to help parents and students plan, implement, and evaluate multidisciplinary interventions. Often, we find that multiple professionals provide overlapping services and fail to communicate with each other, leading to discontinuity and service disruptions—a very inefficient use of resources. Brokering and coordinating resources and services provides an integrative service delivery model that can meet current needs and transition with the student in the future, such as when Amy goes off to the university in the next town, next state, or across the country.

Finally, it was unclear whether a comprehensive psychological evaluation was ever conducted, one that explored Amy's personality and mental health issues in depth. What type of eating disorder (e.g., binge eating disorder, bulimia nervosa, anorexia nervosa) and anxiety disorder (e.g., generalized anxiety disorder, panic disorder, social anxiety disorder, agoraphobia) were in evidence? What gave the hospital clinicians the impression that Amy was displaying symptoms of a borderline personality disorder? Ordinarily, psychological evaluations are conducted at the time of intake during hospital stays. It would be unfortunate if such evaluations existed within Amy's hospital records but were not shared (after appropriate written parental consent and permission were obtained) with the professional school counselor and school psychologist. This is another instance of disintegrated services that would be addressed through use of a collaborative-interdependent model (Erford, 2019).

Supplemental Readings and Supplemental Activities

Supplemental Readings

Erford, B. T. (Ed.). (2019). *Transforming the school counseling profession* (5th ed.). Columbus, OH: Pearson.

Family Educational Rights and Privacy Act (34 C.F.R., Part 99; Final Rule, 2008). Retrieved from http://www.ed.gov/legislation/FedRegister/finrule/2008-4/120908a.pdf

Haddock, L. R. (2014). *Borderline personality disorder.* Retrieved from https://www.counseling.org/docs/default-source/practice-briefs/borderline-personality-disorder.pdf

Kress, V. E., & Paylo, M. J. (2015). *Treating those with mental disorders: A comprehensive approach to case conceptualization and treatment.* Columbus, OH: Pearson.

Supplemental Activities

Learning Activities

- Develop and videotape a 1-minute infomercial explaining the collaborative-interdependent model to help parents, teachers, and community organizations understand how helpful these services can be.

- Collaborative consultation supports an integrative approach that places a premium on collaboration across systems of care. Look on the internet or in the local library for information to report on the social institutions that you will need to be aware of as a professional school counselor. Create a list of community-based institutions that might be helpful in solving more complex problems in a given school (violence, drugs, teen pregnancy, etc.).

- Conduct a mock collaborative-interdependent consultation session for a student who (pick any of the following): has Tourette's syndrome; has attention-deficit/hyperactivity disorder; comes from a "broken" home; has a father with alcoholism; is a latchkey child; achieves grades in the C-to-D range but scores in the top percentile for functional tests; has been caught among a group of students smoking marijuana in the bathroom.

- Lower High School is located in a culturally diverse suburban area. There has been a recent increase in teenage pregnancy at this high school. Describe how you would work with the students, teachers, community organizations, and parents to reduce the recent increase in teenage pregnancy. What stakeholders might you want to involve when advocating for a student who is homeless? What resources will you want to secure for the student and his or her family?

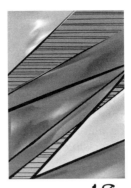

Chapter 18

Did You Bring a Suicide Note?

Tracy L. Jackson

Background

As a school district coordinator, it is my job to provide clinical supervision to the numerous school counselors employed by the district. One day, a middle school counselor called me to say that her principal would not allow a student with suicide ideation back into school unless the student had a note from a therapist stating that he or she was no longer suicidal. I told her that we could not do that and to allow the student to return to school. About a month later, a high school counselor called me, also stating that her principal would not allow a student with suicide ideation back into school unless the student had a note from a therapist stating that he or she was no longer suicidal. Again, I told her that we could not do that and to allow the student to return to school.

Unbeknownst to me, there seemed to be an unwritten policy that the district's administrators were adhering to that prevented students with suicidal ideation to return to school unless they were cleared by a therapist. Later that week, I received a phone call from the irate high school principal. She stated that he did not want the student to commit suicide during the school day and that requesting a note from a therapist ensured that the responsibility would not lie with the school. I explained to her that we could not deny FAPE (free and public education) to students and that refusing admittance until they received a note was not in the best interest of students, for they could miss valuable instruction time, their attendance recorded would be marred, and possibly leaving them home alone while a parent worked was more cause for alarm. After that phone call, I contacted the city's emergency mental health agency and spoke to them about providing notes for students. The director told me how the agency had received numerous requests for notes and that they refused to provide them. She then requested that some type of communication be forwarded to the school district to alert them that written notes confirming that a student no longer had suicide ideation was neither ethical nor permissible.

Incident

A parent called my office, furious that the school counselor told her that her child, Sharon, could not return to school unless she was seen by a mental health provider or doctor. This doctor must also provide a note stating that Sharon no longer had suicidal ideation and was believed fit to return to school. The school counselor also told the parent that this was the building administrator's policy, and Sharon would have to stay home until she returned with a note. After writing all the information down, I told the parent that I would contact my director and return her phone call.

Discussion

Sharon returned to school the next day on the bus. She did not have a note from a mental health provider stating that she was no longer suicidal. When the school counselor asked her if she had visited a doctor, she stated that she had but that her doctor would not write her a note. Her mother needed to go to work and could not stay home with her, so she sent her to school. Reluctantly, the school counselor needed to alert the building administrator that Sharon had returned to school without a note.

Questions

1. How can one handle his or her building administrator, knowing that students with suicidal ideation should return to school as opposed to possibly sitting at home alone?
2. How can one advocate for students when there is no formal policy in place?

Response 1

Malik S. Henfield

Working with building administrators can be quite difficult at times. Much of the difficulty can arguably be attributed to a lack of understanding of the role and function of professional school counselors. This case, for instance, represents a clear example of an instance in which the school counselor ought to advocate on behalf of the student by helping the building administrator understand that students experiencing suicidal ideation have the right to be in school. *What* needs to be done is clear, but *how* to do this in a way that an administrator can respectfully understand may prove more difficult.

A building administrator may be unaware of a school counselor's training standards and, as such, be oblivious to the fact that the counselor has a healthy understanding of not only counseling but also educational and counseling laws and ethics. As such, this situation may present an opportunity to advocate simultaneously for students and the school counseling profession. It would be important for the school counselor to begin by relaying as much factual information to the administrator as possible. The unwritten nature of the policy that the district utilizes, as well as its trickle-down implementation in the school building, is a topic that cannot be ignored and must be addressed. It would behoove the administrator to get a better understanding of the precariousness associated with abiding by informal policies that may, indeed, potentially harm students and, moreover, not be defensible in a court of law. It is of utmost importance that schools are compliant with all educational regulations, including those related to Section 504 of the 1973 Rehabilitation Act and the Individuals with Disabilities Education Act (IDEA). Unfortunately, in this case, district culture seems to have taken precedence over salient legalities.

Given their background training, it is well within a school counselor's scope of practice to advocate on behalf of students by bringing this to the building administrator's attention. To increase the likelihood of being taken seriously, however, it makes sense to approach the administrator armed with specific regulations that clearly demonstrate that preventing students from coming to school because of suicidal ideation is not only unethical but also illegal. The next step would be to demonstrate leadership by volunteering to be a part of the solution. To that end, the school counselor ought to volunteer to lead or, at minimum, serve on a committee charged with developing suicide prevention and intervention policies and procedures that meet the legal guidelines. In the absence of a comprehensive, systemic plan, it would be helpful to consult resources that can assist with developing programming, such as classroom guidance lessons, a group counseling curriculum, individual counseling techniques, and professional development activities, meant to advocate and meet the needs of any students who may be struggling with suicidal ideation.

Response 2

Laurie A. Carlson

Effectively navigating the counselor–principal relationship, particularly in a situation like this, takes intention and finesse. This first question is best addressed through deliberate actions that serve to educate administrators about the specialized training and appropriate roles of the professional school counselor as well as assure administrators that you as a school counselor will assume responsibilities in helping the student return to school as quickly and safely as possible. An administrator who understands that school counselors have the training to respond to suicidal crises and the desire to participate in, and perhaps even lead, student support teams will be much more comfortable allowing the school counselor to take on a leadership role when addressing such situations. Most administrators will be well aware of legal mandates regarding access to free and public education for all students, including those students affected by the IDEA and Section 504. They may, however, not be aware of state statues particular to suicide prevention in the schools. The American Foundation for Suicide Prevention has an online guide to state statutes for suicide prevention in the schools at http://afsp.org/wp-content/uploads/2016/04/Suicide-Prevention-Statutes-Schools-2.pdf. It is also important for administrators to know how school counselors are equipped to support those legal expectations.

It is critical that the student who has just experienced a suicidal crisis be supported in safely returning to precrisis life activities. I believe that administrators fundamentally understand this, but their sense of what is right for the student becomes clouded by their sense of what they perceive to be in the best interest of the institution. The school counselor can help ease an administrator's misgivings and facilitate student return by actively participating in the re-entry process. This participation should be negotiated on the basis of the specific needs of the student and his or her family but would likely include responsibilities such as meeting regularly with the student; maintaining contact with the student's parents and/or therapist; and providing appropriate linkages between other members of the educational team, including teachers. These responsibilities might be part of a formal Section 504 plan but also may be part of a separate re-entry or safety plan. Helping the suicidal student himself is only one aspect of appropriate school counselor response. The second is broader advocacy through involvement in school policy and this leads to systemic change for all students.

After the school counselor has helped to address the needs of this particular student through active participation in a re-entry plan, there is then the institutional capacity to develop formal policies regarding such instances. With the increasing recognition of mental health needs in our country's youth, it is important now more than ever to have written policies in place that not only support students in an equitable manner but also protect systems and professionals so all students can continue to benefit from comprehensive and high-quality educational experiences. Recently, I also learned about a similar policy regarding a therapist letter required for a student to return to school. As a school counselor educator, I was interested in where this policy actually came from and how a district managed to meet their mandate to educate all children while denying attendance in such a manner. With a little research, I was somewhat surprised to find this protocol listed in the Model School District

Policy on Suicide Prevention distributed by the American Foundation for Suicide Prevention. I was further intrigued to discover that the American School Counselor Association is listed as a co-author of the document. The actual language from item 2 on the re-entry procedure states, "The parent or guardian will provide documentation from a mental health care provider that the student has undergone examination and that they are no longer a danger to themselves or others" (p. 6).

Professional school counselors should step up and provide leadership in developing school policies, particularly in relation to the academic, social–emotional, or career needs of students. Implemented well and clearly articulated, policy can serve to protect students and institutions while ensuring equity and best practices. Conversely, if not implemented well and if only informally articulated, such as the one introduced earlier, policies can put forth barriers to students and contribute to ongoing inequities. Policies without clear purpose are those most likely to fall into the last category. When considering the current policy, it is paramount for those who are involved in creating this policy to consider its purpose and to then ensure that such a policy is clearly written and implemented with fidelity to meet the intended purpose. Requiring such a document from a mental health professional can, in theory, meet multiple but divergent purposes, including legal protection for liability against the school to ensure a broad support network for the student. If implemented well and clearly written, then perhaps a legal liability disclaimer signed by the parent would be more appropriate; otherwise, why, include the stipulation that the document indicate no further danger instead of merely documenting that the student is receiving outside services? These are the kinds of difficult nuances that should be considered as the education team creates school policy.

Supplemental Readings, Online Resources, and Supplemental Activities

Supplemental Readings

Granello, P. F., & Juhnke, G. A. (2010). *Case studies in suicide: Experiences of mental health professionals.* Upper Saddle River, NJ: Pearson.

Juhnke, G. A., Granello, D. H., & Granello, P. F. (2011). *Suicide, self-injury, and violence in the schools: Assessment, prevention, and intervention strategies.* Hoboken, NJ: Wiley.

Online Resources

Model School District Policy on Suicide Prevention: Model Language Commentary and Resources
https://afsp.org/wp-content/uploads/2016/01/Model-Policy_FINAL.pdf

Preventing Suicide: A Toolkit for High Schools (HHS Publication no. SMA-12-4669) Center for Mental Health Services, Substance Abuse and Mental Health Services Administration
http://store.samhsa.gov/shin/content/SMA12-4669/SMA12-4669.pdf

Supplemental Activities

Learning Activities

- Collaborate with organizations that have suicide prevention expertise, and invite them to come to the school and lead professional development activities.

- As part of a classroom guidance series on suicide prevention, have students create a trifold filled with resources for educators and teachers interested in learning more about suicide prevention.

Chapter 19

Professional Dilemma: Unteachable Teacher?

Jason Durrell

Background

I am a middle school counselor. The public school where I work is in a suburban setting with an affluent population. Our student body consists of 800 students made up of 95% Caucasians and approximately 5% minorities, consisting of African Americans and Asians (which includes our Indian population), all served by two school counselors. Seventy of our students are on IEPs (individualized education plans for learning disabilities). Approximately 40% of the entire student population is identified as gifted in one or more of the four core subjects (reading, math, science, and social studies). Our school is continuously rated "excellent" or achieves an "A" on the state's building report card.

In working with these students, I am often faced with the question, "Can I switch to a different teacher?", which usually stems from the teachers "demanding" that the student turn in work, study, and be prepared for class. Some middle school students have an oddly routine thought process in that the grass is always greener, a new teacher will inspire great motivation in them, and their work will exceed that of Einstein and Picasso combined. As I treat every student equally who comes to me with their new plan for greatness, and I listen to the student's concerns, my typical response focuses around the learning point that, "We will all have teachers or coworkers we must work with and get along with so that we can reach our goals together. In high school and college, there may only be one teacher who will teach the class you want to take. What would you do then? How can you be a success despite the people around you?" In

159

response to my questions, students usually pepper in astute comments like, "I would drop that class" (I respond with "Give up your dreams?") or "Quit my job and go somewhere else." This discussion is followed by some guided reflection, and the student and I develop a plan on how the student can be more successful and remain in the teacher's class.

Incident

However, there is also a recurring theme in our school that happens a few times during the year, when a student will ask to change to a different teacher because the teacher is being "mean, insensitive, and doesn't care about me or my work." I often know which teacher the student is talking about before he or she divulges the teacher's name. Thinking of one teacher, I don't socialize with her very much, as it appears that we don't have much in common. Generally speaking, I assume that she is good-natured in her actions and is honestly trying to be the best teacher she knows how to be. Although she is pleasant most of the time, I have seen her get frustrated with students, and her underlying emotions come to the surface quickly in the form of an adolescent tantrum. At such times, I have heard her say, "Well, you'll have to figure out how to do this. I can't help you."

The teacher doesn't seem to realize that her personal opinions of students are being relayed to them through her actions. I've talked with her professionally about a few of her students over the years. At first, she participates in developing a plan with the student and is genuinely excited to be a part of the process and appears hopeful that things will change with the student. This optimism fades quickly, however; within weeks, the student is back in my office prepared to lobby again for a change of venue for this class.

The teacher has over 15 years in teaching English/language arts in middle school. Throughout her teaching tenure, the results of her students' performance suggest that most students accomplish a year's worth of growth in the year that they have her. However, there are also those students with whom she has difficulty, and there does not appear to be the same consistency in those students accomplishing a year's worth of growth. The principals are aware of her work ethic and have stated that some students point out, "We just do worksheets. We don't learn" when referring to her class.

Discussion

I've consulted with my fellow school counselor in these situations, and both of us have made a few recommendations to this teacher to help her improve her own frustration (and indirectly help the students in her class). We've suggested that she take more time to get to know the students who are struggling in her class, talk to the struggling students' other teachers to see if they are having similar issues, and reassess the students to see what specific learning skills they may be deficient in and help them with those. Again, it seems like her old habits creep back in, and she is back to her edgy self. This is a sensitive subject, as it appears to be the teacher's own personality that is causing the conflict in these situations.

Questions

1. Is it time for me to have a heart-to-heart conversation with this teacher about how she is handling challenging students? She is strong-willed and socializes with other teachers, so I'm not too optimistic that she will change.
2. How might this situation be conceptualized in terms of outcomes, data, and evaluation within comprehensive school counseling programs?
3. How might a school counselor use an evaluation and/or data to help facilitate change for this teacher?
4. Is this a situation in which the principal should step in? What data might be good to include in presenting the situation to the principal?
5. Should I put all the struggling students in this teacher's class so she HAS to improve how she works with challenging students?
6. Are there other ways that this situation could be improved (if it can't be solved)?

Response 1

Richard E. Cleveland

This scenario presents a student population that is comfortable with advocating for themselves (e.g., requesting a class/schedule change), even when such requests seem influenced by developmentally expected misconceptions (e.g., teacher "demands"). The school counselor in this scenario approaches these situations with more than just professional tact, recognizing the potential for growth in such interactions. A similar approach used with the teacher colleague would reflect a systemic response in which, more than merely helping students function in the school, consultation with the teacher might lead to changing the classroom environment itself (Dinkmeyer & Carlson, 2006). However, before articulating ideas toward data-based consultation, two items require brief attention: school counselor role and consultation focus.

Undoubtedly many school counselor conversations may be considered "heart to heart," but the aforementioned scenario suggests a conversation entering the realm of administrative responsibilities. The American School Counselor Association (ASCA, n.d.-b) website (under "Information for Administrators") provides resources specifically addressing counselor and administrator interactions. Discussing the role of the school counselor, a chart titled "Appropriate [and Inappropriate] Activities for School

Counselors" lists the item "assisting with duties in the principal's office" as inappropriate (ASCA, n.d.-a). School counselors do not have the authority or the responsibility for staffing decisions. We do, however, have the authority and the responsibility to advocate for all students and help them experience success within the pre-K–12 environment. The listed "appropriate" duty, "helping the school principal identify and resolve student issues, needs and problems" (ASCA, n.d.-a), reflects action that is centered around students and their concerns. This is instructive, as it highlights an important point. In some situations, although the tasks and/ or actions undertaken by counselors may seem similar, if not identical, arguably what differentiates the "appropriateness" is the focus of those actions. The current scenario illuminates this distinction.

Whether consultation occurs one-on-one with the teacher or in conjunction with administration, consultation can provide support both professionally (resources for curriculum, pedagogy, dealing with "difficult" students, etc.) as well as emotionally (validating feelings, listening to the teacher's emotions and thoughts, acknowledging areas for growth through a strengths-based perspective rather than a critical one, etc.). Teaching is recognized as a stressful occupation with a significant chance for burnout, where emotional exhaustion may lead to callous depersonalization of students (Tatar, 2009). The suggestion to intentionally place more challenging students in this teacher's class would be both unprofessional and unethical if acted upon. As the scenario points out, the teacher in question here is experiencing a level of personal and professional frustration to a degree that is negatively affecting their teaching duties (e.g., pedagogy, relational interactions with students). A parallel is emerging in which the frustration level of the school counselor is similarly surfacing. Rather than giving criticism, this is pointed out, as it provides an opportunity for demonstrating empathy. Feeling reflections such as, "It sounds like you're frustrated," might (with requisite care and respect) lead to counselor self-disclosure such as, "I feel frustrated when I hear students complaining about the workload and see them struggling academically. I feel helpless when I hear that our collaborative strategies aren't working in the classroom for those students; especially when I hear you talk about wanting these kids to be successful in high school and beyond." Having demonstrated their "trustworthiness" (Tatar, 2009), counselors may engage in more candid discussion with the teacher, reframing the "problem" and continuing efforts advocating for students' success.

Data, both in terms of student outcomes and comprehensive school counseling program (CSCP) evaluation, should have a presence in our advocacy for students, and the present case is no exception. Clearly, data regarding this situation already exist, as the counselor's concern has grown through the culmination of anecdotal evidence, data from failed student intervention plans, and discrepancies in students' academic growth. However, in thinking about developing and collecting outcome data relevant for the present scenario, it is again important to consider our focus; that is, whatever data we provide should be framed around students, their needs, their concerns, and (ultimately) what they require to experience success. Toward that end, two themes are offered, guiding school counselor data-based consultation. First, school counselors as consultants must balance the perspectives (and potential discrepancies) of multiple informants (Johnson & Hannon, 2014) with meso- and macrosystemic views. The counselor in this scenario has already begun this effort, comparing individual student's academic growth with grade-level trends. In addition to academics, school-wide needs assessments provide macrolevel contextual data relevant to the overall school climate. Integrated with CSCP and Response to Intervention (RTI) frameworks (ASCA, 2012a, 2014a, 2014d), such data may supply environmental data evaluating this teacher's classroom in comparison with the overall school.

Second, data-based consultation may incorporate site and/or district data points regularly collected for required educational standards (school improvement plan, Common Core State Standards, etc.). Utilizing a behavioral-intervention perspective, consultation may encourage the teacher to identify goals for student work (quantity, quality, etc.) on the basis of already articulated outcomes. Progress toward desired goals could then be scaffolded as needed for individual students.

Response 2

Laurie A. Carlson

It is evident that the school counselor in this situation is passionate about his students and cares deeply about their educational experience. Such situations involving teacher interaction with students are complex and can be extremely challenging as the school counselor tries to balance advocacy for students with maintaining healthy, collaborative relationships with colleagues. "Heart-to-heart" conversations are always appropriate; however, centering those conversations on how she is handling challenging students would likely not be helpful and steps across the boundary of appropriate counselor roles. Certainly, it would be appropriate for the school counselor to have a "heart-to-heart" conversation with the teacher about academic progress of students who have come forth and expressed challenges in the teacher's class. Even though this would be an appropriate response, it should not be the first course of action.

As a school counselor and now counselor educator, I tend to base interventions on the five ethical principles; for me, one of the foundational principles is autonomy. Whenever possible, it is best practice to empower students to advocate on their own behalf and help them overcome the challenges they face so that a sense of efficacy is increased. Two approaches that have worked well for me are solution-focused brief counseling (SFBC) and transactional analysis (TA). Key strategies within the SFBC approach that are particularly helpful in such cases are scaling and looking for exceptions. Utilizing scaling questions helps a student to operationalize what is not working well in the current situation and then move beyond that to what it would look like when things are going well. Often, when a student visualizes healthier communication with a teacher, things can improve, as the student's psyche may manifest the perceptual possibility. The strategy of looking for exceptions helps students uncover behaviors and communication patterns that have worked well for them in past similar situations. It helps them to realize that a more positive relationship is attainable and that there are, likely, particular behaviors that they are overlooking in the current situation but that they have used with some success already. TA is helpful because it focuses on the analysis of communication patterns and helps a student to understand that communication is bidirectional; that is, the student has some power over the effectiveness or ineffectiveness of it. The way that the student responds to the teacher when communication begins to break down can either destabilize or stabilize the situation. The strength of this approach in this situation is also supported by the fact that many of these students are identified as gifted and talented, able to understand theoretical concepts and transfer their learning from one situation and environment to another. Furthermore, it seems that this would be an appropriate approach in that the counselor identifies some of the teacher behavior to be in the form of an "adolescent tantrum." Likely, her "adolescent tantrum" is in response to a tone of "critical parent," and the last thing that needs to be introduced into the situation is a counselor who approaches the challenge from the perspective of a "critical parent." One final comment on the approach of dealing with the issue through student intervention is that these strategies can be taught to all students through classroom guidance lessons, further increasing their impact on students.

A school counselor should consider the use of process, perception, and outcome data in relationship to such concerns. Process data would include reporting of the amount of time the school counselor spends helping students navigate such issues as well as the number of students affected. One would want to be sure not to overlook individual work with students, but even more important would be process data related to delivery of these strategies in small-group and classroom settings. It would be difficult, and perhaps even unethical, to collect perception data specific to one particular teacher; however, appropriate larger scale collection techniques may include surveys that allow students to reflect on and rate relationships with teachers in general. Finally, with regard to outcome data, one could continue to measure and monitor the achievement disparities noted in the case or even record changes in referrals and student requests for course changes.

Utilization of data for instructional improvement should be common practice in any school, as the educational team works to meet school and district improvement plans. Regular staff development activities that involve data review and program revision create a culture in which continuous improvement is not only mandated but also celebrated. The school counselor's role in this process is to assist administrators in understanding evaluation results and in helping to facilitate faculty decisions around those results. It is critical that the school counselor not be perceived by the faculty as "another administrator," yet the faculty need to understand that school counselors have the requisite training and skills to analyze and interpret such results. When it comes to facilitating change for any particular teacher in relationship to student assessment outcomes, that facilitation tends to be most effective through a collaborative process with input from not only the school counselor and administrator but also from fellow teachers. Identifying and problem-solving student achievement gaps is the responsibility of all faculty.

It seems as though this concern is going to be best addressed through a multipronged approach. I would contend that, aside from helping the administrator facilitate a broad-based discussion regarding achievement gaps with the entire faculty, the school counselor focuses on those student-based interventions articulated in the response to Question 1. As students become more empowered to create positive and helpful relationships with all teachers, challenges with this particular teacher should also be positively affected. It seems highly unlikely with the level of concern brought forth that the principal is not already aware of this teacher's challenges. If the school counselor is concerned about the mental health or safety of the students affected—or perhaps even that of the teacher—then, of course, the appropriate action would be to express that concern to the principal.

Putting all the struggling students in this one teacher's class is not only unethical but also harmful to the teacher and students. Ethical behavior is grounded in the bedrock principles of autonomy, beneficence, nonmaleficence, equity, and justice. Deliberately setting students and a colleague up for potential failure is not acceptable under any circumstances.

There are two other possibilities that come to mind here. The first would actually be a helpful strategy, regardless of the outcomes from any of the previous strategies. Students, parents, teachers, and counselors would all benefit from thoughtful and clearly articulated school policy related to appropriate class changes. The policy should not only include acceptable circumstances for a requested change but also outline an appropriate process that must be followed. Ensuring that students try to discuss the issue initially with a teacher and secondly with a parent before they even come to the school counselor helps to limit the number of inappropriate or "convenience" requests. Having the teacher, parent, and student sign off on a communication record ensures that these steps are followed and helps to create a collaborative environment around each student's education. This process would ensure that there has been a dialogue between the student and key adults and may include space for endorsement of the change.

The second and final thing to consider is the way that students are distributed into classes in the first place. If students self-select, a school counselor should ensure that students are making informed selections based on not only the subject area but also their learning styles and academic goals. Perhaps, finding a way to help students gain exposure to different learning environments before class selection could help. If there is little student autonomy in class selection, and the school counselor, along with other faculty and administrators, "place" students in classes, then it seems that there should be adequate consideration again of students' learning styles, personalities, and academic goals without first placing them with a particular teacher.

Supplemental Readings and Supplemental Activities

Supplemental Readings

American School Counselor Association. (2012). *The ASCA National Model: A framework for school counseling programs* (3rd ed.). Alexandria, VA: Author.

American School Counselor Association. (2014a). *ASCA mindsets & behaviors for student success: K-12 college- and career-readiness standards for every student.* Alexandria, VA: Author.

American School Counselor Association. (2014b). *The school counselor and multitiered systems of supports* [Position statement]. Retrieved November 21, 2015, from https://www.schoolcounselor.org/asca/media/asca/PositionStatements/PS_MultitieredSupportSystem.pdf

American School Counselor Association. (n.d.). *Information for administrators.* Retrieved November 20, 2015, from http://www.schoolcounselor.org/administrators

Clemens, E. (2007). Developmental counseling and therapy as a model for school counselor consultation with teachers. *Professional School Counseling, 10*(4), 352–359.

Dimmitt, C., Carey, J. C., & Hatch, T. (2007). *Evidence-based school counseling: Making a difference with data-driven practices.* Thousand Oaks, CA: Corwin Press.

Dinkmeyer, D., & Carlson, J. (2006). *Consultation: Creating school-based interventions* (3rd ed.). New York, NY: Routledge.

Johnson, K. D., & Hannon, M. D. (2014). Measuring the relationship between parent, teacher, and student problem behavior reports and academic achievement: Implications for school counselors. *Professional School Counseling, 18*(1), 38–48.

Kaffenberger, C., & Young, A. (2013). *Making DATA work* (3rd ed.). Alexandria, VA: American School Counselor Association.

Pelsma, D. M. (2000). School counselors' use of solution-focused questioning to improve teacher work life. *Professional School Counseling, 4*(1), 1–5.

Tatar, M. (2009). Teachers turning for help to school counsellors and colleagues: Toward a mapping of relevant predictors. *British Journal of Guidance & Counselling, 37*(2), 107–127. doi:10.1080/03069880902728564

Tatar, M., & Bekerman, Z. (2009). School counsellors' and teachers' perceptions of their students' problems: Shared and divergent views. *Counselling & Psychotherapy Research, 9*(3), 187–192.

Supplemental Activities

Learning Activities

- *"Beliefs, Vision, Standards":* After being introduced to the American School Counselor Association National Model (ASCA, 2012a), students are divided into small groups and asked to create a fictional school name, level, and mascot. Students are then instructed to discuss and articulate four beliefs, common to all group members, regarding education. Students share out to the whole class. Next, student groups are instructed to articulate a vision statement for their school counseling program based on their written group beliefs. Again, students share out to the whole class. Finally, students are instructed to create five student outcomes for their school counseling program. Student outcomes must: be measurable, be developmentally appropriate for their site level, and be related to their beliefs and site vision statement. When completed, students engage in a share-out with the whole class.

- *"SMART Action":* Students engage in this activity based on a fictional site or their current field experience (e.g., practicum or internship) site for reference. Students are instructed to identify a discrepancy based on their review of school-wide student outcome data (again, either fictional or real, depending on site). From the identified discrepancy, students are instructed to create three action plans (ASCA, 2012a; Kaffenberger & Young, 2013) guiding their site comprehensive school counseling program. All three action plans must address the identified discrepancy, must utilize SMART (e.g., Specific, Measurable, Attainable, Results, Time) goals, and must separately focus on each level of the Response to Intervention (RTI) framework (e.g., one action plan for the bottom tier, one for mid-tier, and one for the top tier). Once completed, students choose one action plan to present to the whole class.

Chapter 20

But She's Going to Be Famous! Addressing Attendance Concerns in Third-Culture Students

Sebastien Laroche

Background

I am an elementary school counselor for a small Department of Defense Dependents (DoDDs) school of 200+ students located on a U.S. military base in Japan. DoDD schools provide an American education and related services to the children of U.S. armed forces service members and other Department of Defense (DoD) employees working overseas. DoDD schools operate under the Education Activity of the Department of Defense and receive all curricular and policy guidance from the DoD headquarters. Furthermore, while DoDD schools follow the guidelines laid out by headquarters, they must also meet the requirements outlined by their particular geographic district and base military branch. Each base functions as its own self-sufficient community, with rules and expectations that vary from base to base. At my school, students are primarily the children of enlisted active-duty Air Force service members and commissioned officers. Many of these students are "third-culture kids" (children growing up in a culture different from the culture of their parents). A majority of the student population at my school is White/Caucasian (43%), with the remaining student body comprising African American, Asian, and mixed-race students. DoD policy states that there will be one counselor assigned to every 300 students at a school. As a result, I serve as the only school counselor at my current location.

Toward the end of the fall semester, I was approached by a kindergarten teacher who requested consultation regarding one of her students' excessive absences. This student accumulated over 30 unexcused absences within a 3-month period. Recently, our district implemented a more stringent attendance policy requiring a conference with parents and began to implement an intervention plan if a student exceeds more than five unexcused absences within a semester. Except for exigent circumstances, absences such as family vacations, modeling auditions, and nonsponsored sports activities without written verification from parent or sponsor are considered unexcused. This policy, in conjunction with my duties as school counselor, obliged me to intervene.

During the consultation, I discovered that our student of concern came from a large family with many siblings, an American father, and a host nation mother. Furthermore, the student's dominant language was not English, and she was mostly absent on the days when she was to receive ESL (English as a second language) services. The teacher's anecdotes also indicated that home support and involvement was low. The teacher requested my presence during parent–teacher conferences that were to take place in 2 weeks. I, too, shared the teacher's concerns and felt that it was in the best of interest of the student to attend. To adequately prepare an appropriate intervention to present to the parent, I left to gather more information.

After my consultation with the classroom teacher, my next step was to speak with her ESL teacher to obtain her input and observations. She shared that she had only worked with the student a handful of times sporadically throughout the semester and could not give an accurate representation of her ability level. An additional records check corroborated what was discussed in terms of the student's background and absences. I hoped before the conference that I would be able to observe the student and have a meaningful interaction with her, so I could obtain as full a portrait of her as possible (it's sad to think that in the 3 months since school started, I've never met or heard of her until now).

An opportunity to meet arrived 2 days later. Our concerned teacher called me down to the computer lab where students were working at literacy-based centers. I introduced myself to the student, who seemed like a very friendly and happy child. Her behavior indicated that she likes school, as she was observed intently concentrating on the various literacy activities and, when appropriate, engaging in jovial conversation with classmates. These observations corroborated the teacher's initial concern; the student is capable of enjoying, achieving, and succeeding in school, if only she had been present on a consistent basis. During whole-group instruction, she was motivated and eager to participate but did not display the proficiency or comprehension skills necessary to provide competent responses. As with many of our ESL students who did not have a disability and whose ethnicity reflected this particular host nation, one of her academic strengths was in math. In conversation, her verbal expression and comprehension were significantly lower than those of the other ESL students in the class who had been receiving services from the beginning of the year. She would parrot answers that other students gave and, at times, elicit gibberish words when she attempted to give her own independent response.

Finally, the time for parent conferences had arrived. The teacher and I met the student's father (the mother was not present). During the conference, the teacher shared with the father the student's strengths and observations of her interactions in the class. I shared that I couldn't provide much feedback, because most of the days that her absences occurred were also the same as her class's scheduled counseling time. We showed the father the attendance tracking data, assessment results (when she was here), and the concepts she has missed since the beginning of the school year. In response, the father explained that the reasons for the absences were due to her many auditions for various media opportunities. Although we respectfully acknowledged the father's choice, we made the point of letting him know how severely the absences were affecting her performance. Dad recognized our concern but made it especially clear that they were seriously grooming the daughter for a future career in TV and movies. As there is not a DoDD policy allowing us to mandate parents to bring their child to school with conditions, all we could do is change the ESL schedule to fall on the days when she was usually at school (Tuesdays, Wednesdays, and Thursdays). We also had to provide the father a warning that if there is little to no improvement in attendance, we would have to hold a meeting in the spring with administration and his supervisor to form an intervention plan (as per the district school policy). Dad acknowledged that he understood, and we left the meeting feeling as though we accomplished nothing.

Incident

By the third quarter of school, our student's inconsistent attendance had worsened to the point where she had missed over half of the total school days so far. Because this is the time when we must ponder grade and classroom placements for the next school year, the consideration of retaining this student was becoming a reality. Since we had previously documented our intervention plan to the student's father, it was time for our student support team (SST) to follow up. First, I notified the father that we had to involve his direct supervisor as per the DoDD attendance policy. Dad was displeased with this fact and repeatedly asked, "Why does it have to go that far? It won't change anything." Eventually, he agreed to the meeting. The SST meeting attendees also included our principal, ESL teacher, and classroom teacher. During the meeting, we shared attendance data and academic progress with the members present. The father was furious throughout the meeting and not willing to look at the information provided to him. He was adamant that this course of action was not fair. His supervisor, who also had children go through our school, attempted to reiterate the school's concerns to the father. The supervisor made multiple attempts to emphasize the negative implications that the constant absences would have on the student and implored the father to reconsider his priorities, but Dad would not have any of it. Dad threatened to withdraw his daughter from school and re-enroll her next year. In response, we explained that, because of her excessive absences, she would be academically ineligible to be promoted to first grade and would have to repeat kindergarten as per our grade placement policy. The father was especially miffed by this fact and excused himself from the meeting. He stated that he would get back to us with a resolution.

Discussion

Two weeks later, I still had not heard from the father. I also received reports that the student had not attended school at all since the meeting. I decided to call the father, and he notified me that he and his wife decided to withdraw their daughter and homeschool her. I responded by letting the father know we would still welcome his daughter's presence at our school and that we are always available for support. The father sarcastically acknowledged my response and bid me farewell.

Questions

1. Should the school have pressed the issue more aggressively at the beginning of the year?
2. How could the school counselor have approached the situation differently?
3. Was this an issue that warranted contacting the Family Advocacy Program (the base version of Child Protective Services)?
4. Would it have been inappropriate to bring the child into the meeting and ask her what she wanted to do?
5. How do situations like this play into the identity development of a third-culture student?
6. What additional data might have helped a school counselor advocate for the student?
7. How could the evaluation/assessment elements of a comprehensive school counseling program systematically identify students like her before attendance problems or academic problems bring the teacher's concerns to the attention of the school counselor?

Response 1
Jared Lau and Chris Wood

Although, at the core of this incident, it could be said that attendance issues for students are a regular concern for all school counselors, this case also highlights some unique challenges that school counselors practicing in DoDD schools experience. For instance, because DoDD schools are located in host countries outside of the United States, the presence of third-culture students is more prevalent than would normally be expected in non-DoDD schools. Nonetheless, this is an especially interesting incident when taking into consideration how skills in analyzing data are relevant to the school counselor's response. Although there is some discussion of information or "data" being presented, it is hard to know how such data were analyzed. Therefore, in framing our responses to the questions posed by the incident author, we will incorporate how school counselor knowledge and skills in analyzing data are relevant to addressing the incident.

Without knowing what "pressing the issue" might look like, we agree that the school could and should have identified the attendance problem earlier. As the district has a new five-absence policy, we wonder why the issue was not identified or addressed until the student had hit 30 unexcused absences. It is clear that the school counselor values relationships with teachers and students. The teacher seeking consultation and collaboration with the school counselor is evidence of belief in the school counselor's competence.

However, the concerns regarding the student might have emerged earlier with a more systematic evaluation of data. Thirty absences in 3 months would indicate that the student missed a third of the available instructional time, and the pattern of missing ESL classes would suggest that, in some specific academic areas, the student is receiving even fewer hours of academic intervention. We wonder why 3 months and 30 absences passed before the student was identified as needing an "intervention plan." Even without the district policy establishing the "five-or-more" absence rule, a school counselor could be analyzing the attendance trends of students to identify individuals with attendance problems. The school counselor mentions that the majority of the student's absences were on days that corresponded with her scheduled "counseling time." Assuming that this scheduled time involves the guidance curriculum portion of the school counselor's program, the evaluation data on the guidance lesson(s) might also have flagged the student's attendance concerns. Moreover, disaggregating school data such as attendance and/or achievement scores (e.g., by gender, race/ethnicity, within each grade level) would identify this specific incident as well as whether there is a subgroup of students within the school who are at risk due to the same attendance problem. We discuss using data analysis within a comprehensive school counseling program and early problem identification more later.

Another recommendation on approaching the incident is the analysis and presentation of data. Specifically, it could be beneficial to explore the attendance data in three additional ways: (a) disaggregation by academic intervention, (b) considering patterns and trends, and (c) in comparison to other students and the group.

First, the school counselor mentions that the student's absences seem to fall on days that caused her to miss ESL instruction and the school counseling curriculum. Although missing 30% of school in the first 3 months should be compelling enough, it could be additionally beneficial to know what percentage of ESL instruction was missed and the guidance curriculum as well.

Second, the patterns and trends with respect to the day(s) of the week and the specific weeks when they occur could be useful to know. The school counselor would seem to have analyzed such patterns, at least visually, to recognize the need to adjust the ESL schedule in an attempt to get the student more of such assistance.

Third, it would be good to compare the student to others specifically in her class/grade level; others in her school; and, if available, her siblings. The presentation of this data analysis might resonate with the parent(s) in a way that becomes a catalyst for change. Also, knowing how the student data compare with those of relevant groups helps provide context for interpretation. For instance, if half of the kindergarten class missed 30 days in the first 3 months of school, this is a very different picture than if no other students had more than four absences. Presenting these data to the parent(s) might provide greater motivation regarding engagement in the educational process.

Moreover, the retention intervention only makes sense if it is warranted by the student's lack of requisite academic achievement. If her academic progress is commensurate with that of her peers or if there are other students with the same academic deficiencies who are being moved on to first grade, then the primary rationale for retention is the "policy."

A full description of the Family Advocacy Program is beyond the purview of this incident response, and readers are referred to the Supplemental Readings, Resources, and Activities. In our view, in isolation, this is not an incident that warrants a report to the Family Advocacy Program or to Child Protective Services. If, however, the lack of attendance was a part of a greater pattern of neglect or there was any evidence of sexual exploitation in her "many auditions for various media opportunities," then contacting the appropriate authorities would certainly be appropriate.

There is evidence to support the practice of conjoint behavioral consultation (Sheridan, Eagle, Cowan, & Mickelson, 2001) and collaborative consultation models (Gable, Mostert, & Tonelson, 2004). Conversely, there does not seem to be much research that warns against including the student in such a meeting. There is not enough room in this chapter for an extensive discussion of different consultation models, so readers are referred to Amatea, Daniels, Bringman, and Vandiver (2004) and Keys, Bemak, Carpenter, and King-Sears (1998), which are listed in the References.

The student described in this incident seems to be both biracial and a "third-culture kid," so her racial/ethnic identity development may be influenced by both. There is some evidence that school belonging is inversely related to emotional and behavioral problems for immigrant students (Georgiades, Boyle, & Fife, 2012). Moreover, the proportionate representation of the student's race/ethnicity in the composition of the school is negatively associated with emotional–behavioral problems as well. In sum, fostering school belonging for the student, positively fostering the racial/ethnic identity development of biracial and third-culture kids, while recognizing how they navigate stages (e.g., resistance and immersion) may be different than students from more discretely defined cultural groups.

As we mentioned earlier, comparing the student's academic performance to that of her peers is one way to understand how her attendance problems may have negatively affected her academic success. However, if the achievement data suggest that she is keeping pace with her classmates, then these data can be used to advocate for the student to progress on to the subsequent grade level. Similarly, her ESL testing data can be used to advocate for services for her as well as to advocate with her parents about the importance of her receiving ESL instruction.

We can answer these questions by illustrating analysis of data from two levels: (a) school-wide data and (b) intervention-specific data, both of which can be part of a comprehensive school counseling program. School-wide data such as attendance, achievement test data, and discipline records can be disaggregated to identify educationally vulnerable individuals and groups within the school. The school counselor's program can use school-wide data to identify individuals and groups within the school in need of specialized school counseling interventions and tailoring of the guidance curriculum. In the incident, the school counselor mentions scheduled time in the classroom. It is possible to have scheduled classroom guidance lessons (and other interventions from the comprehensive school counseling program) that are designed based on closing-the-gap activities (American School Counselor Association [ASCA], 2012a). Relatedly, the school counselor can track (and analyze) the data related to elements of the school counseling program, such as the guidance curriculum. ASCA provides templates to assist in comprehensive school counseling programs, including a "School Counseling Curriculum Results Report." This report is a table for tracking data such as the number of students served, students' perceptions/feedback about the curriculum, and outcome data (i.e., achievement, attendance, behavior).

At the school-wide level, the school counselor can use data to demonstrate how the guidance curriculum (and other elements of the school counseling program) positively affects the school and, at the individual level, the student. We already discussed the need to compare the individual academic achievement data of the student to those of the group. This comparison can also include comparing the students' individual data (e.g., from the results report discussed earlier) on other outcomes such as career/college readiness standards (ASCA, 2014a). Data on the ASCA Mindsets & Behaviors for Student Success can be related to career hopes of the student discussed in the incident. At this individual level, the standard "Demonstrate the ability to balance school, home and community activities" is perhaps "not yet met" by the student described in this incident and is very relevant to her future career as a media star.

In sum, although the challenges presented and questions raised by this incident are numerous, there are still options available to school counselors to help address and answer the questions. In particular, school counselors are encouraged to develop comprehensive school counseling programs that can gather and analyze data to help them make informed and data-driven decisions. Through the development and implementation of a comprehensive and systematic school counseling plan, school counselors can be better prepared to utilize data to help inform practices and decision making, particularly as it pertains to student performance and achievement.

Response 2

Caroline A. Baker

The case presented here is complex, with layers of cultural, developmental, and career concerns and considerations. Culturally, the school counselor is working within a system of American policies and worldview on a military base situated in a Japanese society. Asian cultural norms differ from those of the United States, despite education practices on the base adhering to the U.S. education system. Furthermore, the client in question comes from a blended family representing both the cultural expectations of an American father and a Japanese mother. Other siblings are present in the home, but there is not much context given for their background culture, educational/career expectations, or developmental status. The school counselor describes the client as a "third-culture student," yet this descriptor may or may not be accurate in defining the context (Bikos et al., 2014; Limberg & Lambie, 2011). The client has entered the school system as a kindergartner, approximately 5 or 6 years old. Her brief life experiences in another country may not represent the criteria for being a third-culture student.

Career development needs also surface as an important part of this case. The school counselor is questioning his role and response to the case, and the client's family has named the career goal of the child as becoming a television personality. This is where the complexity of the cultural context of the family could be influencing the attendance issues. ASCA (2012a, 2014a) advocates for career counseling being one of three domains (academic, career, and social–emotional) and seeks the success of all students in relation to these domains, and Japanese culture also maintains the importance of career education and academics (Gong et al., 2013; Tsukuda, 2001). However, family structure and roles may determine the response to the education system and career planning (Bikos et al., 2014; Gong et al., 2013; Lim & Nakamoto, 2008; Roberts et al., 2014). Keeping cultural, developmental, and career needs in mind while working with the entire family seems important in this case study.

In this case, the school counselor reported how the school followed base policy by scheduling a meeting with the father to review the student's performance, as well as the school's concerns, and made schedule accommodations to account for absences. This seems like a reasonable approach to the early situation, yet it did not remediate the problem. Upon the latter part of the school year, when truancy issues and academic progress were of greater concern and urgency, the father responded in a way that indicated he was unprepared for the resulting consequences. It is important to consider informed consent practices around school requirements, possible consequences, and who might be involved (e.g., the base supervisor) so that the parents have the information to make decisions.

Furthermore, understanding the mother's role and the perspective to engage her in the process seems like it could clarify the family's views more thoroughly. Bringing the student into the meeting may or may not be helpful to the case, depending on the family dynamics and her developmental understanding of career decision-making and the school context. Collaboration and consultation, two themes of the ASCA National Model (2012a), not only with the parents and other school staff but also with the Family Advocacy Program, would assist in knowing mandated reporting boundaries and resources for use by the school counselor.

As discussed earlier, the term "third-culture student" may not be most accurate in this case. Of greater importance seems to be the career development identity of the student and how she will be empowered with academic skills that will translate into a future career in entertainment or other fields. Student data around attendance, school performance, and teacher observations would help in earlier identification of and response to student issues. Knowledge about family culture and educational needs could help to engage the family with the school to foster a more collaborative relationship. Finally, career data knowledge around employment rates in different industries such as entertainment might enhance the conversations had with the father.

From collaboration with other agencies and staff to utilizing the data available around patterns of attendance, using the ASCA National Model (2012a) empowers school counselors to proactively serve all students. In this case, the school counselor reported that attendance data revealed the client had missed all the counseling days, which means that the school counselor had limited awareness of her situation. Seeking those data can help to determine follow-up meetings with the student and earlier detection of patterns.

Supplemental Readings, Online Resources, and Supplemental Activities

Supplemental Readings

Achieve. (2013). *Implementing the Common Core State Standards: The role of the school counselor*. Retrieved from http://www.achieve.org/publications/implementing-common-core-state-standards-role-school-counselor-action-brief

American School Counselor Association. (2008). *ASCA school counselor competencies.* Retrieved from http://www.schoolcounselor.org/asca/media/asca/home/sccompetencies.pdf

American School Counselor Association. (2012). *The ASCA National Model: A framework for school counseling programs* (3rd ed.). Alexandria, VA: Author.

American School Counselor Association. (2014). *ASCA mindsets & behaviors for student success: K-12 college- and career-readiness standards for every student.* Retrieved from https://schoolcounselor.org/asca/media/asca/home/MindsetsBehaviors.pdf

American School Counselor Association. (2018). *ASCA National Model templates.* Retrieved from https://www.schoolcounselor.org/school-counselors-members/asca-national-model/asca-national-model-templates

Coleman, H. L. K., Cho Kim, S., & Yang, A. (2008). Cultural identity enhancement strategies for culturally diverse youth. In H. L. K. Coleman & C. Yeh (Eds.), *Handbook of school counseling* (pp. 563–583). New York, NY: Taylor & Francis.

Department of Defense. (2015). *Instruction: Family advocacy program (FAP).* Retrieved from http://www.dtic.mil/whs/directives/corres/pdf/640001p.pdf

Fields, T. H., & Hines, P. L. (2000). School counselor's role in raising student achievement. In G. Duhon & T. Manson (Eds.), *Preparation, collaboration and emphasis on the family in school counseling for the new millennium* (pp. 135–162). Lewiston, NY: Edwin Mellen Press.

Galassi, J. P., & Akos, P. (2007). *Strengths-based school counseling.* Mahwah, NJ: Erlbaum.

Gray, J. (2015). Counsellors without borders. *Therapy Today, 26*(2), 26–29.

Gysbers, N. C., & Henderson, P. (2012). *Developing & managing your school guidance & counseling program* (5th ed.). Alexandria, VA: American Counseling Association.

Hines, P. L., Lemons, R., & Crews, K. (2011). *Poised to lead: How school counselors can drive college and career readiness.* Retrieved from http://edtrust.org/wp-content/uploads/2013/10/Poised_To_Lead_0.pdf

Holcomb-McCoy, C. (2004). Assessing the multicultural competence of school counselors: A checklist. *Professional School Counseling, 7*(3), 178–186.

Limberg, D., & Lambie, G. W. (2011). Third culture kids: Implications for professional school counseling. *Professional School Counseling, 15*(1), 45–54.

Miville, M. L. (2008). Race and ethnicity in school counseling. In H. L. K. Coleman & C. Yeh (Eds.), *Handbook of school counseling* (pp. 177–194). New York, NY: Taylor & Francis.

Recognized ASCA Model Program (RAMP). (2003). *RAMP up your school counseling program.* Retrieved from: https://www.schoolcounselor.org/school-counselors/recognized-asca-model-program-(ramp)

Sink, C. A., & Stroh, H. R. (2003). Raising achievement test scores of early elementary school students through comprehensive school counseling programs. *Professional School Counseling, 6*, 352–364.

Trickett, E. J., & Formoso, D. (2008). The acculturative environment of schools and the school counselor: Goals and roles that create a supportive context for immigrant adolescents. In H. L. K. Coleman & C. Yeh (Eds.), *Handbook of school counseling* (pp. 79–93). New York, NY: Taylor & Francis.

Tsukuda, N. (2001). *Country report: Career guidance in Japan.* Retrieved from http://www.spc.org.sg/9thARACD/CAREER%20GUIDANCE%20 IN%20JAPAN.doc

Wilkerson, K., Perusse, R., & Hughes, A. (2013). Comprehensive school counseling programs and student achievement outcomes: A comparative analysis of RAMP versus non-RAMP schools. *Professional School Counseling 16*, 172–184.

Online Resources

Journal of School Counseling
  http://jsc.montana.edu/

Professional School Counseling journal
  http://www.schoolcounselor.org/school-counselors-members/publications/professional-school-counseling-journal

Supplemental Activities

Further Questions for Reflection and Discussion

- The critical incident takes place in a Department of Defense (DoD) school. What aspects of the incident are unique to this setting?

- What would be different if the incident took place within a traditional school in the United States?

- Would you consider working in a DoDDs school? Why/why not?

- What is the definition of "third-culture kids"?

- The student discussed in the critical incident is not the standard definition of a "third-culture" kid: Why not? What relevance could that have for the incident?

- Research DoDD schools on the internet. How many are there, and in what countries? Do they all have school counselors? Are there any American School Counselor Association (ASCA) RAMP designees that are in DoDD schools?

Learning Activities

- Look at the data available on your state's school and district report cards. These are usually available via the state Department of Education website. What sources of data can you identify? How might those data be relevant in this specific case?

- Look at the EZAnalyze resource/tool. How could the school counselor have used this in the incident?

- Using the data format for achievement data in your state, practice using EZAnalyze by entering data into Microsoft Excel and creating a graphic comparing the data.

- Look at the CACREP (Council for Accreditation of Counseling & Related Educational Programs) standards for assessment (http://www.cacrep. org/section-2-professional-counseling-identity/). What specific standards apply to what the school counselor is being called upon to "do" in recommendations from the incident response authors? For example, the incident response asks the school counselor to compare the student's attendance to the rest of the class (and/or the entire grade level). What knowledge does this require?

- Create some hypothetical data to practice data analysis on EZAnalyze. Using hypothetical data (e.g., state achievement test categories), conduct data analyses and subsequent graphics (bar charts, etc.) in preparation for a parent–teacher conference.

- Look for additional assessments that might be used in this incident. What aspects of psychosocial development could be assessed as related to the presenting concern of attendance? Review the ASCA Student Competencies and College/Career Readiness Mindsets & Behaviors for potential areas of further investigation.

More Learning Activities

- Spend time reviewing the *ASCA Mindsets & Behaviors for Student Success* (2014a) to become familiar with the standards around the three domains.

- Consider personal understanding and beliefs around base culture, host country culture, and student backgrounds and needs on military bases.

- Collect resources that may support the comprehensive school counseling program and include cultural information and expertise.

- Research the student population—third-culture kids. What considerations are relevant for school counselors in working with this population?

Chapter 21

Assessment:
Case of the Ninth-Grade Gap

Justin R. Fields

Background

I worked in a large urban high school that served approximately 1,700 students in a suburb outside of a large Midwestern city. Typically, our population comprised 40% students on free or reduced-price lunch. My school was making a more concerted effort to incorporate the use of data teams into our professional climate and professional development. Data teams involve the building of small professional learning teams within a school to focus on critical issues; collect and analyze data; and incorporate learning into lesson planning, assessment decisions, and educational programming across our school. In an effort to better serve students and to bolster the presence of the school counseling department within the school and staff community, my department, which was composed of four school counselors, initiated a data team project. We reviewed attendance data, graduation rates, standardized test scores, college application data, and class failure data. We noticed that many of our students who were not graduating on time had often had poor performances during their freshman year. After speaking with administrators, we decided to address ninth-grade promotion. In other words, we wanted to improve the amount of ninth-grade students who were prepared to progress to the tenth grade by earning credit in all their ninth-grade core classes (English, Math, Science, and Social Studies). We noticed that when students were failing more than one core course as ninth graders, they were at a greater disadvantage to be able to ultimately graduate on time.

As it was the end of the school year, we were able to review the data of students who had failed more than one core course as ninth graders.

We collected data regarding their high school attendance, discipline, grades, racial/ethnic background, and socioeconomic status (SES). We also reviewed the data from the same students' eighth-grade year, including middle school standardized test scores in addition to academic, discipline, and attendance data.

With the use of these data, we developed what appeared to be the profile of an eighth-grade student whom we could predict would struggle as a ninth-grade student at our school. For example, the profile highlighted a student who was absent over 10 days during their eighth-grade year, was not proficient on two or more eighth-grade proficiency tests, was referred to the administration for discipline over five times as an eighth grader, and earned failing grades in two or more core classes during the eighth-grade year. We proposed an intervention to create a specially designed set of ninth-grade core subject class sections. In addition to these sections teaching the standard course curriculum, we wanted to incorporate classroom, small-group, and individual interventions that could teach and build essential skills related to studying, personal responsibility, communication, and conflict resolution. Because of this intervention, our goal was to positively contribute to school and interpersonal success. Within this set of class sections, we wanted to include as many incoming ninth graders as possible who fit the criteria in our developed profile. Our administrators committed to providing special staffing to these sections to provide extra opportunities for intervention, tutoring, and instruction.

Incident

Upon further analysis of the demographic profile of the students who fit our profile, we noticed an interesting trend. Specifically, over half of the students who fit the profile were Latino, African American, or low income. A concern was raised by the counseling group about the ethics of moving forward with this intervention as it was designed. To move forward would create special sections that would be almost half composed of minority or marginalized students. Specifically, the concern was whether we would be creating a tracking system of traditionally marginalized students and limiting diversity across other classrooms.

Discussion

By moving forward with the collected data and the proposed intervention, we would be limiting the diversity across our freshman classes and taking away from one of the strengths of our school culture. In addition, the perception of this intervention could also be that our school was isolating many marginalized students into specific groups, which could cause many negative reactions. Furthermore, by putting a lot of academically and behaviorally low-performing students into a few sections, it could put a heavy burden on the teachers assigned to teach these sections.

However, this intervention, to the best that we could determine from the available data, would allow us to provide a year-long targeted intervention to a student group with high needs. Ideally, this intervention could assist students academically and increase their ability to progress to the tenth grade with all their required credits.

Questions

1. Was our strategy to develop a profile of a student who would typically struggle as a ninth grader in our school valid? What alternate approaches could have been developed/utilized?
2. Would you move forward with the proposed intervention of creating specially designated core class sections to support this group of students? Or, given the identification process we developed, would you propose an alternative intervention (or interventions)?
3. Do you share the concern that this profile development creates a potentially harmful tracking system that will group a large percentage of marginalized students away from the larger class population?
4. What other ways would you propose to efficiently and adequately intervene with this profile of students who typically struggle as incoming ninth graders?
5. Does the trend uncovered in the data analysis need to be addressed at the group and/or grade level, or do you believe that the data have uncovered a much more concerning systemic trend that needs to be addressed first with our administration and teachers at the school-wide level?

Response 1
Christopher A. Sink

Regrettably, the circumstances presented in the case study are not uncommon in urban high schools. Despite nearly 2 decades of so-called school reform, whether it reflects the No Child Left Behind Act (2001) or the subsequent Race to the Top (U.S. Department of Education, 2009) legislation, there remains a significant correlation between students' test scores and their families' SES (Reardon, 2011; Sirin, 2005). Specifically, research on schools serving more affluent families report higher average student achievement than those schools educating students from low-income families. In a nutshell, the well-documented academic gap related to the vignette can be described as follows: On average, economically advantaged students score near or above the state standards, while the opposite is true for economically disadvantaged students. This reality is even starker in low-income urban secondary schools with a high proportion of minority students receiving a free or reduced-cost lunch. Not to be overly pessimistic here, but research suggests that once the achievement gap opens between affected low- and high-income groups, it does not completely close, even with additional academic support, mentoring, and tutoring. The long-term impacts for low-achieving students cannot be overstated. In fact, this inequity leads to an ever-widening opportunity gap between the "haves" and the "have nots." For instance, far fewer "low-achieving" youth attend postsecondary education or training and have good paying jobs. The likelihood of mental health problems and criminal involvement also increases.

The case study indicates that significant group differences in various student and school-related outcomes occur even in less disadvantaged urban high schools. What is particularly commendable about this scenario is that the school counselors collaborated, as recommended in the American School Counselor Association (ASCA, 2012a) National Model and numerous accountability publications (e.g., Young & Kaffenberger, 2011), to not only document the gap using various outcome data but also start thinking about an action plan based on the findings. The counseling staff recognizes that over 50% of their ninth graders of color or from low-income families are not as likely to graduate on time as other more advantaged students. Moreover, the former group are more likely to exhibit behavior problems and receive disciplinary referrals.

The proposed action plan includes a few recommended interventions, including several that are aligned with Positive Behavior Interventions and Supports (PBIS; Flannery, Fenning, Kato, & McIntosh, 2014) or Response to Intervention (RTI) programs (classroom, small group, and individual). The plan does not merely focus on the academic side of the problem but also includes, as many researchers suggest, developing and reinforcing high school students' social and emotional learning (SEL) skills (e.g., Williamson, Modecki, & Guerra, 2015). To counselors' credit, the plan emphasizes the improvement of students' study skills, responsibility taking, interpersonal communication, and conflict management.

The case study offered five insightful follow-up questions. Rather than being answered separately, they are grouped into similar topics and responded to accordingly.

The first two questions address student appraisal strategies or the proposed ways to gather and interpret student school-related data. Undoubtedly, the school counselors took valuable steps toward understanding the gist of situation. The question of the validity of their evaluation work, however, is more complicated to answer, given the term's multiple meanings. Albeit oversimplified, there are two major interrelated forms of validity in play here: (a) validity related to the assessment (testing) tools and (b) validity associated with the research methods (processes and procedures) utilized to collect the profile data. The first type of validity is not as important as the second, given the aim of their action research. The counselors are not collecting data on individual students for placement into designated programs such as special education; if they were, placement tests must possess construct validity and strong reliability (Type 1 validity). Rather, they are collecting aggregated group data, which applies to the second type of validity. In other words, their methods of collecting student information must use valid procedures and process, such as avoiding bias in what kinds of data are solicited, maintaining student anonymity, careful administration and scoring of measurement tools, and so forth.

More specifically, in situations like the one described in the case study, where researchers' (the counselors') objective was to reveal student performance trends, investigators need to determine whether data patterns hold for an entire group or for a smaller subset of students. The counselors gathered readily available quantitative information (called archival data) that was narrow in scope. Data sources, however, should be more comprehensive in nature before appropriate analyses and interpretations can be attempted. For example, to augment the numerical trend data, qualitative information could have helped the counselors further grasp the complexities of the situation.

Measurement expert Jerome Sattler (2014) speaks to this recommendation, indicating that the four pillars of assessment should be used when studying client/student attributes across varying contexts. Whenever feasible, observations, interviews (e.g., with students, parents/caregivers, teachers), formal measures (e.g., standardized test scores), and informal appraisal tools (e.g., classroom work and grades, attendance, disciplinary records) should be included in the process. Thus, to improve the validity of their student assessment data (i.e., gain a more complete picture of the situation), it is best practice to also conduct (a) unobtrusive and low-impact classroom observations of the ninth graders, and (b) several focus groups with key school stakeholders (teachers, administrators, and students). Ideally, parents/caregivers would also be selectively interviewed to gain their perspectives. If the counselors could revisit the data-gathering process and add other sources of information, they would be in a better position to answer the second question.

Potential ethical considerations are addressed by this question. Before carrying out the action plan, the counselors wrestled with the potential ethical dilemma of singling out a certain group of underachieving, at-risk youth and affording them "special" interventions. Although they did not specify which of the ASCA (2010b) or American Counseling Association (2014) ethical codes might be violated, the situation warranted consideration of the possible detrimental effects of "isolating" already marginalized students into special class sections. Personally identifying any student or groups of students, whether they are struggling or not in class, can be problematic. It has been commonly observed that adolescents feel more vulnerable in school settings where they are surrounded by their peers. However well meaning the additional attention might be, lowering already fragile self-concepts can occur when educators spotlight adolescents' academic deficiencies. Research shows that students of color are more likely to be negatively affected when removed from their regular classes and given special services (e.g., Campbell-Whatley & Comer, 2000).

Whether the proposed action plan (tracking at-risk students into particular classes) will generate any long-term negative student, classroom, or school-level consequences, thus calling into question the ethics of this scheme, is unknown at this point. If the counseling staff all agree that implementing their plan is the best course of action, the process obviously requires a great deal of sensitivity and ingenuity, attempting to minimize any real or potent threats to students' self-concept and related personal qualities. Generally speaking, though, the tracking of high school students, especially adolescents of color and from low-SES backgrounds, does not reverse the pattern of low academic performance and graduation rates (Werblow, Urick, & Duesbery, 2013).

Questions 4 and 5 address intervention issues regarding this case. Unfortunately, schools and their organizational structures, processes, and procedures are not flexible enough to adapt to each student's unique needs. As a result, rushed and unpiloted *large-group* interventions, whatever the student issue may be, normally have little measurable success. Research continues to show, however, that well-designed and implemented systemic or *whole-school* approaches to student academic and behavior problems can be effective. Perhaps the application of a research-based, multitiered approach such as PBIS or RTI would be helpful over time (Burns & Gibbons, 2013; LaVigna, 2012). Assuming that the high school has one, both options can be readily integrated into its comprehensive guidance and counseling program (e.g., ASCA [2012a] National Model; Ockerman, Mason, & Hollenbeck, 2012).

Other workable recommendations for evidence-based interventions are widely accessible online and in educational and school-based counseling literature. For instance, to augment whatever systemic intervention approach (e.g., RTI or PBIS) they select, counselors should address *all* ninth-grade students in their existing classrooms, assisting them to develop the essential academic and interpersonal skills to more successfully navigate the schooling process and maximize their achievement motivation and efforts at learning. Perhaps many of the marginalized students alluded to in the vignette are less adept at negotiating and collaborating with their peers during learning activities, as well as with emotional self-management when faced with challenging educational environments and less than sensitive and caring teachers and administrators. These issues must be addressed in the plan. Furthermore, adolescents must acquire the necessary skills to appropriately advocate for themselves when confronted with seemingly unreasonable workloads, the lack of parent/caregiver support, inadequate school and social services, and so on.

After intervention at the classroom level, the ninth graders who require additional academic and SEL support could be invited to participate in what might be referred to as "positive leadership" groups. These psychoeducational small groups composed of varying academic and SEL skill levels (e.g., include five moderate- to high-needs learners with one or two stronger students). Participants discuss and role-play essential

SEL strategies, such as help seeking, responsibility taking, interpersonal communication, and conflict management. In summary, because abundant evidence indicates that SEL skills support academic achievement at all grade levels, classroom and small-group interventions should be integrated with any academic support provided to low-achieving students (e.g., Durlak, Weissberg, Dymnicki, Taylor, & Schellinger, 2011; McCormick, Cappella, O'Connor, & McClowry, 2015; Williamson et al., 2015). Some additional follow-up questions are provided for readers, as well as a number of supplemental resources and readings, at the end of this chapter.

Response 2
Richard T. Lapan and Catherine Griffith

The school counselors at this site are to be commended for their commitment to the academic mission to the school and engaging in a data-based decision-making process as a means of facilitating improvement. The existence of a data team is an excellent incorporation of the ASCA National Model in planning and evaluating activities within the school counseling program. The resulting profile has the characteristics of early warning indicators with the usual red flags: attendance, poor test scores, discipline problems, and failure to pass key courses in middle school. These findings motivated the school counselors to consider a more preventative approach by addressing the issue of students not graduating on time well before their final year of high school.

Where this approach wavers, however, is at the connection point between the issues that the data indicate and what an adequate response from the school entails. In this instance, they've seen an essential trend in the data and then generated a solution from only their perspective and embeddedness as high school counselors, when the data really highlight a fundamental systems issue for the whole school district to consider. The uncovered data trend needs to be addressed at every level, including a presentation to the school board. This is a system-wide crisis that everyone involved with this school district needs to actively address to develop and then implement a comprehensive set of interventions with the efficacy to really solve the problem. High school counselors acting on their own is not nearly enough.

Furthermore, by proposing separate course sections for these students, the counselors at this site are advocating for the use of "school tracking," the practice of separating students into groups for multiple subjects according to overall achievement levels (e.g., above average, average, and below average) with the intention of allocating resources to best meet the needs of each track. On the surface, school tracking appears to be a promising method of tailoring schooling so that students receive curriculum according to their current needs. Students who excel can further advance in the curriculum, and students who need additional support will receive it. Advocates of school tracking note that the method allows teachers to conveniently structure their lessons more specifically based on ability and speculate that students will have higher self-esteem by working with peers at a similar ability level. However, school tracking has been shown to be a problematic practice that negatively affects students of color, those with special needs, and students from low-SES backgrounds. These students are disproportionately allocated to lower achievement tracks and are subsequently more likely to drop out of school than students placed in college-bound tracks. Little research supports school tracking as benefiting anyone but the "gifted," higher track students, whereas students in lower tracks are more likely to lose confidence in their abilities. That the identified students in this particular case were much more likely to be Latino, African American, or low income is problematic in that it speaks to larger systemic issues in the community, and school tracking is likely to only widen that achievement gap.

Physical separation of students who need differentiated instruction, however, is not the only means of addressing this issue. Flexible grouping, an alternative, is a means of temporarily grouping by learning style, readiness, and subject interest. It can last for brief periods within a lesson or for longer stretches within a semester. For example, a teacher may divide their classroom into three mixed-ability groups: (a) students who need to review prior information before getting started on the lesson; (b) students who are ready to begin learning the new materials; and (c) students who are ready to engage with the new materials in a more challenging manner. Methods of instruction could include the whole class, small-group instruction, students working alone in teacher-directed activities, and even student-led collaborative groups. Students, therefore, are not separated from normal instruction for long periods of time, and the method encourages movement from group to group, so students are not necessarily trapped within a set skill level for a long period of time if they are advancing. Students are in a constant flux of informal grouping and regrouping as their needs change.

Furthermore, we would recommend a more systemic approach at the high school level. One of the four high school counselors, for example, could be assigned the responsibility for developing and coordinating a transition program for eighth to ninth graders identified by data as likely to struggle. This program could focus on assisting each of these "at-risk" students to develop a 4-year individualized learning and graduation plan that connects what students are learning in school to personally valued and desired career pathways. Work-based learning opportunities could be identified that students could take in the 11th and 12th grades and built into this 4-year plan. This counselor could also develop personalized working alliance relationships with each student and their families, who could be brought in to assist in this positive future planning before students start in the ninth grade. The counselor could offer a supportive transitions advisory system for these students during their first semester at the high school. A tiered model in the ninth grade could be implemented that includes credit recovery options, flexible grouping strategies (as outlined earlier), and one-on-one tutoring when necessary. The overarching principles of this comprehensive effort should also include a fundamental commitment to multicultural counseling and building trusting relationships with each of these students and their families. A shared vision and set of possible and personally valued goals should be developed for all involved.

The social–emotional components initially proposed by the school counselors in this case allude to a multitier system of supports, through incorporating classroom, small-group, and individual components, presumably based on the level of student need. However, we think that this approach could be much more effective if also implemented at a school-wide level. Not only would all students benefit from social–emotional skill building, but the commitment to school-wide prevention would also all but certainly cut down on the need to offer more time-consuming intervention strategies.

Finally, as this situation reflects issues at a larger level, we suggest that the school counselors enlist the support of the high school principal and then call a summit across the district (including the superintendent, middle school and elementary counselors, and principals) to discuss the trends in the data and then design a truly developmental and preventative systemic approach. This issue necessitates a multitiered systems response, with multiple safety nets for students throughout their pre-K–12 years. A coordinated approach is needed to link elementary, middle, and high school counselors and teachers together to reduce the very high number of young people leaving eighth grade with substantial supports to make it to graduation.

Supplemental Readings, Online Resources, and Supplemental Activities

Supplemental Readings

Galassi, J., & Akos, P. (2007). *Strengths-based school counseling: Promoting student development and achievement*. New York, NY: Taylor & Francis.

Holcomb-McCoy, C. (2007). *School counseling to close the achievement gap: A social justice framework for success*. Thousand Oaks, CA: Corwin Press.

McKillip, M., Rawls, A., & Barry, C. (2012). Improving college access: A review of research on the role of high school counselors. *Professional School Counseling, 16*(1), 49–58.

Moore, J. L., III, & Lewis, C. W. (2012). *African American students in urban schools: Critical issues and solutions for achievement* (Educational Psychology: Critical Pedagogical Perspectives, Vol. 4). New York, NY: Peter Lang.

Oakes, J., & Guiton, G. (1995). Matchmaking: The dynamics of high school tracking decisions. *American Educational Research Journal, 32*, 3–33.

Parks, A., & Schueller, S. (Eds.). (2014). *The Wiley-Blackwell handbook of positive psychological interventions*. Malden, MA: Wiley Blackwell.

Rowell, L., & Hong, E. (2013). Academic motivation: Concepts, strategies, and counseling approaches. *Professional School Counseling, 16*(3), 158–171.

Silbereisen, R. K., & Lerner, R. M. (Eds.). (2007). *Approaches to positive youth development*. Thousand Oaks, CA: Sage.

Werblow, J., Urick, A., & Duesbery, L. (2013). On the wrong track: How tracking is associated with dropping out of high school. *Equity & Excellence in Education, 46*(2), 270–284.

Williamson, A. A., Modecki, K. L., & Guerra, N. G. (2015). SEL programs in high school. In J. A. Durlak, C. E. Domitrovich, R. P. Weissberg, & T. P. Gullotta (Eds.), *Handbook of social and emotional learning: Research and practice* (pp. 181–196). New York, NY: Guilford Press.

Wilson, W. J. (2012). *The truly disadvantaged: The inner city, the underclass, and public policy*. Chicago, IL: University of Chicago Press.

Online Resources

Ability grouping, tracking and grouping alternatives [Video]
https://www.youtube.com/watch?v=tItvMjRxL_c

American School Counselor Association (ASCA)
https://www.schoolcounselor.org/

National organization with multiple resources (see, e.g., American School Counselor Association Mindsets)

ASCA Urban Professional Interest Network
https://www.schoolcounselor.org/school-counselors-members/about-asca-(1)/professional-interest-networks

Collaborative for Academic, Social, and Emotional Learning (CASEL)
https://casel.org/

Effective social and emotional programming for preschool, elementary, middle, and high schools

Center on the Social and Emotional Foundations of Learning
http://csefel.vanderbilt.edu/

Practical strategies for social and emotional learning for teachers and caregivers (pre-school)

Counselors for Social Justice
https://counseling-csj.org/

Edutopia
https://www.edutopia.org/

Information and resources for parents who want to help their children develop academically

The Ronald H. Fredrickson Center for School Counseling Outcome Research & Evaluation (CSCORE)
www.cscor.org

Includes an array of articles addressing evidence-based practice in improving students' academic achievement both generally and specifically among students of color and of low SES)

Technical Assistance Center on Social Emotional Intervention for Young Children (TACSEI)

http://challengingbehavior.cbcs.usf.edu/TACSEI/index.htm

Evidence-based practices for social–emotional programming geared toward school staff; includes audio-visual presentations

WINGS: Helping Kids Soar

https://www.wingsforkids.org/

Resource for teaching 30 SEL skills that are categorized under 5 clusters of emotional intelligence

Supplemental Activities

Further Questions for Reflection and Discussion

- What other types of gaps between student groups might need to be addressed by the counseling staff?
- How might elementary or middle school counselors *assess* the potential achievement gap in their schools?
- Would the suggestions made above apply?
- How might elementary or middle school counselors address the achievement gap in their schools?
- Would the suggestions made above apply?
- If a low-income school had a well-implemented ASCA (2012a) National Model in place, would you still find achievement and opportunity gaps among groups of students? Explain.
- What role might positive, strength-based counseling methods (e.g., motivational interviewing, appreciative inquiry) play in addressing these issues?

Learning Activities

- *Group work dialogue starters:* (1) Were you placed in a "school tracking" system during your pre-K–12 years? If so, what advantages or disadvantages did you experience as a part of this system? (2) This response proposes a district-wide meeting including the superintendent, school counselors, and principals at the elementary, middle, and high school levels. What steps would you take to organize this event?
- Interview school counselors on their thoughts about the achievement gap. How do they notice this issue manifesting at their school, and what steps have they taken to address it?

Chapter 22

"Other Than That, Mrs. Lincoln, How Was the Play?" Career Development

Allison List

Background

I was a school counselor for 7 years in a school district housed within the second largest city in the state. Our district continuously populated around 63,000 students, with an almost even split between White and Hispanic students, and about half of the population were receiving free and reduced-price lunch (FRL). I worked as both an elementary and a middle school counselor, with the bulk of my years being in the middle school setting. The middle school I worked at has a staff that is dedicated to education. Teacher turnover is uncommon, and many of the teachers once attended that middle school themselves. Over half the staff have been teaching at that school for over 20 years. In that time, they have seen the population change and shift into a student body that is almost unrecognizable from when they first started. For example, the original population of this middle school was middle- to upper-class Caucasian non-Hispanic students. Over the past 10 years, the school has shifted to an almost direct split between students who are Caucasian non-Hispanic and those who are Latino/Latina. Almost three-quarters of the student population are eligible for FRL. Eight years ago, the school experienced an overhaul, and a new principal was brought in, as well as a new focus for the school. The new school's focus adopted a curriculum called pre-advanced placement (pre-AP) in each curricular core area. A teaming approach was adopted, meaning that teachers looped with their students for both seventh and eighth grades. Students became immersed in postsecondary planning conversations with their teachers and counselors, participated in college-bound assemblies, and identified early in the year the college or university that they would like to attend; the results were written, hung up in the hallway, and revisited at the end of each academic term. Each grade level was split into two teams, which were named after Pac-12 schools. Students learned the team school song and were given permission to wear their team t-shirts on Fridays, which was a much sought-out break from the daily uniform. Other Pac-12 school logos were painted all over the school, promoting college-bound exposure. While teachers implemented the school's new vision with fidelity, they often voiced concerns regarding not being able to do their job because most of the kids didn't care about learning their postsecondary options in middle school, and most weren't aware of what GPA or credits meant in the middle school setting. One student in particular reminded me of the complicated nature of not only adolescent development in the middle school years but also how students who are struggling find their place within a school system that puts the majority of their focus into a student's future.

I first met Marisol when she was 13. She is Latina, the oldest of four siblings, and lived in a single-parent household. Her mother was pregnant at the time and engaged. Marisol was failing most of her classes, except for art. She was sent to the office for being defiant and disrespectful. When the administration started to question her regarding her behavior, she was unresponsive and started shutting down. They called and asked whether I could speak with her. She and I had never met before, as she was not on my assigned caseload; however, my counseling colleagues and I were flexible in seeing whichever student walked through our door. Over the course of an hour, Marisol disclosed that she had been sexually assaulted when she was 12 by her mother's ex-boyfriend and was using drugs and alcohol to self-medicate. She shared that meeting with our male administration was uncomfortable for her. Marisol alluded to an abortion being the result of the sexual assault and that she had kept both experiences hidden from her mother. As we were working through this process together, Marisol pleaded that I not disclose this information to anyone, as she and her mother were undocumented. She was afraid of what would happen to her family, given the political climate, as they fled from Mexico after the drug cartel murdered her father. Marisol feared what would happen, but she desperately wanted her mom to know about the sexual assault, as she had been carrying this burden for over a year, and her relationship with her mom was deteriorating. She also expressed wanting to do well in school but not knowing how to get started, as she did not have good relationships with her teachers. Throughout our meeting, my phone rang numerous times from her teachers wanting to know when Marisol was returning to class because she had missed too much school already.

Incident

The reporting for this incident presented many ethical considerations, even though I was a mandated reporter. Not wanting to report to authorities to protect their statuses, yet wanting to share some information with her teachers to help them gain some perspective and explain why Marisol was not engaged was taxing. Being a mandated reporter, I started with the police department, because of the nature of the report. I spent hours on and off the phone with the process and voicing my concern for the well-being of the family, being careful not to disclose their status. This was a Friday afternoon, and the police said that they would contact Marisol's mother by Monday to let her know what had happened. They told me that if I would be more comfortable contacting Marisol's mom, to do so as soon as possible. Knowing the current state of Marisol's distress and the safety concerns I had for her over the weekend, I called her mother through a translator and asked that she come down to the school. Marisol wanted to be present in the meeting but asked that I help her share the information. This was a challenge, as I had to use an interpreter. Marisol's mother confirmed fleeing from Mexico and an aggressive ex-boyfriend. Marisol's mother was in shock over the event shared but stated that she felt relieved in a way, because she knew something was wrong and it seemed to be more than teenage angst. She supported the call to the police department and asked for counseling resources for her daughter. Marisol's mother also expressed concern with her grades, as she was on the honor roll in elementary school.

I spoke to the family at length about the limitations of confidentiality. I asked whether we could generate a vague statement to give to Marisol's teachers regarding her current behavior because, knowing the staff, I understood that some information was warranted to help her teachers gain insight as to whether Marisol would be successful in the classroom. The family agreed. Together, we created a blanket statement that said something like Marisol is currently dealing with a traumatic event in the family and that they may see certain behaviors as a result of that. Marisol had let me know that she had already confided to her art teacher that she was having a hard time. I continued to work with Marisol and her family throughout the school year. Additionally, I referred out to a day treatment facility, psychiatric testing, drug/alcohol counseling and followed up on court-ordered mandates that were the result of two drug possession arrests on our school campus.

With each behavioral incident, her teachers became more discouraged and frustrated. The statement that her family and I generated helped for about a week, but as assignments stopped being turned in, I decided to observe in her classes.

Discussion

The distress and complicated nature of combining mental health support and academics was blatantly clear. I sat defeated, as I realized this was how Marisol felt on a daily basis. In the comfort of my quiet small office,

Marisol and I could make headway, but those skills were not able to be translated into a jam-packed English class where students were standing up and giving a speech on what college they are going to, what they plan to study, and how much they needed to increase their Measure of Annual Progress (MAP) score to get there. The mere thought of postsecondary planning wasn't even something that existed for Marisol, let alone a class assignment. How could I show Marisol's teachers that their perception of her not caring was all a mask to hide the grief, trauma, and fear that she has experienced?

Questions

1. How can school counselors bridge the gap between social–emotional support and academic systems?
2. How can school counselors help teachers and the administration understand the fine line between upholding a school's mission and supporting the social–emotional needs of students?
3. Would you have handled the situation any differently in terms of informing her teachers?
4. Why do you think Marisol was able to confide in her art teacher?
5. How can counselors address the power of relationships to staff members who tend to not be comfortable with that aspect of teaching?
6. How can postsecondary planning be affected for students who have experienced trauma? What sorts of approaches could be used to plan for their future?
7. Knowing the staff has experienced a shift in the student population, what sorts of professional development would be useful to help them connect the pieces of the school's goals and the demographics of students?

Response 1

Wendy Hoskins and Katrina Harris

The American School Counseling Association (ASCA) built a model based on three counseling components: personal–social, academic, and career (ASCA, 2012a). Often, practitioners see the three counseling areas as separate. However, successful school counselors spend time working within two or more areas at the same time. To bridge the gap between social–emotional support and academic systems in this critical incident, the counselor would utilize social–emotional skills while discussing student academic issues, particularly in relation to the sensitive nature of what is blocking the student's academic success. Taking time to listen to the student's values and belief systems can help the counselor find common ground and similar "language" to develop a shared understanding of the academic system.

Sometimes, the best way to advocate for students is to educate stakeholders about the roles and functions of school counselors. Be proactive and create opportunities to present at school board meetings, faculty gatherings, and parent–teacher conferences. Educate members of the school system about how counselors can work with students to discuss personal–social needs and how positive results can enhance student academic and career goals. Providing a framework of how counselors can help students move toward the mission and goals of the school through addressing social–emotional needs can have long-lasting benefits.

Teachers, by nature, are curious about students and their welfare. Creating a safe space for students includes developing a healthy communication among school personnel, students, and caregivers. By drafting the initial statement to teachers with the student and her mother, the school counselor has encouraged open lines of communication, and the student becomes empowered by advocating for her academic needs (Astramovich & Harris, 2007). Moving forward with this critical incident, continue with periodic updates developed with the parent and student for school personnel. Next steps for the school system can include educating stakeholders and enhancing empathy regarding the underlying nature of "disruptive behaviors," often tied to unresolved trauma or crises.

As this critical incident highlights, student demographics are changing often faster than the demographics of the school personnel. Highlighting similarities or differences among school personnel versus the student population can be an eye-opening start for increasing stakeholder understanding. Multicultural awareness and culturally appropriate action should be considered and integrated in all aspects of the greater school system throughout the year. Utilizing an annual multicultural program evaluation provides a framework for helping all students move toward the school's mission and desired educational outcomes. Components of a culturally competent program evaluation model begin with developing an assessment geared toward understanding the specific needs of the student population. Then, throughout the year, school counselors can help develop curricular activities, classroom guidance, and counseling components that address the highest needs. Collecting data regarding effectiveness, communicating results, and garnering stakeholder feedback will help school personnel reassess the school's strategic plan, mission, and goals (Astramovich, Hoskins, & Coker, 2013).

Stakeholders are not always aware of the benefits they can provide to students in need, yet members of the school community can provide the bridge for students seeking hope and a resilient future (Flom & Hansen, 2006). In connecting with students outside the classroom, being a role model or mentor can be uncomfortable. However, children need a trusted adult to turn to. They may choose us regardless of whether we are prepared for that role. School counselors can educate stakeholders regarding the ties between positive educational experiences and the personal–social needs of everyday life.

Having a positive relationship with school personnel can provide students a feeling of connectedness and belonging that can result in higher educational aspirations and achievement.

Trauma is tricky. Trauma does not necessarily stay in the forefront of all actions or emotional responses. There may be periods of time when an individual may seem "trauma free." However, the long-lasting effects of trauma also change as the child's worldview changes. School counselors need to be prepared to listen and process past trauma as a child matures and sees the event through her or his new lens. In this critical incident, dating, hormonal changes, identity issues, and thoughts of leaving a safe space may bring new trauma-related responses. School counselors need to be aware of triggers such as the anniversary of the original traumatic incident, environmental factors, and other individuals involved. Knowing that there can be long-term repercussions from trauma, a framework with targets and goals can help a student feel grounded. Develop an individualized postsecondary plan to be used as a guide that includes small realistic goals showing progress and a feeling of accomplishment. When trauma is revisited and a student experiences a momentary setback, there is room to breathe, evidence of past successes, and future goals built in to help the student get back on track.

Response 2

Cass Dykeman

Allison List presented a complex case that is not atypical for the 21st century school counselor. In this case, several worlds collide—an intersection of race, ethnicity, SES, generational differences, immigrant status, and gender with trauma.

In terms of Question 1 (emotions/academics gap), the first thing a school counselor can do is become educated about adverse childhood experience (ACE) and its prevalence in today's K–12 students. A wide variety of experiences are included under the ACE term such as: (a) parental divorce, (b) living with an addict, and (c) physical abuse. For a complete list see: https://www.cdc.gov/violenceprevention/acestudy/pdf/BRFSS_Adverse_Module.pdf. The deleterious impact of ACEs on learning is known and cumulative (Bethell et al., 2017). The greater the number of ACEs, the more learning is affected. In the United States, 54% of adolescents have one ACE, and 28% have two or more (Soleimanpour, Geierstanger, & Brindis, 2017). There are exceptions that school counselors know all too well, but most school teachers want to be successful. As the educator in the school building who spans the worlds of mental health and pedagogy, it is incumbent on the school counselor to help teachers see that the path to classroom success can't be detoured around the emotional precipitants of ACEs.

With regard to Question 2, two barriers exist for the school counselor attempting to help teachers see the interrelationship between a school's academic mission and the emotional support of students. These barriers exist even after a school counselor is successful in educating teachers about how ACEs affect learning. The first barrier is practical; teaching students with ACEs requires frameworks and skills not taught in conventional teacher education programs. These frameworks and skills are called *trauma-informed teaching*. The influential psychologist Albert Bandura (1997) noted that we are most likely to engage in behaviors when we perceive we can be effective. Without training, the likeliness that teachers will engage in trauma-informed teaching is nil. The resource section at the end of this critical incident response contains information on the specific frameworks and skills of trauma-informed teaching.

The second barrier is related to teachers themselves. It is known that avoidance is one of the primary ways we all cope with painful emotions. The problem with avoidance as a coping strategy is that it kindles distress rather than reduces it. In America's classrooms, not only students have a history of ACEs: Many teachers have ACEs as well. Moreover, whether a teacher has ACEs or not, the teacher can experience vicarious traumatization from working with students with ACEs. Thus, unless education on trauma-informed teaching includes strategies on dealing with vicarious traumatization, this in-servicing will go nowhere.

In reference to Question 3 (informing teachers about student information), youth have a fundamental moral right to privacy. However, youth can have a different sense of privacy and different privacy needs than adults. When a school counselor believes that teacher knowledge of specific information may benefit the student, simply ask the student for permission to share that information and give the rationale for such sharing. If the student gives permission, two benefits accrue: First, teachers gain a greater context to understand a student's behavior; second, the goal and task negotiations that occur about what information can be shared and with whom it can be shared can build the working alliance between the youth and the school counselor. Although youth have a fundamental moral right to privacy, there are exceptions to school counselor–student confidentiality. It is incumbent on the school counselors to make these limits known to students before engaging in counseling. For what these exceptions are, I refer school counselors to counselor educator and attorney Ted Remley's works on counseling ethics (Remley & Herlihy, 2016; Remley, Rock, & Reed, 2017). It is an unwise school counselor who doesn't have texts like these ones always within his or her reach.

Referring to Questions 4 and 5 (power of relationship), school counselors are well aware of the influence of working alliance upon their success. What most school counselors don't know is that, in his seminal article on working alliance, Ed Bordin (1979) held that his theory has equal applicability in the classroom. Subsequent research has proved him correct (Toste, Heath, & Dallaire, 2010). As noted earlier, most teachers want to be successful. School counselors who offer in-service support to teachers about working alliances can build relevancy for attending to relationships in the classroom.

Pertaining to Questions 6 and 7 (trauma and postsecondary planning), the preeminent career theorist Donald Super emphasized *planfulness* above all other career activities. Indeed, he even coined the word itself (Savickas, 1994). Planning requires the availability of a wide range of memory functions. However, ACEs consume much of these memory functions (Ford, 2005). Thus, a school counselor is doomed to fail at career planning with ACE students if concomitant trauma work is not done. Even if a school counselor can get a student with untreated ACEs to college, the academic, mental health, and occupational outcomes are problematic (Karatekin, 2017; Schilling, Aseltine, & Gore, 2007). One approach to trauma counseling that works with youth and both fits a school context and has proven multicultural effectiveness is narrative exposure therapy (Ruf et al., 2010).

Supplemental Readings, Online Resources, and Supplemental Activities

Supplemental Readings

Brinson, J. A., & Smith, S. D. (2014). *Racialized schools: Understanding and addressing racism in schools*. New York, NY: Routledge.

Substance Abuse and Mental Health Services Administration. (2018). *Adverse childhood experiences*. Rockville, MD: Author. Retrieved from https://www.samhsa.gov/capt/practicing-effective-prevention/prevention-behavioral-health/adverse-childhood-experiences

Online Resources

Narrative Exposure Therapy (NET)
http://www.vivo.org/en/ueber-vivo/

Resources for Schools to Help Students Affected by Trauma Learn
http://www.traumainformedcareproject.org/resources/bibliography%20of%20resources%20for%20schools%20to%20be%20trauma%20informed.PDF

Trauma-Informed Care for Children Exposed to Violence: Tips for Teachers
https://www.justice.gov/sites/default/files/defendingchildhood/legacy/2011/09/19/tips-teachers.pdf

Trauma and Learning Policy Initiative (TLPI)
https://traumasensitiveschools.org/

Supplemental Activities

Learning Activities

As a school counselor, you will be tasked with developing postsecondary information sessions, workshops, podcasts, or videos to be offered periodically throughout the school year. Consider the following topics and determine how you will disseminate the information:

1. *College bound!* There is increased demand for K–12 schools to gear students toward postsecondary education and training opportunities. How many students at your local school could be first-generation college bound? Is this an exciting prospect for the students? Will the family be proud? Are the at-home conversations more about how to get by the next day rather than future planning? How do students balance conflicting messages about their future? How will you find the answers to these questions and disseminate helpful information?

2. *Career day!* Your career awareness goal is to include a higher percentage of professionals that reflect the student demographics working in a variety of careers and representing various postsecondary educational institutions. What information do you need to accomplish this goal? How would you garner assistance and support from administrators and teachers to create and set up the event? What challenges might you face in your community?

3. *Take your education with you!* To help displaced or undocumented families understand that education can be possible and portable, you may need to think outside the traditional "brick-and-mortar" box. What options for postsecondary high school education and training are available in your locale? How many of these options are only for individuals who plan to stay locally? What systems or agencies can help transient individuals achieve their postsecondary goals? What options can they consider around the globe or online?

4. *Stakeholder buy in!* Program evaluation can help inform stakeholders and develop a better school counseling program. How will you utilize program evaluation as a sales pitch to stakeholders regarding your role and effectiveness? What aspects of program evaluation will be most beneficial to share with stakeholders? Describe how you will integrate program evaluation to bolster student success and college readiness.

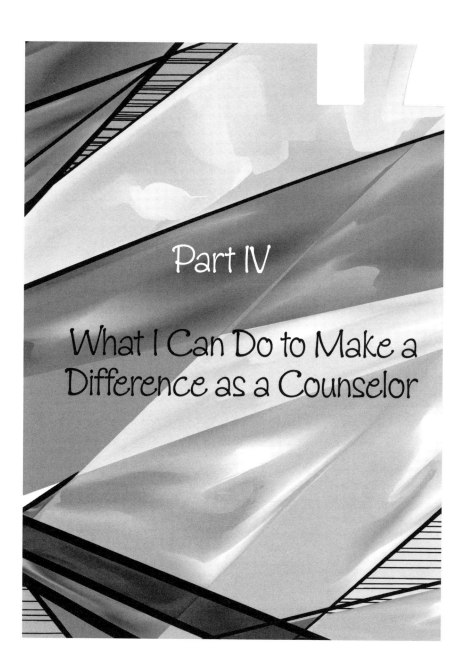

Part IV

What I Can Do to Make a Difference as a Counselor

Chapter 23

I Need to Know About Adverse Childhood Effects

Jodi L. Saunders

Background

Lucas is a 6-year-old African American boy who, teachers have determined, needs to repeat kindergarten because of poor social and emotional skills and behaviors. Although he is bright and developmentally on target with core academic skills such as number and letter recognition, he is developmentally delayed socially and emotionally.

Incident

Often, when his adoptive mother, Ms. Karis, drops him off at school, Lucas does not want her to leave and feigns illness (e.g., headache, cough). This is presented as Lucas's reasons for needing to stay with Ms. Karis. Lucas is a complex, underweight guy whose behaviors and emotional state are also somewhat unpredictable because of his severe attention-deficit/hyperactivity disorder (ADHD). In one instance this year, when his kindergarten class was passing another on the sidewalk, Lucas suddenly reached out and shoved a little girl from the other class into the bushes. Still, his teachers described Lucas as one of the kindest, most helpful, and good-hearted children in the class. In addition, Lucas is extremely hypervigilant in new or public situations, often standing in one spot and turning slowly with his eyes rapidly scanning the room. As Ms. Karis dropped Lucas off for the first day of kindergarten this year, she explained that he would need to be introduced to everyone in the room. Ms. Karis stated that Lucas would then relax a bit and would also remember every person's name in the room . . . forever. Lucas's teacher described him as very shy and a child who preferred to play alone or with only one other person. His teacher indicated that Lucas did not seem to know how to join a group (ask if he could play, etc.), despite being taught on several occasions.

Although Lucas's mother agrees with Lucas repeating kindergarten, she is concerned about how to best help him. A meeting with Ms. Karis revealed that Lucas was placed into foster care with her at the age of 15 months. He was found in a dilapidated house during a drug raid in the middle of the night amid weapons and drug paraphernalia. His mother stated that when Lucas was placed with her, he did not speak, grabbed food off the counters, and was sadly independent—putting himself to bed, refusing to be held, and never crying even when seriously injured. Although, obviously, Lucas and his adoptive mother had made great gains regarding attachment, issues still manifested. Lucas's hypervigilance appears to be a coping mechanism developed at a very young age to stay as safe as possible. As a child, Lucas had tested positive for various drugs when removed from his biological parents' home. Doctors were concerned of the likelihood of further neurological consequences, such as ADHD.

Although Lucas was placed into foster care at 15 months, the case extended over time and visits continued with his biological family for nearly 2 years before termination of parental rights was determined. Ms. Karis, the adoptive mom, was also the foster parent for Lucas. She reported working closely with psychiatrists and pediatricians and participating in an intensive parent–child interaction therapy to assist Lucas and his new family. Ms. Karis also reported attempting to engage him in group activities such as sports clubs or similar community activities, but Lucas refused to leave her side and appeared content to watch the activities instead of engaging in them. Mom reported that, although Lucas still talked about his "other mom" and his "grandfather" (having both positive and negative memories), before every visit with his biological family, he had expressed fear that he would not be returned to his foster (now adoptive) mom. Ms. Karis also reports that Lucas was removed from a location and a culture (African American, poverty, substance abuse, unsafe neighborhood) very different from theirs (Caucasian, college-educated professionals, no substance use, neighborhood with no safety concerns) and is concerned about the impact of those changes as well. Ms. Karis has approached the school counselor for resources, help, and a partner in helping Lucas succeed in school; in the community; and, particularly, with peer interactions.

Questions

1. How would you assess Lucas's needs and how best to respond to them?
2. What resources or activities other than therapy could be beneficial?

3. Do you believe that Lucas would benefit from grief/loss therapy? If so, what techniques or activities would be most helpful? If not, what approach would you recommend? What other supports might be helpful in helping Lucas work through his losses?

4. Are there resources, activities, or other approaches that you feel would be helpful in assisting Lucas in "catching up" developmentally in the social and emotional realms?

5. What impact do you believe that the change in location, culture, etc., has had on Lucas?

6. How would you describe Lucas's struggle with relationships, specifically addressing the possible causes and solutions?

Response 1

Amanda Dreisbach Rumsey and Catherine Y. Chang

The case of Lucas is complex and requires collaboration between the family, school, and community. As a school counselor working with Lucas and his family, you will want to be mindful of his cultural heritage, the cultural heritage of his adoptive family, and your own cultural background. All these factors will affect how you interact with this family and how you conceptualize this case. As a school counselor, the first step I would take in assessing Lucas's needs would be to talk to Lucas and observe him. I would also consult with Lucas's teacher; his adoptive mother, Ms. Karis; and, if possible, his previous psychiatrists or psychologists. I would carefully consider how the information may affect his current functioning, identify strengths and weaknesses, and determine whether there are information gaps.

Lucas has identified strengths such as being kind-hearted, helpful, and independent. He also has a supportive parental figure and is intelligent. These strengths should be considered when identifying strategies to respond to Lucas's needs. Lucas's early childhood experiences—which included living in an unsafe environment with questionable parental attachment or bonding and the presence of drugs in his system—likely had an impact on his social and emotional development. His current bonding with Ms. Karis, although challenging at times, can be seen as a positive step toward developing attachment. Lucas's diagnosis of severe ADHD would also be a factor to consider. I would collaborate with Ms. Karis and Lucas's doctor to support Lucas getting the appropriate medical and/or behavioral interventions for ADHD and keep in mind that retention would not change the symptoms of ADHD. I would also want to encourage Ms. Karis to consider seeking outside counseling, both individual and family counseling, to support Lucas's social and emotional development.

I would consult with Lucas's teacher to determine what interventions had already been tried and identify new strategies for support. In addition to Lucas's teacher, I would involve a team of people including, but not limited to, myself (school counselor), Ms. Karis (adoptive mother), the school psychologist, and a school administrator, and I would use the tiered Response to Intervention (RTI) framework to evaluate the data and proceed with a plan for intervention. The RTI process is "a method for identifying at-risk learners at an early stage, matching them to appropriate research based interventions, and flexibly providing these students with additional support as needed" (Wright, 2007, p. 10).

When thinking about what resources or activities other than counseling would be helpful, I would want to consider Ms. Karis's previous unsuccessful attempts at involving Lucas in group work. Lucas seems to enjoy being helpful and is on target with core academic skills. In the classroom environment, giving him helping roles such as organizing books, sharpening pencils, or feeding a class pet may be a way in which he could feel helpful and remain positively engaged. Lunch with a "buddy" could be a useful tool that I would try by picking one or two other students to come to the counseling office for an occasional lunch with Lucas. In the community, I would recommend involvement with expressive arts activities such as visual art, movement, drama, and music. These activities may provide nonthreatening ways to support the development of social and emotional skills. I would also consider a structured physical activity, such as swimming, karate, or gymnastics, that Lucas could begin to get involved with that was more individual in nature but included other people. This type of activity may support Lucas's physical growth and development while also providing an outlet for energy.

Lucas would likely benefit from participation in grief or loss therapy, particularly if it was done with a play-therapy approach, along with other interventions. With his young age and developing attachment with Ms. Karis, I would not support placing the entire focus on the grief and loss but would want to include family counseling and social skills training activities as well.

Lucas is likely to need continued support to assist him in "catching up" developmentally in the social and emotional realms. He will benefit by participating in activities that are geared for self-awareness, self-management, social awareness, relationship building, and responsible decision making. This will require a safe and stable environment with collaborative strategies in place to support Lucas's growth. These strategies might include classroom interventions that his teacher initiates, as well as additional supports from other school personnel and from Ms. Karis at home. Some strategies might include: strategic grouping in class, use of the positive reward system, increased opportunities for helping roles, and explicit instruction of positive social behaviors with reinforcement.

The cultural changes that Lucas has experienced as a result of leaving his biological family and joining his adoptive family are likely to have a greater impact on him later in childhood or as an adolescent. He may have conflicted feelings when he considers the changes in his environment and attempts to understand his own identity within those two separate cultures. Lucas's poor social and emotional skills and challenging behaviors can be directly linked to what we know about his history. His experience of living in an unsafe environment has contributed to his hypervigilance in new situations. He has learned that he must independently assess a situation for safety and does not have the freedom to be carefree in new environments. His attachment to Ms. Karis demonstrates that he does have the ability to connect and build relationships; however, he is not yet able to trust completely. His relationship with his biological parents is one of confusion and loss now. Together, these experiences demonstrate that, with support, Lucas may be able to develop healthy boundaries and attachment in his relationships, but caution should be applied when working with Lucas. He needs to have adults who demonstrate stability, safety, and consistency so that he may begin to trust. As he develops, and healthy boundaries and attachment are supported, his self-awareness and peer relationships will likely improve.

Response 2

Tom Keller, Brandie Oliver, and Nick Abel

The case of Lucas will require a professional school counselor to use a wide variety of skills, including consultation, collaboration, and counseling, all viewed through a culturally responsive perspective. The challenges that Lucas encountered in his first 6 years of life have, not surprisingly, influenced his development. According to Erikson (as cited by Fiore, 2011), children who fail to form secure attachments early in life are prone to mistrust, which is evident in Lucas's reluctance to participate in new situations or join group activities. Later stages of Erikson's model detail how children develop autonomy and begin to understand that they are responsible for their own behavior—both traits that seem to be lacking in Lucas's development. Through a lens of social learning theory, we might also point out the fact that appropriate social–emotional skills were likely not modeled for Lucas during the formative years, which may have also contributed to his issues with social interaction (Broderick & Blewitt, 2015).

Despite Lucas's many developmental issues, we are concerned about the choice to retain him in kindergarten. Research has shown retention to be only a marginally effective intervention at best, and an overtly harmful one at worst (National Association of School Psychologists, 2011), with studies linking the practice to increased behavioral difficulty, poor peer relationships, and decreased self-esteem (Jimerson, 2001). Additionally, African American males are disproportionately retained when compared with students from other ethnic backgrounds (National Center for Education Statistics, 2010)—an ongoing equity issue that our schools must address.

Although Lucas's case is challenging, we feel that a team of concerned individuals collaborating on a variety of interventions aimed at increasing his prosocial behaviors could make a difference for this young man. In the following text, we discuss how a school counselor could lead such an effort by utilizing his or her skills in consultation, collaboration, and cultural responsiveness.

Our first step in this case would be to engage in direct consultation with Ms. Karis. In this role, the school counselor (consultant) would arrange to meet with Ms. Karis (consultee) to develop an intervention or series of interventions that could be implemented at home to address Lucas's developmental issues, such as attachment. In this case, one possible intervention might be a reward system under which Lucas could have lunch with his mother (or other trusted adult) on Fridays during weeks when he did not have issues in school (morning separation, behavior referrals, etc.). Another strategy Ms. Karis and the classroom teacher might try is systematic desensitization, whereby the mother is gradually less involved with the morning dropoff over the course of several weeks, until the point is reached at which she need not even enter the school building. As interventions are tried, the school counselor would work collaboratively with Ms. Karis and the classroom teacher to assess the effectiveness of each intervention and develop new possibilities, if necessary.

This case would be too much for any school counselor to handle alone. Instead, it would clearly require the collaboration of many individuals, including the school counselor, teachers, administrator(s), parent(s), existing care providers, and community organizations. Although the school counselor might "run point" on organizing and coordinating a team of individuals, he or she cannot and should not be the sole source of support for Lucas, Ms. Karis, and/or the classroom teacher. If the school has a student assistance team (SAT) or an RTI team, Lucas's case should immediately be referred for discussion and development of a multitiered system of support that would likely include ongoing behavior monitoring, positive behavior intervention and support (PBIS) strategies, reward systems, and counseling interventions. Ms. Karis should play a significant role in any team that examines Lucas's case, as her insights into his early development (including interventions tried at home and in previous educational and social settings) would be invaluable. In addition, we would advise the counselor to seek a "consent to share information" from Ms. Karis so that all the professionals involved in Lucas's case (physicians, therapists, etc.) could be contacted and involved in planning and monitoring the effectiveness of interventions. These professionals might also be consulted about Lucas's ADHD (and any other underlying disabilities) that might qualify Lucas for special services and accommodations under the Individuals with Disabilities Act (IDEA) or Section 504 of the Rehabilitation Act of 1973.

Understanding the cultural dimension in this case is a critical component. Although we are unsure of the cultural makeup of the school community, we do know that Lucas is being raised in a home environment that is culturally different from his previous home environment on many levels (e.g., socioeconomic status and race). Another key piece of information absent from this case is whether there is a male role model in Lucas's life. One strategy that we recommend is to find a mentor for Lucas, preferably an African American man. Mentored youth have shown improvement in outcomes in behavioral, emotional, social, and academic domains spanning development (DuBois, Portillo, Rhodes, Silverthorn, & Valentine, 2011). Throughout Lucas's development, the counselor can help Ms. Karis understand the unique identity development process, including his racial identity development, and invite Ms. Karis to assist Lucas in developing and nurturing connections to his culture of origin as he grows up with a foot in both worlds. Although grief may be a natural part of this process, we believe that it is important to assist Lucas in the meaning-making process of his loss. Meaning making assists the student with identity development after a loss, making sense of the loss, and finally searching for benefits following a loss (Neimeyer, 2005). These three components within meaning making would all be beneficial to Lucas as he continues coping with the losses he experienced early in life and works to build healthy relationships and interact cooperatively with others.

Supplemental Readings and Online Resources

Supplemental Readings

Brigman, G., Mullis, F., Webb, L., & White, J. (2005). *Consultation in schools; Building counselor skills for working with parents, teachers, and other school personnel.* Hoboken: NJ: Wiley.

Merrell, K. W., & Gimpel, G. (2014). *Social skills of children and adolescents: Conceptualization, assessment, treatment.* New York, NY: Psychology Press.

Wright, J. (2007). *RTI toolkit: A practical guide for schools.* Port Chester, NY: Dude Publishing.

Online Resources

ASCA SCENE
http://scene.schoolcounselor.org/home.
This is a networking site for professional school counselors and is a great website to share ideas and lesson plans and ask questions.

Center on Response to Intervention: An American Institute for Research
http://www.rti4success.org/
This center provides support for those who want to learn more about and implement RTI.

Intervention Central
http://www.interventioncentral.org/
This website provides teachers, schools, and districts with resources for helping struggling learners.

Positive Behavioral Interventions and Supports
https://www.pbis.org/school/rti
This website provides information and resources related to Response to Intervention (RTI), which is a systematic way to document the performances of students who need additional services, and provides interventions based on the students' needs.

Positive Parenting
   http://positiveparenting.com/

This website is a great resource to share with parents and includes parenting advice and online parenting classes.

Chapter 24

The "We" in Cyberbullying

Stephannee Standefer

This incident examines whether the school counselor knows how to build effective working teams of school staff, parents, and community members to promote the academic, career, and personal–social development of students. The topic of the incident addresses a multilevel stakeholder effort to decrease bullying/relational aggressions among students and increase students' sense of safety both inside and outside the school building.

Background

It was the third time in a week Ms. Sandoval, the school counselor, was called into the administrator's office for an "emergency" meeting. Emergency meetings meant that a student's safety was in jeopardy (e.g., fights, drugs, sexual incidents, theft). The meetings usually consisted of the principal, school security (police officer), deans (assistant principals), the school social worker, and the school counselor. The Reid Middle School has over 700 students, three deans, one police officer, one school social worker, and one school counselor.

Incident

Ms. Sandoval entered the office to find a frightened female student, LeVida, sitting in front of the administrator, Ms. Peersnot. On the administrator's computer screen were pictures of a text conversation that was documented as taking place over the past 2 days between LeVida and another student, Jamila. Probes into the incident revealed that over 500 text messages were

213

exchanged between these two young women in the past 2 days. LeVida and Jamila were fighting over a young man, Bob. Jamila threatened to "cut your [LeVida's] face up so when he [Bob] looks at you all he sees is scars" and warned LeVida to "stay away from him or I [Jamila] will change your life forever." LeVida returned the challenges by stating, "I ain't scared of you, b#@$h, you better pay attention to what you eat. Rat poison don't have no taste."

LeVida's mother discovered the texts. The mother sent screenshots of all the texts to Ms. Peersnot. As the head administrator, Ms. Peersnot called the emergency meeting as soon as the students entered the building. The school team began the process of investigating the incident, which included creating a safety plan for LeVida, Jamila, and the young man, Bob. The intense nature of the threats required police intervention. The team also needed to determine how to appropriately discipline the students according to the school's code of conduct. Furthermore, we needed to address the students' parents; LeVida's mom was demanding an immediate answer. We also needed to inform the teachers to be on the lookout for these students and inappropriate behaviors in class or hallways.

This incident would take hours to process. It was the third serious incident this week. The school counselor had a mound of paperwork to complete, a pounding headache, and was feeling tired and overwhelmed from the events of the week. As she returned to her desk as the school day closed, she found an email from the history teacher, Ms. Roth. She was sure there was "tension" between some students in her class this morning. She wanted to know whether Ms. Sandoval would be available to consult with her on how to proceed. She believed that this "tension" was impeding the students' academic efforts and wanted to address it immediately.

Discussion

Last week at our monthly "Coffee with the Principal" parent night, parents expressed concerns about student safety both at home and in the building. The use of online technology applications like Snapchat, Instagram, and Facebook took bullying and relational aggressions to another level. Students were also texting constantly. Parents were hearing things from their students that they did not know how to address. They were looking to the school counselor for answers, guidance, and support.

Bus drivers were also reporting in-bus incidents that they did not know how to control. The bus transportation company wanted to meet with the school staff to create a process to equip the bus drivers to deal with incidents on the bus. The principal asked the school counselor, Ms. Sandoval, to participate in this process to ensure that the bus drivers were considering the student's developmental abilities. The principal valued the school counselor's contributions and wanted to include her in the planning for this process.

Last, there is an overall concern from all the stakeholders regarding the students' ability to be academically successful in a culture where they are more concerned about physical and emotional safety.

Questions

1. How would you conceptualize these issues from a school-counselor-as-consultant perspective?
2. How would you prioritize the many layers of student academic, career, and personal–social development of students in this scenario?
3. Who are the stakeholders? How would you engage them in your conceptualization? What steps would you take to secure their involvement?
4. What are some of the systemic strengths and limitations in this scenario? What strengths could you leverage? What do you perceive to be barriers in your plan?

Response 1

Brandie Oliver, Nick Abel, and Tom Keller

As former school counselors, we empathize with Ms. Sandoval as she deals with a large student–counselor ratio (700:1) and a seemingly nonstop parade of crises. Although this case is complex, one thing is perfectly clear: No school counselor would be able to solve this issue alone. A systemic problem this large requires collaboration among a group of dedicated individuals led by a skillful team builder and visionary. We believe that a school counselor skilled in consultation, collaboration, advocacy, and the implementation of a comprehensive school counseling program (CSCP) would be the ideal person to lead such an effort.

The biggest issue here is the widespread concern in the school and community about bullying and the general school climate. Although concerns about academic and career development are understandable, it stands to reason that students would have difficulty reaching their potential in these domains when social–emotional issues so frequently threaten their sense of safety at school. As such, our primary focus would be improving school climate to reduce the frequency of conflict and bullying among students. While there is no one-size-fits-all approach to issues like these, a multitiered response in the context of a well-designed CSCP (such as one based on the American School Counselor Association [ASCA] National Model [2012a]) makes the most sense to us.

Like many school counselors, Ms. Sandoval is caught in the unenviable position of frequently responding to crises rather than preventing them. Also, although the current situation feels overwhelming, it may provide the jumping-off point needed to design and implement a CSCP—which would ultimately make her job feel more manageable. A first step would be for Ms. Sandoval to form an advisory team to guide the development of her CSCP, including how to best respond to larger issues of school climate. Advisory teams frequently consist of key school personnel, such as teachers and administrators, but should also include stakeholders such as parents, community leaders, employers, and students. In this scenario, Ms. Sandoval is fortunate that a caring, concerned group of adults already exists, including parents, bus drivers, an administrator who trusts and values the opinion of the counselor, and at least one teacher who understands that classroom climate affects student learning. Ms. Sandoval may find that all she needs to do to secure cooperation from these people is ask. That said, if her initial efforts fall flat, she might look for incentives to get folks involved. A meal, snack, or coffee might be all that is needed to entice participation. Perhaps a community organization would offer a grant to fund this work and reimburse team members for their time. A nationally known speaker or film screening may pique the interest of concerned individuals.

Once Ms. Sandoval has secured cooperation from key stakeholders, the team's first task would be to gather data to identify areas for improvement and to establish a baseline for measuring the effectiveness of their interventions. In this case, school data such as office referrals, attendance, and suspensions/expulsions would be very useful, but surveys and focus groups targeting students, parents, and other stakeholders would also be important in identifying needs and tracking perceptions of safety and climate. On the basis of these findings, the team could create specific, measurable, attainable, realistic, time-bound (SMART) goals for addressing the issues they uncovered and then move to planning interventions.

The complex issues in this scenario call for a multitiered response focused both on prevention and on responsive services and allowing Ms. Sandoval to operate as both consultant and counselor. At the highest level are school-wide interventions aimed at improving climate, such as comprehensive bullying prevention and intervention training for all students, staff, and school personnel to ensure a common understanding and response to this issue—all to prevent major disruptions to school safety. Once a common language, a definition, and procedures are in place surrounding bullying and peer maltreatment, other comprehensive interventions can be implemented. One example to improve school climate would be the implementation of a restorative justice approach to disruptive student behavior. Ms. Sandoval can take the lead to train and build the capacity for this school to adopt the restorative justice framework to better prepare school personnel to handle conflict and work to focus on relationships as the core element in the school. Another intervention at this level might be a community event on cyberbullying or online safety, during which parents and families are given information and tools to keep an eye on their children's digital footprint in an effort to prevent minor issues from spiraling into major conflicts. Ms. Sandoval might also develop a series of preventative guidance lessons on topics such as cybersafety, conflict resolution, and empathy education, that she could either teach herself or ask classroom teachers to deliver during advisory periods, homerooms, or other common times.

The next level of interventions would target high-risk groups of students (or families) in need of additional training and skill development. Possible interventions at this level include peer mediation or teacher facilitation of low-level conflict resolution (preferably through a standardized method such as restorative justice); counseling groups aimed at general skill building in areas such as anger management; self-management; and building relationship skills through cultural awareness education.

The final tier of intervention in this scenario would include direct services provided by the school counselor, social worker, or other trained helping professional to students who are involved in major conflicts. Scheduling weekly sessions with the students most in need of direct services would serve to reinforce skill building and provide time to debrief specific examples of conflict in the students' lives. Incidents involving ongoing bullying or threats to safety would still be referred to school administration, but our hope would be that the aforementioned steps reduce the frequency of these issues while improving the overall feeling of safety among the student body—ultimately leading to an increased emphasis on academic and career development.

Response 2

Chris Janson

From the perspective of the school counselor, Ms. Sandoval, the surface concerns within Reid Middle School involve school climate and culture as well as contentious and even threatening communication facilitated by emergent social media and its impact on relationships among youth. However, below those considerable issues there exists an even more stubborn obstacle to healthy and effective schools: the predilection of those within educational systems to believe that they are the true experts regarding student and local concerns rather than the youth, families, and communities who live those issues and thus know them best (McKnight & Block, 2010). To find successful and sustainable solutions to the concerns and issues within Reid Middle School, Ms. Sandoval should lead efforts to reframe the school's relationship with students, their families, and local community members to facilitate their development of strategies and solutions.

Certainly, the challenges to student safety in Reid Middle School likely affect the domains of student development that school counselor professional organizations focus on most: academic, career, and personal–social development (ASCA, 2012a). At the same time, however, there is another domain of youth development that has been relatively neglected, and it can also serve as the most powerful instrument of positive and constructive change at Reid Middle School. This domain could be referred to and labeled in many ways, but here let us refer to it as *the political* in a classic Greek sense. Our concept of the political comes originally from the Greek *politkos*, which can translate roughly to "of, for, or relating to the people." For youth, the development of the political self involves growing toward a place of agency or the ability to exert influence over their communities, the organizations (like their school) housed within them, and the relationships that constitute the true stuff of life.

In Reid Middle School, Ms. Sandoval could work with others in and around the school—students, caregivers and family, staff, and community members—to design and facilitate a community learning exchange (Guajardo, Guajardo, Janson, & Militello, 2016) in which all involved contribute their perspectives regarding school culture, the bullying that has grown within it, and solutions and strategies to address both. Community learning exchanges (CLEs) are constructed around five axioms that guide their design and the work within them: (1) Learning and leading are dynamic social processes; (2) conversations are critical and central pedagogical processes; (3) the people closest to the issues are best situated to discover answers to local concerns; (4) crossing boundaries enriches the development and educational process; and (5) hope and change are built on the assets and dreams of locals and their communities (Guajardo et al., 2016, pp. 24–27).

To honor the axioms that the people closest to the issues are best positioned to resolve them and that hope and change are constructed around the gifts and assets of those very same people, Ms. Sandoval, Ms. Peersnot, and Ms. Roth would identify a smaller team of students, the caregivers and family of students, and community members to assist them in designing and then facilitating these CLEs. The invitation to be involved would be carefully crafted to emphasize that they would play a fully involved role in the design and facilitation of the exchange. This diverse team would then reach out to others, inviting them to be a part of an innovative gathering developed to improve the school culture, reduce bullying, and support each participant's growth as leaders and learners.

At the center of all this would be Ms. Sandoval. As a professional school counselor, she is a collaborator by training, philosophy, and her position at the very fulcrum of both informal and formal data within the school (Janson & Maxis, 2015). By broadening her collaborative reach beyond simply school staff to include families, community members, and most important, the students themselves, she can begin to tap into local knowledge and wisdom within the community. Doing so is essential in addressing the challenges facing Reid Middle School and its students, and in the process, it would not only deepen the partnership between the school and the community but also quite possibly strengthen both in the process.

Likewise, as counterintuitive as it is, students themselves are quite often those least likely to be involved in school improvement efforts (Cook-Sather, 2006). When schools recognize, honor, and use student perspectives and voices, relationship and power dynamics among the adults and youth in schools shift and open up space for students to experience and recognize "the political potential of speaking out on their own behalf" (Lewis, 1996, p. 44). Ms. Sandoval can be instrumental in how Reid Middle School re-imagines how schools can respond to challenges. By organizing a truly collective effort, she and the other school leaders can frame leadership and learning as fluid and dynamic social processes rather than stagnant top-down practices; engage in pedagogical conversations rather than administrative mandates; cross boundaries that separate staff from student from community rather than reinforcing them; and recognize and marshal the assets and insights of youth, families, and community rather than insisting on their own expertise.

Such an approach is not without its challenges. Foremost, it demands shifts in school–community relationships and challenges the traditional paradigm in which educators advocate "for" youth rather than "with" them. The shift in power dynamics alone is not something that comes easily to educational organizations or the educators within them. However, the axioms of CLE work, and stories of their impact on individuals, organizations, and communities can provide assistance in changing how schools and educators engage and advocate. CLEs are not a formula, however, nor can they be. However, they can provide a beacon for those who choose democratic and empowering efforts to "make the road by walking" (Machado, 1978).

Supplemental Readings, Online Resources, and Supplemental Activities

Supplemental Readings

Freire, P. (1997). *Pedagogy of the oppressed.* New York, NY: Continuum.

Guajardo, M. A., Guajardo, F., Janson, C., & Militello, M. (2016). *Reframing community partnerships in education: Uniting the power of place and wisdom of people.* New York, NY: Routledge.

Horton, M., Freire, P., Bell, B., Gaventa, J., & Peters, J. (1990). *We make the road by walking: Conversations on education and social change.* Philadelphia, PA: Temple University Press.

Horton, M., & Jacobs, D. (2003). *The Myles Horton reader: Education for social change.* Knoxville, TN: University of Tennessee Press.

McKnight, J., & Block, P., (2010). *The abundant community: Awakening the power of families and neighborhoods.* San Francisco, CA: Berrett-Koehler.

Online Resources

Abundant Communities
 http://www.abundantcommunity.com/

Community Learning Exchange
 http://communitylearningexchange.org/

Highlander Research and Education Center
https://www.highlandercenter.org/

Llano Grande Center for Research and Development
http://llanogrande.org/

Supplemental Activities

Further Questions for Reflection and Discussion

How can schools and school counselors learn more about the strengths, assets, and gifts in the community surrounding their schools? Explore the differences in process and outcome when one advocates "with" rather than "for" others and other communities? How can schools listen better to student perspectives to inform school processes, policies, practices, and culture?

Learning Activities

Neighborhood/community learning walks
- Use of circles (learning, study, etc.)
- Community asset mapping
- Community elder interviews

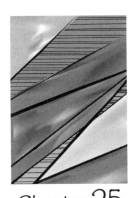

Chapter 25

Ambassador Between
Two Nations

Lisa Grayshield

Background

Mr. Powers, a new middle school counselor receives a note from the sixth-grade teacher, Ms. Ayala-Rivera, that she is concerned about Michelle, because she is missing a lot of class and is often late to school. Michelle is a member of the local federally recognized tribal community that is located approximately 45 minutes from the school. Ms. Ayala-Rivera reported that Michelle is bright and talented and gets along well with her peers. She further reported that Michelle received all As on her first quarter report card and mostly Bs and Cs in the second quarter. The teacher said that if Michelle continues to decline, she will barely pass her classes in the third quarter. The teacher's primary concern is that she has noticed a trend with her Native American students. Like Michelle, others have started the year doing well academically and then about midway through the year show an academic decline or drop out of school.

Ms. Ayala-Rivera has been teaching at the school for more than 30 years and can recall the names of numerous Native American students she has taught in her classes. She has witnessed that many of the Native American students dropped out of high school. Ms. Ayala-Rivera has seen generational patterns, such as in the case of Michelle of school defined "truancy."

In the past, the incidents of truancy were addressed on an individual basis and often without success. The same excuses were similar: The child missed the bus, and there was no vehicle to get him or her to school; students were sick; they had a clinic appointment; and the family or children had to attend a cultural event that took all night long and the children were tired. Absentee policies in the past were not as strict as the current

221

policy. The school truancy policy allows no more than three excused absences per academic quarter without a doctor's note. The nearest Indian Health Hospital is 2 hours away. In the first quarter, Michelle used all three excuses within the first month of the first quarter in addition to a week off for a tribal ceremony that she attended with her grandparents. In the second quarter, Michelle used all three absences in the first 3 weeks, and Ms. Ayala-Rivera sent home a note requesting to have a parent–teacher conference. Michelle's parents did not respond, and before the quarter was finished, Michelle had missed 3 additional days.

Incident

It is now the beginning of the third quarter, and Michelle has already missed 2 days. Ms. Ayala-Rivera asked the school counselor, Mr. Powers, to contact the parents and again request a parent–teacher conference. Ms. Ayala-Rivera further requested that the principal be involved in the meeting to further impress upon the parents the importance of school attendance. She felt that drastic measures should be taken to ensure that Michelle's parents understood the implications and the law regarding school absence and truancy. Ms. Ayala-Rivera conveyed to the school counselor that, in the past when she reported an attendance problem, very little was done because the school attendance policy was enforced by the town's legal system. Michelle was American Indian, and she lived on the reservation. Without the assistance of the tribal authorities, the legal system has very little jurisdiction over the reservation population. Tribal authorities rarely address school attendance issues with grade school and middle school children, because they had much more pressing issues, and very few tribal police to enforce truancy laws.

Ms. Ayala-Rivera disclosed to Mr. Powers that she had taught Michelle's mother in her class only 16 years earlier. Michelle's mother was very young when she gave birth to Michelle. As Ms. Ayala-Rivera recalled, Michelle's mother did not complete high school. Ms. Ayala-Rivera stated that the "Indian parents on the reservation do not value education, and if something is not done to force Indian parents to get their children to school, the kids will continue to drop out of school and be a problem for society."

The new school counselor, Mr. Powers, is a recent graduate of a CACREP (Council for Accreditation of Counseling & Related Educational Programs)-accredited counseling program and has some training in multicultural issues. The counselor is not a American Indian, but he did grow up in the local surrounding community and has some knowledge about the local tribal people. The school counselor recognizes that the relationship between the tribal community and the school has never been very strong. He agrees with Ms. Ayala-Rivera regarding the issue being bigger than anyone cared to admit in the past. The school often blamed the American Indian parents for their lack of value in public school education. The American Indian parents blamed the school for their lack of respect for native culture and often blamed the teachers for not caring for their children.

Ms. Ayala-Rivera has generally been considered "a good teacher" by the American Indian children and parents and is often the teacher requested for their children. When the school counselor phoned Michelle's mother, he found that she was unaware that Ms. Ayala-Rivera was so concerned. The mother believed that Michelle was doing well in Ms. Ayala-Rivera's class. She was aware that Michelle's grades had dropped a little but did not believe that Michelle was having any problems. The mother agreed to schedule an appointment with the school to talk about Michelle's attendance.

Discussion

In preparing for the meeting, the counselor recalled an article, "Barriers and Best Practices for Indian American Students" (Grayshield, 2006) in which there was reference to a presidential executive order (13336) stating that American Indian children have a right to an education that is culturally and linguistically appropriate. Although this charge was profoundly important in the lives and education of American Indian children, in practice, public schools find the law difficult to implement because of the limited number of American Indian teachers and so many pressures on teachers to ensure that students make adequate yearly progress due to accountability standards.

Mr. Powers considered numerous issues in preparation for addressing the systemic Native American student attendance issues and Michelle's immediate needs. In preparing to have a meeting, Mr. Powers reflected on his need to consider the following: (a) the teachers' and parents' biases, or difference in values; (b) the sociopolitical context, with respect to preparing children to become productive members of society, finish school, go on to college, and get a job to support their families; and (c) the historical context of American Indian education as well as that of the relationship between the local school and tribe in addressing the issues.

Questions

1. How can the school counselor provide relevant and pertinent information in which a structure can be established that promotes respect and responsibility on both sides?
2. What steps can be taken to locate and compile resources to help the district and the family to accommodate the cultural values of the family, the demands of the school policy, and the needs of Michelle?
3. What resources are available to assist with addressing the challenges of school attendance? Does the tribe have resources, tutoring programs, attendance policies, or cultural programs?
4. What resources are not being considered? Could these be considered in fostering an ongoing positive relationship with American Indian children, their parents, their communities, and the school to improve achievement and success?

Additional culture-specific questions for consideration:

5. What are the differences in values between the American Indian community and the public school community, and are they really that different? Are there tribal ceremonies and designated events that conflict with children attending school?
6. What has been done in the past to address this issue? Have the school community and the tribal communities made attempts to foster a good working relationship on behalf of the children and their education? If so, what happened? Is there anything that can be learned to make progress in this endeavor?
7. What have other school/tribal communities done to successfully build a partnership that allows for this support?
8. What is the historical context regarding the school/tribe and larger surrounding community for this particular tribe?
9. Why are the current policies for attendance not being followed or addressed with American Indian children?

Response 1

Heather J. Fye

As Mr. Powers prepares for a meeting with Michelle's family and the school, it is imperative that a collaborative structure is established that promotes respect and responsibility for both sides. It may be helpful for Mr. Powers to inquire what both sides plan to address at the meeting. When negotiating the official meeting date and time, it is important for the school to be sensitive to the time, date, and availability of Michelle's family.

When Michelle's parents arrive to the official meeting, it is important that school staff acknowledge the parents' willingness to meet and overall support of Michelle's education and growth as an adolescent. As the meeting begins, it will be important to establish an environment that is collaborative, open, safe, and inviting for all sides. Mr. Powers may assist both parties during the meeting to draft a goal to be established and implemented into the future regarding Michelle's educational needs. During the meeting, it may be helpful to gain an understanding of what is perceived as helpful of Ms. Ayala-Rivera and build upon the rapport she has built with several parents. Statements related to blaming the school for a lack of respect on the parents' part and the parents not caring on the schools' part should be redirected to open discussions about past frustrations and moving forward, along with dissipating the current belief that kids will continue to drop out and be a problem for society. Overall, it is crucial that steps be taken to establish trust and strengthen the relationships between Michelle's parents, the tribal community, and school, and it may take time.

Mr. Powers may want to inquire with Michelle's parents and the tribal community about the potential benefits the school may provide for Native

American families and their community. What strengths and resources may already be in place for the tribal community? Who may be able to assist Michelle with schoolwork if her parents are unable? Who is the contact person for the tribe whom Mr. Powers or another school personnel may be able to consult? It is important that the school respect the tribal community values, including their Native American history. It may be helpful for Michelle's family and the tribal community to understand the policies affecting the attendance and provide them with a voice, possibly inviting the tribal leaders to meetings. It would be important to highlight both that the family is unique and that school has unique responsibilities.

An important step in ensuring success between Michelle, her family, the tribal community, and school is to continue building and maintaining trust and rapport with all parties. Mr. Powers should meet with Michelle individually and discuss her educational and postsecondary options and life goals, friendships at school and home, learning needs, and cultural influences. It may be helpful for Mr. Powers to reach out to Michelle's family and ask about cultural influences (e.g., would they prefer that a leader attend the meeting with the family at school?). The school would benefit from a holistic understanding of the culture of the tribal community and potential dates for tribal ceremonies. The school may want to review their attendance policy in relation to the increased understanding of the tribal culture. May the school be able to receive funding to assist Native American students with supplemental learning? What programs may be available for students missing class (e.g., after-school program, supplemental or online learning)? What resources may be available that encompass a culturally and linguistically appropriate education? May the school be able to provide transportation for students who attend after-school programs to make up attendance? Overall, it is important for the school to continue building rapport and narrowing the gap between Native American children, their families, and the school district. Additionally, it is important for Michelle's family to understand the importance and challenges of the school to uphold their attendance policy and how educational achievements may help Michelle with her long-term goals.

It would be important for the school to gain a greater understanding of the potential strengths and resources that the family and tribal community may already have in place. The school may collaboratively work with the tribal community to utilize and build upon their resources. If the family or community has access to a computer and internet, supplemental work missed for excused events could be completed at the convenience of the student. Incorporating a tutoring program with school-assisted transportation may assist Michelle in making up missed days. Mr. Powers should access what is happening within the educational environment and curriculum, along with the tribal events, around the time when Michelle and other students' attendance dropped. Is this a trend? Is there something happening culturally that it would be helpful for the school to be aware? What are the family's expectations of education? Mr. Powers may assess the current state of Native American culture and education in the curriculum. Faculty development meetings, increasing cultural competencies, and including Native American culture and history in the curriculum may be steps that the school takes to reach out to all students. Last, Mr. Powers may be able to provide guidance lessons to supplement increasing cultural competencies within the school climate.

There has been little emphasis on many of the issues that have affected Michelle and others to attend school. Little is being considered about the bus routes (e.g., Is it a long ride? How early is the pickup?), available funding for Native American children for appropriate education, the strengths and resources available to the students and families, respect of culture, intelligence, and willingness of Michelle to receive education. The closest Indian Health Hospital is 2 hours away and nearly impossible for families to reach to receive medical excuses. Additionally, the legal system and tribal police do not appear to work collaboratively with families on the students' truancy issues. As collaborative trust and respect is built for all parties, it is hoped that the attendance issues will decrease for students at the school.

Response 2
Chelsey Windl

Although Mr. Powers mentioned having grown up in the area, he remains a part of a different culture that has undoubtedly influenced his beliefs and values. Before meeting with Ms. Ayala-Rivera, Michelle, and her mother, it is imperative that he evaluate his personal beliefs and values, as well as any biases he holds regarding the Native American population, because it may impede his ability to remain neutral and address the problem at hand. He must go into the meeting with an open mind and a willingness to learn about their culture, as should all of the attendees. It may be beneficial to speak with both sides individually to discuss this before the meeting. It is imperative that they all work together to find a solution, not to place blame one another. If this comes about, it must be addressed by the school counselor.

When scheduling the meeting, Mr. Powers must be flexible and find a time that is convenient for Michelle's mother. It may be helpful to allow her to invite another individual from their tribe. This may make her feel more comfortable and less outnumbered, and it may provide an additional perspective from the Native American culture. When Michelle's mother arrives, it may be beneficial for Mr. Powers to acknowledge her presence, as it shows that she values her daughter's education and future. He may also want to highlight some of Michelle's strengths. Her teacher, Ms. Ayala-Rivera, may speak on this as well. It is important that school personnel involved express that they are concerned with her attendance and dropping grades because they believe in her and want her to be successful; they really do have her best interest at heart. Mr. Powers may want to inquire about the mother's hopes and fears for her daughter as well. This may elicit a deeper conversation about their culture and allow for a better understanding among school personnel.

Mr. Powers will address Michelle's attendance record, the school's attendance policy, and the importance of attending classes regularly. She is missing out on valuable learning time, and it is affecting her performance. It is important that the family understands the policy and the reasoning behind it. The group can then discuss any barriers to Michelle's attendance and brainstorm ideas on how to manage them. By the end of their time together, the group must create a goal to address Michelle's truancy issue and identify steps to reaching this goal. The school and Michelle's family must ensure that they will continue to communicate and work together to make this happen. The school counselor may also want to mention that they see similar trends with other Native American youth at their school and would like to help them as well. Michelle's family may be able to provide some insight on how to work effectively with their tribe to address this.

At this time, the school and the tribal community obviously do not have a very good relationship, and change is needed. For this to happen, both parties must be willing to collaborate. The school reaching out to tribal leaders and creating an advisory committee comprising Native American youth, parents, and other members of the tribe would be a great start.

It is imperative that Mr. Powers and other school personnel recognize the influence of culture on their Native American students. Tribal events are incredibly meaningful for them, and they should be able to attend them; however, it is causing them to miss school and is negatively affecting their academic performance. What can the school do to work around this? The school should communicate with the tribe to determine when these events occur. Perhaps they can adjust the attendance policy or the students' schedule to accommodate for them.

For Native American youth like Michelle, it is essential that they know they are supported and understood at school. Therefore, it is necessary for Mr. Powers to meet with her one-on-one to discuss the challenges she is facing. It is likely incredibly difficult for her to meet the demands of both the school and her tribe. Together, they can work on how to balance this. They may talk about cultural influences as well as her career aspirations and plans for her future, friendships and relationships with her classmates, and so forth. It could be that Michelle does not want to attend school; maybe she is being picked on by other students, but Mr. Powers would never know this unless he takes the time to meet with and build a relationship with her. This should be done with all students, but it is even more important for minority youth.

It would be helpful to know what resources are already available to Native American youth, both at school and on the reservation. School personnel and tribal members can work together to ensure that these resources are being utilized in a way that is effective for these students. For instance, it would be good to know whether youth have access to computers and the internet while on the reservation. If so, could the school find a way for students to participate virtually through Skype or another means if they are unable to make it to school? Does the school provide tutoring? If so, are Native American youth using this resource? A tutoring program could help them improve their grades; catch up on missing work; and, if allowed by the school, serve as make-up time for their absences. If there is a tutoring program and Native American students aren't partaking of it, it will be important to identify possible barriers to their attendance. Perhaps this program is only offered after school, and the bus system does not allow for them to participate in such activities. In this case, the school could work on getting these students transportation, offer tutoring during the school day, or even bring tutors to the reservation. As mentioned previously, the school may be able to alter their attendance policies to work around tribal events. Perhaps, they could even allow for these students to have a study hall or begin their school day slightly later to allow for travel time, especially if the reservation is far away.

It is extremely important for these students to feel accepted and invested in their school. It is important for diversity to be celebrated. One way to do that is to bring their culture into the school environment. This can be done by adding Native American history to the curriculum, developing a club surrounding multiculturalism, and having school-wide assemblies or celebrations for major tribal events, just to name a few ideas. Not only will this help to make the Native American students feel more connected to the school, but this could also be an amazing learning opportunity for the other students. It may cause them to be more understanding of the Native American student population and create a more positive school climate.

The scenario describes several unavailable or inconvenient resources for the Native American population. It mentions that, to receive health services, they must travel for 2 hours. This issue is twofold; this could be the reason why the students are unable to get a doctor's note for an absence, and the lack of medical care may increase the likelihood that they become ill. They may not receive necessary treatment and medication. What are the living conditions like on the reservation? Do they have adequate housing, healthy food to eat, and so forth? If students' needs aren't being met, this could affect their overall health and ability to perform in school. Could the school take a more holistic, wraparound approach to address the needs of Native American youth like Michelle?

Another thing to consider is the involvement of the tribal police. It would be extremely helpful for the school and the tribal authorities to work together on this issue. Of course, this will require the two groups to build a solid relationship with a sense of respect and trust first, which will take some time. Transportation to and from school may also play a huge role in the truancy issue. It is important to take into account the time when they are being picked up, the length of the ride, and so forth.

Finally, a resource that seems to be overlooked is the staff of teachers like Ms. Ayala-Rivera, who already have positive relationships with the

Native American students. The school should use this to their advantage. Mr. Powers could ask her what she does for these students and ask the students what sets her apart from other teachers. The school can then use this information to train other teachers to be more culturally sensitive, which may improve the school climate and make coming to school more enjoyable for Native American students.

Response 3
Nick Abel, Tom Keller, and Brandie Oliver

Starting with Michelle, it is imperative for the school counselor to understand that each student, and family, is unique. In each situation, the counselor should invite the student and family to share their particular challenges while also emphasizing the strengths and assets of their family members, structure, and cultural worldview. This approach creates an environment that promotes sharing and collaboration among all parties. Time must be devoted to developing rapport before moving to the often challenging "work" portion of a meeting. Perhaps, Michelle and her family could be asked about their hopes for Michelle's life. Where do they envision her in 5 or 10 years? Is high school and/or college graduation a part of that dream? If so, those are dreams for the school staff to build upon, and the importance of middle school education can be emphasized in that equation. In short, Michelle's family must be made to feel like a valued member of the discussion. They should be invited to share as often as possible, offer solutions during the brainstorming portion of the meeting, and be considered partners in confronting this challenge rather than adversaries who have broken the law and need to be threatened. Relevant laws and school policies must be explained, but the counselor should do so only after rapport has been established and the family has had ample opportunity to share and ask questions.

The counselor's first step should likely be to connect with elders and respected leaders within the tribal community. As mentioned earlier, an issue like this will require the cooperation of concerned and culturally sensitive individuals from both the tribe and the school who have taken the time to build rapport and trust and to discuss the challenges in an open and honest manner. The school should take an emic approach by inviting the Native American population to share about their culture, including challenges faced by their population (particularly school-age youth), the strengths and assets of their community, possible solutions they envision to this particular problem, opinions of the school, hopes for the future, and so forth. The school needs to speak honestly about its concerns (particularly as they relate to attendance and dropout rate), explain the law and school policy, and offer resources and ideas to tackle the issues. Both parties might reach out to other schools and Native American populations in neighboring communities or states to discuss these issues, share solutions and resources, and/or form larger working groups to tackle systemic challenges. The counselor might also do a web search or post to a counselor email list or idea exchange (such as ASCA SCENE) for ideas, resources, research, and so forth.

In working collaboratively with the tribe to tackle these issues, the school should inquire as to the availability of tribal resources such as those listed earlier. If the tribe does not have additional help or programming available for school-age children, perhaps the school could work with the tribe to establish a presence on the reservation via tutoring or after-school programs such as sports or clubs. As the school counselor continues to learn Michelle's story, he may discover that she could benefit from truancy programs and supports that are offered at the school. For example, it may be possible that Michelle could benefit from a friendship or social support group that the school counselor offers on a regular basis. In the event that Michelle suffers from anxiety related to her school attendance, the counselor could also provide individual counseling to help build coping strategies for Michelle to help alleviate her anxiety.

In addition to the aforementioned suggestions, the school might consider evaluating the academic curriculum and the knowledge, awareness, and skill sets of the school community as they relate to serving Native American youth and families. According to the 2014 Native Youth Report (Executive Office of the President), one of the root causes for low Native American academic achievement is the lack of culturally relevant curriculum and culturally competent staff who understand how to reach this population. To rectify this, it is recommended that schools work to incorporate Native American history and languages in the curriculum. To cultivate a more collaborative approach, the school and Native American community could work together to construct new classes/units, select new textbooks (if applicable) and materials, and provide ongoing professional development to all school employees. A good starting point might be to hold a community forum on or near the reservation to gather their opinions on various issues related to education and the local school community.

Supplemental Readings, Online Resources, and Supplemental Activities

Supplemental Readings

American School Counselor Association. (2012). *The ASCA National Model: A framework for school counseling programs* (3rd ed.). Alexandria, VA: Author.

American School Counselor Association. (2016). *ASCA SCENE*. Retrieved from http://scene.schoolcounselor.org/home

Attendance Works. (2014). *Chronic absence and Native American students: Unique challenges*. Retrieved from http://www.attendanceworks.org/chronic-absence-native-american-students-unique-challenges/

The Center for Native American Youth. (2011). *Center for Native American Youth at the Aspen Institute.* Retrieved from http://www.cnay.org/Home.html

Executive Office of the President. (2014, December). *2014 Native youth report.* Retrieved from https://files.eric.ed.gov/fulltext/ED565658.pdf

The President. (2004). Executive order 13336 of April 30, 2004: American Indian and Alaska Native education. *Federal Register, 69*(87). Retrieved from https://www.gpo.gov/fdsys/pkg/FR-2004-05-05/pdf/04-10377.pdf

Quick Find On-line Clearinghouse. (n.d.). *Topic: Native American students.* Retrieved from http://smhp.psych.ucla.edu/qf/nativeamericans.htm

Reid, A. (2014). Native American identity formation in relation to educational experiences. *Social Sciences Capstone Projects, 28.* Retrieved from http://commons.pacificu.edu/cassoc/28.

Online Resources

National Indian Education Association
http://www.niea.org/

Regional Education Laboratory (REL): Native American Education Research Alliance, REL Central
https://ies.ed.gov/ncee/edLabs/regions/central/NAERalliance.asp

U.S. Department of the Interior: Bureau of Indian Affairs
http://www.indianaffairs.gov/

U.S. Department of the Interior: Bureau of Indian Education
https://www.bie.gov

Supplemental Activities

Further Questions for Reflection and Discussion

Additional culture-specific questions for class discussion (provided by the scenario author):

- What are the differences in values between the American Indian community and the public school community, and are they really that different?
- Are there tribal ceremonies and designated events that are in conflict with children attending school?
- What has been done in the past to address this issue?
- Have the school community and the tribal communities made attempts to foster a good working relationship on behalf of the children and their education? If so, what happened?
- Is there anything that can be learned to make progress in this endeavor?
- What have other school/tribal communities done to successfully build a partnership that allows for this support?
- What is the historical context with regard to the school/tribe and larger surrounding community for this particular tribe?

- Why are the current policies for attendance not being followed or addressed with American Indian children?

Learning Activities

- Invite an expert on Native American issues to visit class (or Skype) to discuss current issues. Work with this person on ways students can advocate for that community. Consider making this a class assignment.

- Assign groups of students to role play the meeting with Michelle's family. Possible roles include parents (and other family members), Michelle, principal, school counselors, tribal elders, and so forth.

- Have students construct guidance lessons that include diversity issues, understanding Native American culture, and advocacy and collaboration efforts with all stakeholders.

- School counselor students who are members of the American School Counselor Association have access to the diversity section of resources that include journal articles, lesson plans, publications, sample documents, school counselor magazine articles, and websites. It may be helpful to review and include this information in class, assignments, and experiential learning activities.

Chapter 26

How Can We Be Stronger Together?

Laura L. Gallo

Background

Anita Blue, a second-year school counselor, works in a small suburban area high school with a population of 750 students in grades 9–12. There is one other school counselor in the high school. The student population in the high school has steadily changed from predominately upper middle class to a growing population of lower socioeconomic status (SES) families. New housing for families meeting the federal low-income guidelines has continued to be developed over the past few years in the Richland school district.

Incident

The changing needs of the student population places stress on teachers, administrators, and school counselors to create new programming to help students. In particular, a growing population of African American and Latino students have enrolled at the high school. Little to no professional development has been provided for faculty and staff related to diversity or understanding different cultures.

Before and throughout this transition, teachers within the school district have worked diligently to incorporate technology into the curriculum. Teachers have provided tutoring modules and online practice quizzes and fully transitioned to online textbooks to increase students' exposure to the wide range of electronic resources. Teacher websites are utilized to keep students informed regarding upcoming tests, homework deadlines, and available study aids. These valuable resources are useful to many high school students, but the growing number of students from low-SES homes creates inconsistent access to the internet and/or to a computer. Teachers are unsure how to address the problem of students not having internet access in the evenings.

In addition, the growing number of students from low-SES homes have transferred into the high school after attending two or more other schools. These multiple transitions between schools have left gaps in students' learning, making schoolwork a struggle. The majority of students who are failing classes are often students from low-SES homes. A common intervention in the past for struggling students has been referrals to after-school help sessions. The larger population of struggling students appears to come from low-SES homes, creating a reliance on school bus transportation. Lack of personal transportation excludes them from the opportunity to stay after school for extra help. In addition, the school counselor believes parents of these students are not participating in parent–teacher conferences, college planning nights, or other night programming because of limited transportation.

When this population of students is asked how they feel about school, they report a lack of support and acceptance. In fact, many report they would rather drop out than come to a school where they feel no one cares about them or helps them. Results of a student survey show a lack of community and cohesion among the student population. Teachers also sense a division between students and feel frustrated with no supports in place for the struggling students. The teachers wonder what else can be done to help these students.

Discussion

The high school principal looks to the school counselor for support in coming up with interventions to help meet the needs of this growing change in the district student body population. The counselor is aware of the many assets the school has and begins to think of ways to utilize these within the school setting. For example, there is a growing population of upperclassmen who transferred into the school over the past 2–3 years. These senior class members come from low-SES or struggling homes. They have demonstrated success in school and have made plans for college. There are also many students in the school who seek volunteer opportunities. The school counselor begins to talk with teachers about which students are performing well in their classes. She also identifies community resources that may be useful in helping meet the needs of students. Last, Anita begins working with the other school counselor in formulating plans for interventions.

Questions

1. What are the different issues this school counselor is facing?
2. How does SES affect the issues facing this school and these students?
3. What is the school counselor's role in creating change within this school system?

4. How could the school counselor serve as a consultant for teachers?
5. What types of interventions or programs could be utilized at this school?
6. How can the assets that the school already has be incorporated into the system?

Response 1
Carrie A. Wachter Morris

The school community is experiencing demographic changes to the student population. For the school to meet the needs of a more diverse student body, it will need to experience a transformation of its own. The school counselor is faced with helping to meet the needs of an increasingly diverse and less affluent student body while also helping students, faculty, and staff learn about and from each other.

With the increased diversity within the school, there is awareness that student needs are no longer being met, but faculty and staff have received little to no professional development related to diversity and understanding different cultures. This may be a good area for the school counselor to tailor professional development and in-service opportunities for the faculty and staff, as well as to build opportunities for consulting with faculty. She could do classroom observations or offer classroom guidance lessons where she modeled specific communication or teaching approaches for teachers or include students in panels or discussions with teachers. By helping faculty see her as an ally in their quest to meet the needs of their students, she could help them learn when to change strategies or help them understand student behaviors within their larger contexts.

Structurally, prior ways of approaching schoolwork and assumptions about the resources of families also need to shift. For example, the focus on expanding and integrating technology has challenges around accessibility for students from lower income backgrounds, and frequent moves for some students have left academic gaps that need to be addressed. With limited transportation options, access to technology outside of school and the current after-school extra-help model is not feasible. Transportation issues also reduce family involvement in student support meetings and postsecondary information sessions. These factors, in combination with a lack of understanding about how to better meet the needs of all students, have contributed to dissatisfaction in students who do not see the school as a place of support and understanding as well as learning. Although new programs could be developed to meet transportation, academic, and other needs, there is a potential resource strain on the school if there is limited funding in the school budget for additional programming and families cannot absorb additional programming costs.

The school counselor's role in creating change starts with continued assessment of the needs of the school community (students, faculty, staff, and families). Those needs may be differential, and multiple interventions will be necessary to help support cultural understanding, create academic learning, and cultivate a supportive school environment. As needs are identified, the school counselor needs to prioritize those needs and work with teachers as a consultant to identify strategic ways to meet them, either with the resources available or through procuring additional resources. The school counselor would not be expected to implement every intervention on her own; she can also connect individuals and groups with other resources or networks that might provide support. Some examples of ways she might take action include the following:

- Procuring grant funding to support new programming or resources
- Approaching community stakeholders to support new programming at the school
- Disseminating information about no- or low-cost access to technology
- Compiling information about food, housing, and clothing resources
- Providing small- or large-group counseling to help students learn about each other
- Working with teachers to create supportive learning environments for all students
- Training students to be peer mentors or peer tutors
- Matching students with volunteer opportunities to support the school community

Given that students have specifically identified a feeling that the school does not care about them, interventions that link students with each other and with faculty and staff might be particularly appropriate. Teachers could build collaborative teaching or tutoring opportunities into classwork. For example, students could pair up and teach each other concepts that had been recently introduced. That way, each student has the opportunity to contribute to learning and take on leadership responsibilities in the class.

The school has a variety of assets that the school counselor could access to build connections within and outside the school building, such as upperclassman peer mentoring relationships with new or struggling students. These older students could help talk to and support their younger peers academically and personally while also talking with their mentees about postsecondary options. Opportunities might exist for communication, collaboration, and peer tutoring without transportation barriers if mentors and mentees lived in the same neighborhoods. Identifying the strengths of the large number of students who would like to volunteer could also help the school counselor and teachers identify students who might be available to tutor students in their homes or their neighborhoods, who might provide social or emotional support, or who might be helpful in building resources or programming for students and families who are struggling.

Response 2

Susannah M. Wood

Anita Blue and her colleague both have significant challenges to work with in their school, as well as several assets and resources that they have identified that can help them with those challenges. When considering how to identify and address the multiple issues facing their school, Anita may choose to revisit some of the models she was exposed to in her master's preparation program such as Dahir and Stone's (2012) steps to advocacy, their PREPARE (philosophy, relationships, equity of power, professional development, accessibility, resources, evaluate) model of consultation, or their CASTT (community, administrators, students, teachers and technology) paradigm of collaboration and resource management. However, given the significant systems in play in Anita's situation, I would suggest utilizing Mason, Ockerman, and Chen-Hayes's (2013) "change agent for equity" (CAFE) model to break down the multiple challenges into manageable pieces. The (CAFE) model is predicated on the idea that the school counselor identifies himself or herself as a leader, advocate, collaborator, and change agent. In having this core identity, a school counselor is "more likely to practice ethical decision-making, multicultural competence and data-driven evaluation" and "maintains an inclusive and systemic view, one that sees both the micro and macro spheres of potential influence" (Mason et al., 2013, p. 8). The model includes four phases: thought, collaboration, action, and evaluation (Mason et al., 2013).

It is in the thought phase that Anita and her colleague could brainstorm what changes need to happen; how ethical, multicultural, and advocacy issues are at play, including opportunity and access; and to what extent they believe in their system's capacity to change. Here, the counseling team can identify the pertinent issues, including the following: (a) career/college preparation of the high school students, especially those from homes with limited financial resources (Johnson, Rochkind, Ott, & DuPont, 2010); (b) equitable access to technology and transportation across all student groups; (c) developing differentiated academic supports to reach targeted student groups within the school day; (d) "widening the net," or collaborative alliances between counselors, administrators, teachers, and other allies to create interventions for student success (Dahir & Stone, 2012); (e) multicultural and social justice professional development for staff; and (f) facilitating partnerships focused on trust, collaboration, and communication between students, families, and the school. Although I have listed what I see as the pertinent issues facing Anita and her counseling team, it would be up to them to prioritize them. They may want to hold off on identifying priorities until they have walked through the collaboration phase, which may bring to light other allies that can help them create the changes they have identified. Given the nature of the challenges, Anita cannot take on all of them alone—to do so would result in burnout and lack of change.

In this phase, Anita and her colleague can consider the following, as suggested by Mason and colleagues: "How and to whom does this change need to be highlighted as critical? How can I take the initiative in promoting change? With whom and with what other efforts can I/we join to promote change?" (2013, p. 13). Anita may want to create a change "team" that could include her administrator; teachers; parents; and other allies such as social workers, school board members, local university representatives, and district personnel who oversee transportation and technology. While the collaboration is essential, the goal here is not to change the stakeholders but, rather, to cultivate the trust and communication needed to engender collaboration and to determine how each party can support each other. In team building, like any other initiative, multiculturally competent school counselors must recognize any area of bias, power dynamics, and blind spots (Dahir & Stone, 2012). Dahir and Stone cite Bucher's (2008) "nine megaskills," which include empathy, perspective taking, and intercultural communication. Given that Anita's community, student members, and school culture are changing, it becomes imperative that the counseling team continue to reflect on how they are communicating with stakeholders and how they are creating a safe and empowering place to team, discuss, plan, and exchange ideas.

The team then can work into the action phase of the CAFE model and determine objectives, identifying effective and efficient ways to promote change, delegate responsibilities, create timelines, and plan for documentation and data collection around the specific planned formed (Mason et al., 2013). Anita can bring in the assets she has already identified into these conversations. The team could consider creating student panels around college/career readiness from high school alumni who identify with the current high school students and include resources from the College Board's "You Can Go!" videos of diverse students who have enrolled in college and found financial aid to support going (http://youcango.collegeboard.org/?navid=bf-ycg).

Anita and her colleague could utilize their role as consultants to work with teachers to identify students who would benefit from specific individual academic supports through tutoring during the school day or small groups that can explore study skills, test taking, and college/career planning. Anita, her fellow counselor, and the teachers may benefit from internal professional development dedicated to advocacy and social change through reading books and reflective activities. Given the disconnect in the relationships between the community and the school, including challenges surrounding transportation, the team could consider going to the housing developments or utilizing local agencies such as the YMCA to host forums on 4-year high school planning, college preparation, and career fairs. The team may also want to pursue partnerships with local community colleges and universities, including schools of education. Working together with faculty members, the school may be able to identify resources in technology through joint grants or technology recycling that can be used to provide computers and laptops to students and families in need. A partnership with university or college faculty could also result in ongoing professional development for school faculty and staff as well as collaboration on data collection.

Data collection, in turn, would serve to scaffold the last stage of the CAFE model, the evaluation phase. Here, Anita and her team will identify how they know that change has occurred or will occur in the future by planning to collect specific data at certain times, such as graduation rates, surveys that assess student knowledge about postsecondary planning, and focus groups from the community. The team should consider how they will disseminate their findings and the future steps the school will be taking through technology and live presentations within the community and/or with the local university.

Advocate, collaborator, leader, resource coordinator, and consultant are all roles that school counselors play. If they wed these to an internal identity as an agent of change, then Anita and her colleague can make substantial progress in addressing the challenges her school faces. By utilizing the CAFE model, Anita can think through the challenges and the assets she has, create a team, identify areas of change, address cultural and systems interactions, plan actions to create change, and evaluate through the use of data the progress made and the impact the changes have had on the school, the students, and the community.

Supplemental Readings and Online Resources

Supplemental Readings

American School Counselor Association. (2015). *The school counselor and peer support programs* [Position statement]. Alexandria, VA: Author. Retrieved from https://www.schoolcounselor.org/asca/media/asca/PositionStatements/PS_PeerHelping.pdf

Cole, R. F., & Grothaus, T. (2014). A phenomenological study of urban school counselors' perceptions of low-income families. *Journal of School Counseling, 12*(5). Retrieved from https://files.eric.ed.gov/fulltext/EJ1034768.pdf

The College Board. (n.d.). *The educational experience of young men of color: Capturing the student voice.* Retrieved from https://secure-media.collegeboard.org/digitalServices/pdf/advocacy/nosca/nosca-young-men-color-student-voice.pdf

Dahir, C. A., & Stone, C.B. (2012). *The transformed school counselor* (2nd ed). Belmont, CA: Wadsworth.

Dockery, D. J., & McKelvey, S. (2013). Underrepresented college students' experiences with school counselors. *Journal of School Counseling, 11*(3). Retrieved from https://files.eric.ed.gov/fulltext/EJ1012298.pdf

Hatch, T. (2014). Advocating for systems change. Advocacy thoughts from Reese House. In *The use of data in school counseling: Hatching results for students, programs, and the profession* (pp. 188–190). Thousand Oaks, CA: Sage.

Johnson, J., Rochkind, J., Ott, A. N., & DuPont, S. (2010). *Can I get a little advice here? How an overstretched high school guidance system is undermining school students' college aspirations.* Retrieved from http://www.publicagenda.org/files/can-i-get-a-little-advice-here.pdf

Martinez, M. A. (2013). Helping Latina/o students navigate the college choice process: Considerations for secondary school counselors. *Journal of School Counseling, 11*(1). Retrieved from https://files.eric.ed.gov/fulltext/EJ1012292.pdf

Schulz, L. L., Hurt, K., & Lindo, N. (2014). My name is not Michael: Strategies for promoting cultural responsiveness in schools. *Journal of School Counseling, 12*(2). Retrieved from https://files.eric.ed.gov/fulltext/EJ1034778.pdf

Online Resources

The College Board's "You Can Go!"
http://youcango.collegeboard.org/?navid=bf-ycg

Communities in Schools
www.communitiesinschools.org

Family Promise
www.familypromise.org

Kids in Need Foundation
www.kinf.org

National Center for Children in Poverty
http://www.nccp.org

National Low Income Housing Coalition
www.nlihc.org

Chapter 27

Am I Biased Too? Bias-Based Bullying

Cassandra A. Storlie

Background

Miguel is an 8-year-old Latino student who is new to an alternative elementary school in the Midwest. He is of medium build for his developmental age and has a very dark-skinned complexion. Miguel has been transferred to an alternative school setting because of the multiple acts of violence toward a peer at his previous public school. Miguel maintains that his fights with peers were all a result of being teased about his dark-skinned complexion and Spanish accent. Miguel comes from a background of low socioeconomic status (SES), and he and his family live in a two-bedroom apartment. He has been diagnosed with attention-deficit/hyperactivity disorder (ADHD) and is compliant with his medication regimen for it. English is not Miguel's first language, and he has difficulty in reading and writing English at the second-grade level. As such, Miguel has been placed in special education classes at the school, despite his strong scores in mathematics.

Incident

It was reported by a reliable source to the current school counselor that Miguel was being groomed to join a local Mexican gang. Latino students, as young as 10 years old, have commonly engaged in gang activity in this community. Community outreach workers have confirmed that Miguel's cousins are leaders in the gang, and multiple thefts and episodes of vandalism have occurred in the surrounding area.

Discussion

Miguel's parents are both undocumented immigrants from Mexico City and came to this country for a better life for their children and to make money to send back to their family members in Mexico. They both work low-paying jobs with long hours that prevent them from being more involved in Miguel's life and the lives of his four siblings. The parents depend on the eldest daughter to care for the younger children at night and after school. Miguel has begun to sneak out after his oldest sister goes to bed, primarily to hang out with his older cousins.

The school counselor met with Miguel after being introduced to him by the principal after the third violent altercation in the alternative school setting. Miguel stated that another "White" student was making fun of his dark-colored skin and he "couldn't take it anymore." Miguel's teachers informed the school counselor that he feels most comfortable talking with adults when he can play video games on a handheld device. The school counselor chose to meet with Miguel and used this technique to help with developing rapport. Miguel was mildly receptive and, with some prompting, began to open up about the fights he had been in at school.

After talking for a few minutes, Miguel questioned why the school counselor wanted to talk to him and felt he was still in trouble from the most recent fight. The school counselor explained the role of the school counselor and the goal of decreasing violence and bullying in the school. Miguel disclosed that he didn't like playing in his neighborhood or going to school because he would be made fun of because of his dark skin. He went on to say that "Kids don't make fun of me when I hang out with my cousins." In exploring more, Miguel reported that rival gang members recently "jumped" his cousins. He further reported that his sister has been making him stay in the house as soon as he returns home from school, and he has been sneaking out more. After some pause, Miguel admitted his cousins were gang members but felt safe with them because no "White people" made fun of his dark skin or accent.

Miguel discussed how he was kicked out of his other school for always getting into fights and then talked briefly about some of the fights he got into with his siblings for calling him "darkie." Shortly after that, Miguel stopped talking and threw the handheld video game down, stating, "I hate it here! I hate this school! Why can't you all just leave me alone?" After a few minutes of attempting to redirect Miguel's anger, the school counselor had to call for assistance because Miguel became violent.

Questions

1. As a leader in this elementary school, what actions can the school counselor make to address the bias-based bullying at this school?
2. What leadership efforts can the school counselor take to educate teachers and school personnel about bias-based bullying?
3. How can the school counselor engage Miguel's family about his violent behavior?

4. In what ways can the school counselor collaborate with community members to address Miguel's needs, and the needs of other Latino students, outside of the school setting?
5. What leadership efforts does the school counselor need to make to address vulnerability to gangs in Miguel's community?

Response 1
Jodi L. Saunders

An understanding of the culture and values of Miguel's family and the local Latino community will not only enhance the probability of success when engaging both Miguel and his family but can also serve to decrease the frustration that school personnel may be experiencing when dealing with Miguel. Although not always, fighting and physical violence can be part of the coping culture of lower SES families and communities (Payne, 2013). In addition, belonging to a gang is a type of support system. In listening to Miguel, he clearly describes the importance of a strong support system to protect him from the bias-based bullying he is experiencing and why he is so vulnerable to the possibility of becoming a member of a gang. In addition, having a solid understanding of the adverse effects of bullying on the recipient is also important. Bullying has been linked to anger and misconduct (Bosworth, Espelage, & Simon, 1999), information that may not only be helpful to school personnel but may also be welcome information to Miguel's parents, who may not understand the possible reasons for his behavior. An opportunity to share information with the family and work together with them, rather than appear to place blame, is more likely to result in a successful collaboration.

In addressing the bias-based bullying on a school and community level, programs that focus on bystanders have been shown to be successful. Since it is estimated that over 80% of bullying occurs in front of witnesses and bystanders, implementing programs that focus on bystander intervention programs in addition to bullying prevention programs is an important consideration. Designing programs, projects, or activities that can serve as healthy support systems to Miguel, the Latino community, and any other individual or group is another important consideration.

On an individual level, Miguel seemed to respond to the school counselor positively as evidenced by his sharing of a lot of difficult information. His outburst at the end of the session was likely because he realized how much he had shared and felt vulnerable, so he needed to pull back and push the counselor away to protect himself. Continuing counseling with the school counselor would be valuable for Miguel.

Response 2
Rhonda M. Bryant and Beth A. Durodoye

Using ASCA National Standard 8.1, effective leadership as a framework, the school counselor leader must not only demonstrate knowledge of leadership strategies that inculcate system change but must also implement a comprehensive developmental school counseling program that reaches all stakeholders, including students, families, and school staff (ASCA, 2005). The case of Miguel offers the school counselor nuanced but exciting opportunities to demonstrate leadership that shapes Miguel's life in a positive manner and reframes his situation in ways that benefit the school and local community.

One of the first actions the school counselor can take to address bias-based bullying in this school involves courageous exploration about how ethos of the school, district, and community may affect how school staff members implement policy and practice, particularly as related to managing minority students' behaviors. Review of school, student, and community data on the alternative school's success in returning children to their home schools; the school's utilization of culturally focused strengths based support; and learning outcomes for students (as related to community educational attainment and earning power) would help frame the counselor's exploration of school ethos. Similarly, evaluating the alignment of the school counseling program as with American School Counselor Association (ASCA) National Standards would also clarify how the school meets the needs of the students, particularly those who have experienced bias-based bullying. For example, does the district support mediation and conflict coaching as useful foundations of managing students' problematic behaviors? Alternatively, does the school adopt a relentless emphasis on structure, zero tolerance, and exclusionary disciplinary practices that preclude students' access to school counseling resources that teach them self-regulation and better executive functioning skills? We are inundated with data reflecting the consequences of ineffective school policies that fuel the school-to-prison pipeline, increase the dropout rate, and lead to teacher burnout.

Understanding the ethos of the school sets the stage for the school counselor to develop strategies to educate teachers and school personnel about bias-based bullying. Several variables can affect how the school counselor develops and presents these strategies. For example, within-group racial and ethnic differences can influence how staff perceive and respond to the school counselor; between-group differences may also influence how staff receive her input.

Indeed, Miguel's situation reflects a stark reality of many students: he is not yet a teenager, but the district has already identified him as a threat, needing placement in an "alternative" school with other students deemed unsuitable for the "regular" school environment. His behavior is not acceptable, but acknowledging the color hierarchy that exists in U.S. and Mexican societies and the inherent unfairness of Miguel's bullying may defuse (to some degree) his frustration with the label "troublemaker" when he is on the receiving end of bullying. Meeting with Miguel's family and community may help the family learn to trust the school counselor. There may be significant religious leaders involved with the family who could help with Miguel.

[11]
Historical hostilities (Vontress, 1979) may also mitigate the community's trust of the counselor and the school staff. However, Bronfenbrenner's (1977) theory of social ecological systems offers one way to conceptualize the school counselor's efforts to reduce bias-based bullying. Because the school is a social system that reflects the macrocosm of society and the microcosm of the neighborhood, the school counselor can initiate teams of community-based leaders, parents, and students that identify cultural strengths that address students' bias-based bullying. Certainly, finding solutions in the community that present cultural values assists in scaffolding services for not only Miguel but also his family, who likely feel overwhelmed by his behavior too.

Building a comprehensive counseling program that is "preventive in design and developmental in nature" (ASCA, 2012b, p. 1) has not always been synonymous with a school–community partnership. Miguel's school counselor, aware of the challenges with gangs in the community, can also collaborate with local agencies that provide outreach to families with undocumented members to ameliorate the challenges with being undocumented and living in a high-need community. It is important that these local agencies include Spanish-speaking staff who speak the dialect associated with that used in the family's community of origin. Other collaborations can include partnerships with local organizations that support safe after-school alternatives for students and mentoring programs.

Miguel's school counselor does face daunting challenges in addressing bias-based bullying in the school and guiding school staff toward a cultural-strengths orientation for implementing school policy rather than one based on a cultural-deficit model. Her leadership efforts are to collaborate with families (not limited to blood relatives but reflective of an extended kin network), community leaders (that reflect the expertise and input of families and students), and a school counseling program that trains students in conflict resolution and peer mediation. Establishing safe zones in the school that allow students to regroup and access a trusted adult can also create a safe school environment. As the school plans learning goals and outcomes based on district, school, and student data, Miguel's school counselor can similarly use data and program outcomes to refine the school counseling program to meet the needs of students and the community.

Supplemental Readings and Online Resources

Supplemental Readings

Bosworth, K., Espelage, D., & Simon, T. (1999). Factors associated with bullying behavior in middle school students. *The Journal of Early Adolescence, 19*, 341–352.

Payne, R. K. (2013). *A framework for understanding poverty: A cognitive approach.* Highland, TX: aha! Process.

Polanin, J. R., Espelage, D. L., & Pigott, T. D. (2012). A meta-analysis of school-based bullying prevention programs' effects on bystander intervention behaviors. *School Psychology Review, 41*(1), 47–65.

Online Resources

Southern Poverty Law Center
  https://www.splcenter.org

Chapter 28

When Systems Fail, What Is Next?

Robin Alcala Saner

Background

Samantha is a 15-year-old student who was hospitalized 2 weeks before the incident because of suicidal ideation. She is from an affluent, two-parent family and was recently diagnosed with depression. Sam (as she prefers to be called) is an above-average student, perhaps showing some perfectionistic tendencies. Her mother informed the school counselor of the hospitalization right away, but there has been little communication since. Although the school counselor, Mr. Gallo, requested it, the parent did not sign a release of information with the hospital staff or therapist.

Twelve days after Samantha's hospitalization (Tuesday), a classmate committed suicide. The day after the suicide, Sam's father contacted the school counselor and said that the hospital staff felt that Samantha was ready for a 3-hour school visit. The school counselor, after collaborating with her colleagues, shared the situation with the parent and requested that Samantha's return be postponed until the current school crisis had subsided. As it is not unusual for hospitals or treatment centers in this region to send students back to school without communication with the school, the counselor requested that the parent share with Samantha's team that there had been a suicide of a classmate and asked the treatment team to process the death with Sam.

Incident

On Friday, Samantha came to school as the day began and went directly to classes. As the school was in crisis response mode, the counselor was

247

unaware of this until she saw Samantha in the hallway. She immediately pulled Samantha into the school counseling office. Samantha shared that she was getting out of the hospital the following day and "just wants to return to school." Samantha appeared calm, but had little affect and seemed detached, which was atypical for her.

Mr. Gallo, the school counselor, contacted Sam's mother and asked her to pick Sam up from school. Concerns were again shared regarding the hospital release and returning to school during the response to the traumatic event. The mother insisted that she wanted Samantha back in school. The mother also stated that the hospital staff were aware of the situation and supported the decision. Samantha was being released from the hospital and was going home with plans to return to school on Monday.

On Sunday, Samantha made a near-fatal suicide attempt and was rushed to the hospital. She remained in the emergency room until a room was available for her in the adolescent psychiatric unit, where she spent 3 additional weeks. Discussion of this attempt and the rehospitalization was rampant through online social media, with many errors and fabrications by high school students. Samantha spent 5 days in treatment and is scheduled to return to the high school 7 days after the most recent suicide attempt.

Questions

1. What steps can the school counselor take to transition Samantha back into school more effectively after her second hospitalization? Who are the key players who need to collaborate to create a safe and successful transition for students from hospitalization and treatment?
2. What were the failures/flaws in the system initially, and how can they be avoided/remedied in the future?
3. What actions can the school counselors in this school district take to improve the system?
4. How can school counselors facilitate improvement in the transition process between home/school/hospital/community?

Response 1

Meredith A. Rausch

There are several steps for Mr. Gallo's response phase regarding Samantha's healthy transition into the school environment. From an ecological perspective, working with Samantha as an individual should be the primary priority, with additional supports provided within her home, school, and outside systems. The first key player and, perhaps, team lead for ensuring the successful transition for students who required hospitalization is the school counselor. The first step for Samantha's transition involves maintaining consistent and open dialogue between Sam and Mr. Gallo. Setting up a time for a daily check-in can assist Mr. Gallo with developing a continual rapport with Sam. This also allows an opportunity to observe any noticeable changes in appearance, affect, or behavior, as well as the chance to respond to any harassment issues that may have taken place among the student body. If Sam currently has a teacher she feels comfortable communicating with, this teacher may be asked to provide mentorship and an additional viewpoint regarding any changes in Sam's demeanor or progress.

Second, Mr. Gallo can work within the school to foster an environment where inappropriate use of online social media is not tolerated. Although this can pose a struggle, particularly with guidelines regarding the inability to monitor the majority of student online activity, Mr. Gallo can utilize classroom guidance to discuss digital citizenship. As another approach to providing system-wide support, a back-to-school night can incorporate messages regarding parental guidelines for monitoring online activity.

The school counselor can work to collaborate across other systems as well. For example, although Mr. Gallo struggled to maintain consistent and thorough communication with Samantha's parents, a working and continuous relationship with parents or guardians of previously hospitalized students should be a priority for the school counselor. When difficulties with communication arise, the administration may be involved to assist in stressing the importance of creating a bridge of open communication with the school environment. This includes making sure that parents understand the importance of having signed consents in place for release of information from hospitals and mental health professionals. Continuity of care across multiple systems will provide opportunities for Samantha's continued success and progress. For schools with crisis teams already in place, these teams should create and follow protocol for student hospitalization for suicidal ideation and attempts—in this example, Samantha and other students could be affected by suicidal contagion due to the other student's completed suicide.

Although, in this example, it was not communicated by the parents, a school counselor should be the first informed once a previously hospitalized student returns to school. One of the most critical times for a previously suicidal patient involves the days and weeks directly following a hospitalization, as many will struggle, and some will make an additional attempt during that time period. In addition, recognizing that suicide is the third leading cause of death for high-school-age individuals is an important factor in helping keep all students safe (Kerr, 2009).The counselor should not be apprehensive broaching the subject of suicide with a student. Opening communication with a student regarding the suicidal ideation or attempt can provide relief to the student based on the idea that the problem can be discussed (Hays, 2017). Revisiting a suicide assessment with a student on a regular basis can provide signals when distress is forthcoming. Asking if the student has a plan and whether it is lethal, available, and specific (Hays, 2017) is necessary for thorough assessment purposes.

Mr. Gallo may want to provide teachers and parents with the common risk factors of suicide, including feelings of helplessness or hopelessness, substance use or abuse, increased stress, a history of suicide, and a sudden improvement in affect (Hays, 2017). In this incident, risk factors include Samantha's perfectionistic tendencies, diagnosis of depression, exposure to suicidality of others, and age. It is important for the school counselor to obtain a parental release as quickly as possible and then hold an emergency faculty meeting. Including teachers who regularly see the student before the start of the school day will better inform staff and provide a greater opportunity for Sam to succeed in her recovery. Mr. Gallo worked to contact Samantha's parents and the hospital but struggled with these communication lines. Controlling communication where possible within the school environment, with other parents, and through the use of a support team comprising individuals with whom Sam feels comfortable talking to, may be able to provide enough to keep Samantha safe even if her parents are uncooperative.

For the school district, working to create crisis management teams within each school building, as well as coordinating the efforts of these teams through quarterly meetings to review protocol and progress, is imperative. Discussing methods of increasing suicide risk assessment and awareness; maintaining a "no tolerance" policy regarding online social media bullying, gossip, and harassment; and coordination of care with outside systems (e.g., hospitals, mental health professionals) are the best ways to provide consistent care for all district students.

Creating a protocol for student transition after recent hospitalization will allow counselors an opportunity to provide thorough student care. School counselors can be the nucleus for this transition. Engaging parents in weekly phone calls or face-to-face meetings, keeping signed copies of releases of information, working with the hospital to ensure continuity of care regarding the student's plan for success, and raising awareness within the community are all important steps for improving this difficult transition. Including these steps in an individual plan for the student and revising the crisis team protocol as necessary during quarterly meetings allows for a more stable and thorough transition process for future students.

Response 2

Danielle S. Bryant

It is evident by the previous events that certain steps must take place to transition Samantha (Sam) successfully back to high school. Establishing the lines of communication with Sam's parents is crucial for success. This connection gives the school counselor an opportunity to determine how the school can be supportive and helpful; this affords the opportunity to gather as much information regarding Sam's progress as possible. The counselor then needs to facilitate a debriefing session with all staff members (e.g., administrator, teachers) who can assist Sam with the transition. It is best to be proactive rather than reactive. To be proactive, it is critical to establish a program to work with the family on transitioning Sam back to school. One important thing to add to this plan is a signed release form authorizing communication with Sam's health care team. Depending on the expected length of time Sam is away from school, arranging to have schoolwork completed while at home can ease the anxiety that falling behind in school may cause. In addition, planned periodic contact with Sam via phone call or a short visit shows that she is important enough for someone other than family to communicate with her. Young people often feel that their parents do what they do because they "have to." How wonderful, then, it would be to receive a card or phone call from the counselor, a person who does not "have to." Think back to a memorable life event. Remember when you received a card, phone call, or gift acknowledging the event from someone other than your parent, spouse, son, or daughter and that feeling of "how nice, that this person actually remembered." The feeling is different when it comes from someone unexpected. It adds an extra layer of "Yes, people care and are thinking about me." When the time comes, hold a back-to-school transition meeting. This meeting should take place early in the week, so that there is enough time afforded for acclimation to school. There is nothing worse than starting something new and allowing enough time to pass so that bad feelings and anxiety about whatever went wrong fester in the mind and that the desire to try it again is given up. In addition to parents, teachers, hospital staff, and the school counselor, all of whom are key players, the most important attendee to this meeting is Sam. Sam should be directly involved in this meeting, because it is about her and because having a part in the decisions will help her to have a sense of control.

On learning that Sam had been hospitalized for suicidal ideation, failure to mobilize the school crisis response team (SCRT) proved to be detrimental to the student, the school, and the community. Mobilization of the SCRT is fundamental in implementing next-step procedures for the situation in accordance with suicide prevention policies and administration protocols. Although both systems want what is best for the student, when two systems work independently of each other, communication and cocollaboration can be difficult. The accuracy of pertinent information and concerns of either system has a greater chance of being lost in translation when there is a third party relaying the messages (see Figure 28.1). The goal of the SCRT is to ensure the safety and support of all students. They set in motion the communication, collaboration, coordination, and cooperation protocols designed to foster resiliency and an atmosphere that encourages emotional, academic, and social success. The initial flaws in the system amount to the breakdown of four essential components: communication, collaboration, coordination, and cooperation. Failure to communicate is how it all began.

Communication is the mutual exchange of thoughts, concerns, and ideas between systems (see Figure 28.2). For information gathering,

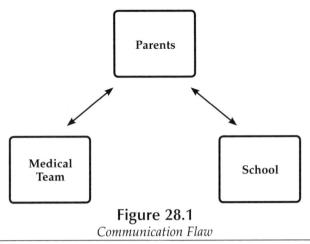

Figure 28.1
Communication Flaw

Note. Arrows denote flow of communication.

knowledge, and understanding to support the next steps toward achieving a goal, communication is vital. That leads to collaboration. Both systems coming together to brainstorm ideas, and to produce and implement strategies through collective system efforts, is necessary and aids in supporting Sam. That then leads to coordination. Organizing the resources, strategies, and the information gathered so that each system can accomplish its portion is the mutual objective in support of the common goal. Finally, there is cooperation. All systems play a part and work together to support each other's individual goal to achieve the ultimate common goal, which, in this case, is to help Sam (see Figure 28.3). Without these components, system failure on one or more levels is imminent.

Although most children grow up without any mental health problems, surveys suggest that fewer children and young people are mentally healthy today than 30 years ago (Mental Health Foundation, 2018). That is possibly due to the changes in society, which affect the experience of growing up. The way we live today is very different from 30 years ago. As with anything in our evolving society, handling and implementing systemic change for the emerging mental health issues among young people in school is a process. The growth of mental health instability among our youth and the disconnect between the mental health system and the school system warrant the need for school counselors to take action to improve the system. One of the actions that school counselors can take to improve the system is to design a back-to-school transition plan that outlines practical re-entry planning procedures. Some of the things that should be included in this plan are school resources, community resources, assessment of need, and communication protocols. The school counselor can also initiate training and professional development, offer suicide intervention and prevention training to all school personnel, and

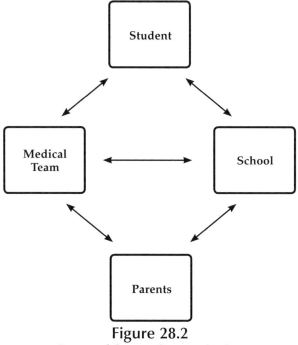

Figure 28.2
Improved System Communication

Note. Arrows denote flow of communication.

then, extend the same training opportunity to the community. Another action that school counselors can take is to compile a comprehensive list of resources and services that is readily assessable for possible collaboration and referral in the event of a crisis.

Facilitating improvement in the transition process is achieved by raising awareness emphasizing the importance of developing and using a transition plan. Utilizing a standardized form for back-to-school transition can accomplish a great deal while keeping all involved in the process on the same page. Counselors can also facilitate improvement by hosting community outreach events in an effort to develop a collaboration between the home, the school, the medical professionals, and other support providers.

Transitioning back to school after mental health treatment can be taxing both socially and emotionally. Imagine that you are a goldfish in a fish bowl in the center of a room full of cats. You may feel like you are the center of attention, as though all eyes are on you, even if they are not. You may even feel like you have nowhere to go, no way to escape, and no support to help ease the anxiety. You conclude that you have two choices. Stay in the bowl, where you know it is safe but the overwhelming, emotional, social, and mental anxiety is always going to be there. On the other hand, you could jump out of the bowl to face

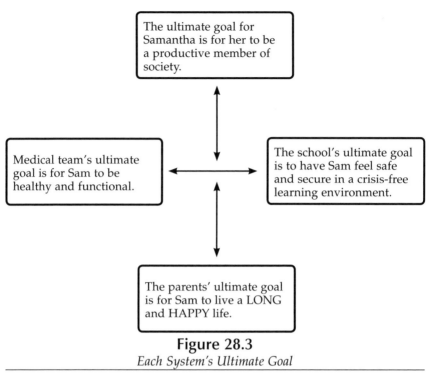

Figure 28.3

Each System's Ultimate Goal

Note. Arrows denote collaborative goal.

the inevitable, because you feel it is hopeless and just want the mental anguish to cease. Now imagine that same scenario, but in the distance, you see hope and think: Does hope see me, can she help me, and will she help me? Deep down, you know she can help, but you do not know how to get her help. You are not sure what to do: You know that you just need to get her attention, but how? Therefore, you resort to doing what is in your power to do: alter your behavior. You act out with suicidal behavior. The behavior could be swimming around the fish bowl as fast as you can. It may be splashing the water as much as possible. Perhaps it is taking unnecessary risks, such as jumping in the air (in a room full of cats) several times, with each leap being higher than the previous one. Regardless of how the behavior manifests itself, it is imperative to understand that suicidal behavior is an attempt to communicate; we just need to pay attention.

School counselors are in a position to assist. They can assist with social and emotional anxiety. They can assist with a crisis, and they can assist with the transition back to school. Sustained healing necessitates addressing the aftermath of the crisis and continuing the process of recovery so that students feel safe and secure (National Education Association Health Information Network, n.d.).

Supplemental Readings, Online Resources, and Supplemental Activities

Supplemental Readings

Hicks, B. B. (1990). *Youth suicide: A comprehensive manual for prevention and intervention.* Bloomington, IN: National Educational Service.

Missouri Professional School Counselors and Counselor Educators. (2015, May). *School-wide crisis management plan guide: A professional school counselor's guide to school-wide crisis management.* Retrieved from http://www.missouricareereducation.org/doc/schcrisis/SchoolwideCrisis.pdf

Shore, K. (2011). *The ABC's of bullying prevention: A comprehensive schoolwide approach.* Port Chester, NY: National Professional Resources.

Online Resources

American Association of Suicidology (AAS)
http://www.suicidology.org

American School Counselor Association (ASCA)
www.schoolcounselor.org

The National Suicide Prevention Lifeline: (800) 273-TALK (8255)
http://www.suicidepreventionlifeline.org

The Prevention Institute
www.preventioninstitute.org/eightstep.html

Signs of Suicide (SOS): (781) 239-0071
www.mentalhealthscreening.org

Supplemental Activity

Learning Activity

Design a faculty in-service education program on suicide prevention and intervention. Your design outline should include the following:

1. The purpose of the in-service presentation
2. The format of the program
    i. *Intended audience:* elementary, middle, or high school staff and/or faculty
    ii. *Delivery method:* presentation supported by PowerPoint, video, and/or handouts
3. Content
4. Topic introduction
5. Topic nuts and bolts
6. Question and answer session

Chapter 29
Please Help Me, but Don't Tell Me How to Raise My Child

Anna Viviani

Background

Tyler Redding, a 10-year-old, Caucasian, male fifth grader has been scheduled for an individualized educational plan (IEP) meeting to address behavioral problems and declining academic progress. Tyler has attended Winnebago Elementary School since starting school at age 5. His behavior and academic standing have been average to above average in previous academic years. Tyler's mother, Mrs. Redding, reported that he struggled with math in second grade, so at Mrs. Redding's request, Tyler has received individual assistance with math for the past 2 years. Additionally, Mrs. Redding said that Tyler was diagnosed with attention-deficit/hyperactivity disorder (ADHD) in second grade and that he is on medication when she remembers to give it to him and when she can afford to purchase the medication. She was unable to provide a prescribing physician or medication name when asked. Both of Tyler's parents are from the local community and went to the same school as Tyler. The Reddings are divorced, and Mr. Redding moved out of state last year because of friction between Mrs. Redding and himself. Mrs. Redding states that Mr. Redding also has ADHD and a math learning disability; however, she does not believe that he was officially diagnosed as a child. Mr. Redding found construction work out of state. Mrs. Redding was laid off from her place of employment last year and moved in with her boyfriend over the summer. Mrs. Redding's boyfriend has 2 daughters (ages

257

9 and 11) who live with him as well. Mrs. Redding has been unwilling to provide custody documents but insists that she has sole custody and does not want Mr. Redding contacted.

Incident

Tyler's behaviors have become increasingly disruptive since the beginning of fifth grade, and, as a result, his grades have declined. Tyler has displayed aggressive behavior toward some peers yet is very protective toward other peers. Tyler often reports that he is tired and doesn't feel good. Tyler reports feeling isolated at home spending significant amounts of time alone in a basement bedroom. He reports walking home from school and going straight to his room, where he plays video games until 2:00 or 3:00 a.m. Tyler states that his mother will bring his dinner downstairs to his room or a small TV area outside of his room. Tyler reports watching TV until very late at night and has recently started to see "ghosts" in the boyfriend's home. Most recently, Tyler has made suicidal threats. This includes a recent attempt when Tyler placed a plastic bag over his head. The attempt was interrupted by one of the girls living in the home. Tyler stated that his mother "doesn't care" about him and "would be happier if [he] were dead," so that she could "get on with her life." In calling Mrs. Redding today to discuss this incident, Mrs. Redding reported knowing about his recent attempt and has locked the plastic bags in the garage. She refused to come to school to pick him up today. In the phone conversation the school counselor had with Mrs. Redding today, a referral to a mental health agency for counseling was recommended; however, Mrs. Redding declined, stating Tyler was "just doing it for attention" and didn't need my help. Historically, Mrs. Redding contacts the school when she perceives a problem but is difficult to converse with and refuses to attend IEP and other official meetings.

Discussion

The school counselor consulted with Tyler's teachers to gain additional insight into his classroom behavior. His teachers reported that Tyler is often "sullen" and "uncooperative," unless he perceives the activity as fun. The morning teachers have reported that Tyler will come to school very tired and often attempts to sleep in the early hours of the day. If the teachers try to involve him in the class work, he will become disruptive to the point that he has to be removed from the room. This is happening several times per week. His afternoon teachers report him as being volatile and easily agitated. Mrs. Barth, his science teacher, states that Tyler is very sensitive to comments by his peers, even when the comments are not directed to him or about him. All teachers are reporting a decrease in attention span, an inability to focus on even small assignments, and an unwillingness to complete any in-class worksheets or homework. Two of Tyler's teachers had both parents in their classes when they were children and feel that "there is nothing wrong with Tyler, he simply has bad parents."

Questions

1. How might the school counselor work with Mrs. Redding to obtain the mental health services Tyler needs? Should Mr. Redding be contacted? At what point does the school counselor contact the Department of Children and Family Services? How can the school counselor advocate for Tyler without alienating the parent(s)?
2. How might the school counselor enlist the teachers, principal, and family to create a more effective team to address the personal, social, and academic needs of Tyler? What services can be provided within the school environment to support Tyler?
3. How can the school counselor provide services to students to assist them with the transitions they are experiencing (e.g., divorce, loss of a parent, bullying)? How will the school counselor identify other students who might be at risk for similar challenges?

Response 1

Sondra Smith-Adcock

Tyler is distressed, likely depressed, and he needs help. His suicide attempt had the potential to be lethal and he must be protected from trying to harm himself again. Tyler's school counselor understands her leadership role as a system change agent, partnering with parents, teachers, and community to help students (Council for Accreditation of Counseling &Related Educational Programs [CACREP], 2009). Ms. Redding, Tyler's mother, states, "Please help me, but don't tell me how to raise my child." Let's assume Ms. Redding's positive intent in this statement. She wants to help her son. She does not want to be talked *at*, but talked *with*. As school counselors, we want to deeply empathize with and problem solve with parents, just as we do with our students. In this way, we encourage parents to become effective advocates for their children (Trusty & Brown, 2005). Building partnerships should be sensitive to the diverse needs of families, and Tyler's is no exception (Bryan & Henry, 2012).

Tyler's suicide attempt and his medication issues need to be addressed immediately. According to the reauthorization of the Federal Child Abuse Prevention and Treatment Act (CAPTA) (42 U.S.C.A. §5106g Act of 2010), neglect is an act or failure to act that might put the child at risk for serious harm (Child Welfare Information Gateway, 2012). Although Ms. Redding's denial of his suicide attempt could be considered a failure to act that puts Tyler at risk, we also have an opportunity to help her realize the importance of following up on a mental health referral. Second, the school counselor might want to contact Tyler's father. The American School Counselor Association's (ASCA's) Ethical Standards for School Counselors (2010b) encourage school counselors to make reasonable efforts to provide critical information regarding students to both parents, unless a court order prohibits it. Little is known, however, about the relationship between Tyler and his father. Efforts should be made to obtain the custody agreement.

When families are facing as much adversity as Tyler's (e,g., financial problems, divorce, mental health issues), it is common for schools to take a remedial rather than a collaborative approach to family engagement (Amatea, 2008; Bryan 2005, Tucker, 2009). In interactions with Ms. Redding, we want to focus on family assets rather than deficits, viewing her as a willing and capable partner (Amatea, Smith-Adcock, & Villares; 2006). Amatea (2008) recommends the following: (a) Acknowledge strengths; (b) treat caregivers as equals, not subordinates; (c) avoid blaming the caregiver for the student's difficulties; and (d) establish consistent, two-way communication. Ms. Redding has stated that she wants to feel heard and that she wants help for Tyler. She has advocated for her son in the past. Instead of blaming, reframe. Ms. Redding may need financial help getting the medications, or she may need additional information about the referral process. Respect her perspective. Hear her out. Advocate for Tyler's mental health care.

It is somewhat troubling that teachers were blaming of Tyler's parents. Blaming parents for the child's difficulties is unproductive and limits the opportunity for any meaningful collaboration (Amatea, Mixon, & McCarthy, 2013; Amatea et al., 2006; Tucker, 2009). The school counselor's leadership in helping teachers to build effective family partnerships is needed. By helping teachers to engage Ms. Redding in a collaborative, mutual decision-making model of communication as opposed to a one-way, educator-as-expert mode, we might mitigate some of her negativity toward the school staff and increase her likelihood of following through with Tyler's mental health referral and other recommendations (Amatea et al., 2006; Tucker, 2009).

Although the referral to a mental health counselor is indicated, Tyler also needs ongoing and multisystemic support within the school setting, including within his classroom. Tyler has confided a number of concerns that imply school-based intervention. When he is tired, why not let him sleep? Find out why he is sleepy. Individual counseling also allows the school counselor to offer Tyler direct support during the school day, to hear problems from Tyler's perspective, and to help him to advocate for himself. Additional responsive services might include small-group work for children of divorce and school-wide psychoeducation on suicide prevention.

Tyler is not alone. Every day, school counselors confront the reality of the number of school children who have problems that impede their academic success (DeKruyf, Auger, & Trice-Black, 2013). Comprehensive school counseling programs are organized around this need (ASCA, 2009). Nonetheless, estimates suggest that fewer than 20% of children who need mental health help receive it (Kataoka, Zhang, & Wells, 2002; Maag & Katsiyannis, 2010; President's New Freedom Commission on Mental Health, 2003). To address this alarming reality, recent calls have been issued for systemic efforts to screen and intervene with childrens' mental health problems and provide treatment both in and outside of schools, and the school counselors' role in this universal screening and treatment effort should be prominent (Erickson & Abel, 2013).

Tyler's story is particularly affecting because he is a young child at risk for suicide. Another issue to consider is how school counselors assess the level of suicidal risk in children. Sadly, suicide is the fourth leading cause of death among young people 10–24 years old (Centers for Disease Control and Prevention [CDC], 2010). Barrio-Minton (2007) outlines risk factors for suicide in children, and Tyler meets several: he is male, he has ADHD (which may mean impulsivity), he feels ignored, he has coped with stressors by attempting suicide before, and he has had an organized attempt. This puts Tyler at an elevated risk. School counselors should be knowledgeable about suicidal risk factors and address them.

Key aspects to managing this incident focus on the school counselor's leadership and advocacy skills. As a systems-change agent, Tyler's school counselor will manage this incident through (a) family–school–community collaboration to advocate for Tyler and (b) a complement of systemic and responsive services to meet Tyler's and his families' needs.

Response 2

Lourdes M. Rivera

This incident highlights the complex and multifaceted aspects of working with children who are experiencing emotional and psychological difficulties in school and at home and the many challenges the school counselor may need to address in coordinating services to support students during difficult transitions. Clearly, Tyler has been having difficulties at school for some time, and these have escalated because of the family's struggles and losses. Based on the information provided, and given the seriousness of the student's emotional and psychological difficulties (recent suicide attempt and continued suicidal ideation), priority must be given to securing the student's safety.

From the information provided, the school counselor has already begun to work with other school staff by obtaining as much information as possible from Tyler's teachers. The school counselor can also take on a leadership role by collaborating with other school staff (e.g., social workers, administrators) to ensure that all appropriate local and school guidelines are adhered to appropriately and effectively to get Tyler and his mother the assistance they need. Working with other staff can facilitate the process of identifying resources available for the family as well. In addition, the school counselor must adhere to ethical as well as legal requirements in the fulfillment of his or her responsibilities. Being knowledgeable of these guidelines and ensuring that all other school personnel are aware of these as well are essential, and the school counselor can take a leadership role to ensure that this is the case.

Ideally, working with the family—in this case, the mother, as she currently has custody—to provide Tyler with the support and mental health services that he needs would be the most effective strategy. The school counselor should continue to make efforts to engage Mrs. Redding, conveying support and understanding for how difficult this situation must be for her. The school counselor should also provide Mrs. Redding with information on the seriousness of the situation and the policies and procedures that must be adhered to by the school in this type of case. Helping the mother understand these guidelines and requirements may foster greater collaboration on her part.

Although every effort to engage the mother should be made, given Tyler's recent suicide attempt and the mother's response to this (i.e., "he's just trying to get attention") and the inconsistency with which Tyler's medical needs have been addressed in the past (e.g., not being able to provide contact information for his doctor or consistency in ensuring that he takes his prescribed medication), the school counselor needs to be prepared to make the necessary report to Child Protective Services. Given the complexity of the issues raised in these types of situations, school counselors need to be familiar with their own states' reporting guidelines for child abuse and neglect. However, when in doubt, the best strategy is to report the case to ensure the child's safety. In this particular case, given the history, unless the mother agrees to work with the school to address Tyler's needs, it would be most advisable to make the report to Child Protective Services.

Once Tyler's immediate safety needs are addressed, the school counselor can continue to take on a leadership role in ensuring that Tyler is provided with a supportive school environment and that his educational and emotional needs are appropriately met.

The school counselor should continue to work closely with Tyler's teachers and other school personnel to monitor his progress and ensure that a safe and supportive environment is provided for him. This can be accomplished in a more formal manner by having regularly scheduled meetings with teachers and staff or encouraging teachers to provide updates and/or checking in with them on a regular basis. By maintaining open lines of communication, the school counselor can help establish positive working relationships with all school staff that can contribute to creating a supportive and safe environment for all students.

In addition to any outside counseling services that Tyler receives, the school counselor should also continue to provide supportive individual in-school counseling for this student. This ongoing in-school support can address Tyler's academic and interpersonal relations with teachers and other students and assist him in making positive progress in his schoolwork. This will also enable the school counselor to closely monitor Tyler's progress and assist him in negotiating the demands and expectations of his school. Efforts should also be made to get Tyler involved in activities and groups in the school to assist him in developing positive relationships with students and other adults. Helping Tyler to engage in these types of activities will help to decrease his sense of isolation and help him develop friendships at school.

As a leader and advocate for all students, the school counselor, in collaboration with other school professionals (e.g., the school psychologist), can provide in-service training to staff and administrators regarding the indicators of abuse, neglect, and suicide. This training can ensure that all school personnel are able to recognize indicators of concern and be able to identify students who may need services. Additionally, in-service training can be provided to ensure that information on school, district, and legal policies are shared with and understood by all school staff. If the school does not have clear, written guidelines in place for responding to suspected child abuse or neglect and/or responding to incidents of suspected suicide ideation, the school counselor can work with other school personnel to ensure that these are developed and shared with all school staff. Early detection and prevention is the responsibility of all school personnel; the school counselor, by taking a leadership position in ensuring that the information is shared, can have a powerful impact.

As prevention is ultimately more beneficial than remediation, the school counselor, as part of a comprehensive school counseling program, can work on developing classroom presentations, lessons, and group activities to educate and inform students about issues they may be experiencing (e.g., divorce, depression). These efforts can help identify students who need services and provide opportunities for students to develop effective coping strategies. As part of these efforts, providing information to all members of the school community (e.g., students and teachers) on resources available for students would also be beneficial. Other strategies can include conducting workshops for parents on relevant issues and challenges that students may struggle with and educating them about resources available to assist them and their children.

Supplemental Readings and Online Resources

Supplemental Readings

American School Counselor Association. (2015). *The school counselor and child abuse and neglect prevention.* Retrieved from https://www.schoolcounselor.org/asca/media/asca/PositionStatements/PS_ChildAbuse.pdf
Bryant, J. (2009). School counselors and child abuse reporting: A national survey. *Professional School Counseling, 12*(5), 333–342.
Bryant, J., & Milsom, A. (2005). Child abuse reporting by school counselors. *Professional School Counseling, 9*(1), 63–71.
Gibbons, M. M. (2008). Suicide awareness training for faculty and staff: A training model for school counselors. *Professional School Counseling, 11*(4), 272–276.

U.S. Department of Health and Human Services, Administration for Children and Families, Administration on Children, Youth, and Families, Children's Bureau. (2015). *Child maltreatment 2013*. Retrieved from: http://www.acf.hhs.gov/programs/cb/research-data-technology/statistics-research/child-maltreatment

Online Resources

American School Counselor Association
  http://www.schoolcounselor.org/

National Center for the Prevention of Youth Suicide
  http://www.suicidology.org/ncypys/about

Chapter 30

How Can We Work Across the Road If We Aren't Included?

Dawnette Cigrand

Background

Silver Oak, a residential treatment facility (RTF) had been servicing at-risk high school students in the Forester rural school district, with a graduating class of around 100 students, for 18 years. Most of these students attended a local alternative school, while some were integrated into the local public high school based on their progress in the program. This relationship between the treatment facility and the school district was going well, so both administrations agreed to partner in an expansion of the group home to include an elementary-school-age program for 5- to 12-year-olds as well.

Incident

The following summer, the administration from the Silver Oak treatment facility proceeded and accepted contracts for elementary-school-age students for the fall semester. The Forester school district did not take part in this process of accepting students into Silver Oak, as they had not taken part in this process in the past. After the Silver Oak administrator, Dr. Marbley, had accepted three students, she asked to meet with the school district staff to discuss these students and their transition to the elementary school.

The school principal, Dr. Abbott; Mr. Clariton, the special education teacher; and Ms. Bouch, the school counselor, were asked to meet with the Silver Oak administrator to develop a transition plan for the students.

265

Through this meeting, Ms. Bouch learned that the three students were considered very "high need," including one student, who was never to be alone with one staff member at the group home; that is, two staff members were expected to be with "Caden" always.

All three students came in with lengthy individualized education plans (IEPs). Caden's was especially extensive, as his IEP came to the Forrester school office in a box previously used for reams of paper. Although Forester Elementary had experienced teachers and staff in place to meet the needs of students already in the district, they had to scramble to hire additional staff to meet the IEP requirements of these students. For the stability of the students and because of the urgency to hire more staff, it was decided that one staff member at the RTF would accompany Caden and act as a paraprofessional to him at school.

Caden, who was entering third grade, had several diagnoses, including reactive attachment disorder (RAD). The main reason why Caden required two staff members with him always was that he could be very aggressive toward staff members, and two adults were needed for safety. Through the RTF, Caleb saw a psychiatrist regularly to manage his medications, and a social worker conducted group counseling with all the students there. My described responsibility was to support him with his behavioral issues at school.

Discussion

Caden's transition to school was rocky at best. In the first week, he had threatened and/or hit staff members, had thrown his lunch tray across the lunch room, and had attempted to run away from the school building. A select group of staff members, including Ms. Bouch, had been trained in the Crisis Prevention Institute's Nonviolent Crisis Intervention and had to implement these restraints at various times during the week. There were many other staff in the building who had not gone through this training but who had interactions with Caden. Through behavior observations in various school settings, it became apparent to the school counselor that several staff members and students were afraid of Caden and his behavioral outbursts. In addition, school staff became aware that Caden was not doing well at Silver Oak. Two staff members had already quit after working with him. School administration wondered whether the RTF had staff who were adequately trained to appropriately serve Caden. If not, the Forrester administrative team wondered how this affected Caden's behaviors at school.

In addition, parents had heard from their children in the district about Caden's violent behaviors and were calling the administration with concerns. As trained professionals, the school team was aware that transitions are very difficult for students with these particular needs and anticipated these types of behaviors initially. Even so, staff and students were intimidated, and parents were worried for their children. As the professional in the building with the most training and experience with students with aggressive behaviors, Ms. Bouch, the school counselor, was asked by the principal to develop training for staff and a plan to work with parents who were concerned.

Questions

1. How would you prepare staff members in the building for students with aggressive behaviors?
2. Would you recommend to the school that it share staff members with the RTF to support this type of student? Why or why not?
3. How would you work with concerned parents in this situation while protecting the FERPA (Family Educational Rights and Privacy Act of 1974) rights of the students in the RTF?
4. At what point would the rights of the student with the IEP conflict with the rights of regular-education students?
5. What is the role of the school counselor in situations such as this one described?

Response 1
Eric R. Baltrinic

It is imperative that all staff members understand and assess their skill levels in serving children with aggressive behaviors. Building on the foundation of the "select" group of staff members trained in nonviolent crisis intervention, training that assists school staff with identifying and responding (not reacting) to Caden's and other students' behaviors is recommended; training in positive behavioral supports (http://www.apbs.org/) may be helpful in this area. It is difficult to see a child struggling with severe issues (RAD), which contributes to Caden's behaviors (i.e., aggressive outbursts). Caden's behaviors can place emotional and psychological strains on school staff. Interventions provided to students by school staff members can be adversely affected when staff members (a) personalize student behaviors; (b) move too quickly to problem solve; or (c) enact disciplinary actions too quickly, which can escalate student behaviors. Prosocial responsive behaviors need to be modeled by school staff to other students, as students need to learn to respond to aggressive behaviors by their peers. De-escalating student behaviors before they become crisis-level behaviors is an ideal outcome; training in collaborative problem solving (see information available at http://www.ccps.info/; http://www.livesinthebalance.org/; and http://www.thinkkids.org/) may be helpful in this area. Extra time and energy is expected by staff (not the exception) when dealing with severe behaviors, so frequently checking in with staff is critical for school counselors to assess the quality and consistency of interventions; training in motivational interviewing (http://www.motivationalinterviewing.org/) may help in this area. Finally, Caden would benefit from having a designated space (e.g., a room or area)—monitored by his classroom aides—to cool down and, at times, to complete his work.

I would not recommend sharing staff with the Silver Oak RTF without an explicit clause in a written contractual agreement outlining that the RTF staff is designated (1.0 full-time equivalent [FTE]) to the school, thus preventing the designated intervention specialist/staff member from being recalled to fulfill other duties at the RTF. Perhaps a short-term contractual arrangement with the RTF staff member could be implemented under the conditions mentioned earlier until another permanent school staff member (e.g., a trained intervention specialist) was hired.

The Forester rural school district is responsible for serving the community. The concerned parents of those students affected by Caden's behaviors would be consulted on a case-by-case basis without disclosing the nature of Caden's problems (i.e., RAD) or his special education status (i.e., IEP service category). IEP service categories are what guide the construction of classroom accommodations, level of restrictiveness in placements, and behavioral interventions, but they do not preclude disciplinary actions when students violate the rights of other students. School staff need to be committed to continuously modifying their interpersonal styles with Caden as needed and assessing the effectiveness of his accommodations and placement. Overall, reducing the restrictiveness of the placement for Caden (e.g., from RTF to regular school placement) needs to be accompanied by more intensive school staff support when considering his integration back into the regular school population.

All students have a right to a free public education. However, students also have the right to access education in relatively safe conditions. Assurances and safeguards would need to be in place to minimize any risks to the general student population from any known or predictable aggressive behaviors from students with IEPs; for example, underscoring the importance of staff knowing how to de-escalate Caden's behaviors and the availability of a safe and isolated space for Caden in times of crisis. However, if Caden is continuously isolated from his school peers, he is being denied opportunities to socialize within the general school population, thus compromising the placement change from the RTF to the regular school setting.

Given the intensity of this case, what is the role of the school counselor in this and similar situations? School counselors can assist Caden and other school staff through:

- The provision of trainings to school staff and administrators on the topic areas described in Question 1 given earlier (e.g., motivational interviewing, positive behavioral supports, and collaborative problem solving, among others);

- The provision of classroom guidance on topics such as personal safety, bullying behaviors, and similar topics that will help students be responsive to students with behaviors similar to Caden;
- Involvement with behavior intervention planning and implementation, including consultation with instrumental school staff members;
- Involvement in parent consultations along with school administrators, and;
- Modeling and providing access to information on school staff members' self-care.

Response 2
Tarrell Awe Agahe Portman

The rural setting of the Forester school district adds a unique dimension to this case. The close working relationship between the Silver Oak RTF and the district in the past appears to be a positive relationship. The nature of Caden's behaviors and the impact on others appears to be a "known" issue in the rural community and has the potential to stigmatize the child and other children at the RTF. This rural culture must be considered in addressing the needs of the student, staff, and community.

If I were in Ms. Wells's role, my priority would be to develop educational materials and professional development for the staff, teachers, administrators, community volunteers, and peer students to understand how to address safety concerns. This would require education at multiple levels. I would prepare classroom social skills lessons to present first with the third graders, followed by small groups addressing social interactions among peers—basically teaching the other students how to react (or not react) to behavioral outbursts. My preparation of teachers would include using resources to help them understand various diagnoses that might lead to aggressive behaviors. The interventions and strategies that could be used to de-escalate or prevent outbursts would be addressed. As the school counselor, I would form a teachers' committee to develop professional preparation events, opportunities, or training that would address the immediate needs as viewed from the teachers' perspectives. I would also advocate for professional development funds to be used for addressing this situation.

My recommendation would be for the school district, RTF, the local division of human services, and any other education support agency to work together to share staff to support Caden. These agreements should be clearly written into Caden's IEP under "support systems," with the percentage of time allocated and specific timeframes in place. Social workers from the Department of Human Services (DHS), remedial specialists, and case managers should be an active part of the RTF treatment plan and included in the school district academic accommodations plan. The IEP also needs to include a behavioral management plan with clearly delineated steps for removal from the school setting back to the RTF when necessary.

Parent training would also be necessary for the district, but I would focus on all children, not just Caden. The community education surrounding the role of prevention and treatment in the community would also prepare people for understanding and responding to this situation. The concerned parents in the community bring their own perspectives toward Silver Oak into the conversation. It may be that many people in the community are already engaged with the children at Silver Oak through other social or religious circles. Educating the community on FERPA rights, services provided by Silver Oaks, and the responsibility of the school district to serve all children is necessary. This may include the school counselor and Silver Oaks staff presenting to various community groups with the intent of gaining acceptance for their contribution to the community. Parents need to be reassured that the education of their children will not be disrupted.

All students have the right to education within a safe, learning environment. Students with IEPs or Section 504 (of the Rehabilitation Act of 1973) plans have additional rights by federal law. When the behaviors of one student affect the learning environment of another student, it is the responsibility of the trained professionals to remedy the situation in a way that has the least educational impact on all students. These accommodations may require a change in staffing; physical location; or time scheduling for classes, recess, or lunch; or they may require another example of "outside of the box" thinking. These decisions are within the domain of the multidisciplinary team, including the treatment professionals and parents. The role of the school counselor in this situation is as a member of the team and as the overall cultural manager of the school climate environment with the school administrator. In this case, the school administrator gave the school counselor a direct responsibility for preparing others for working with a particular child's behaviors. The school counselor should consult, research, and develop a plan for fulfilling this request. However, the school counselor is only one member of the team and not a "superhero" (American School Counselor Association, 2010b).

Supplemental Readings, Online Resources, and Supplemental Activities

Supplemental Readings

Ingram, B. (n.d.). *Trauma informed approaches to classroom management.* https://achieve.lausd.net/cms/lib/CA01000043/Centricity/Domain/260/Trauma%20Informed%20Approaches%20to%20Classroom%20Management.pdf

Mazher, W. (2018). Teaching students with learning disabilities to cope in middle school. *The Clearing House: A Journal of Educational Strategies, Issues and Ideas.* Published online March 1, 2018. doi:10.1080/00098655.2018.1436822

Mumbauer, J., & Kelchner, V. (2017). Promoting mental health literacy through bibliotherapy in school-based settings (conceptual). *Professional School Counseling*, 21(1), 85–94. https://doi.org/10.5330/1096-2409-21.1.85

Trauma and Learning Policy Initiative. (2005). *Helping traumatized children learn: A report and policy agenda.* Retrieved from https://traumasensitiveschools.org/tlpi-publications/download-a-free-copy-of-helping-traumatized-children-learn/

Online Resources

Children, Violence and Trauma—Interventions in Schools
https://www.youtube.com/watch?v=49GzqPP7YYk

Trauma-Informed Practices: Resources for School Counselors
http://forhighschoolcounselors.blogspot.com/2017/06/trauma-informed-practices-resources-for.html

Supplemental Activities

Learning Activities

- Visit a residential children's home or treatment center for a tour. Write a journal entry, before touring, immediately after the visit, and a week after the visit. What are your reflections of the environment in relation to a school system.
- Conduct online searches for consultation models. Select one and work through the various stages using the incident presented. Create a virtual presentation to present to a mock school counseling conference. What would you choose to focus on? Why?

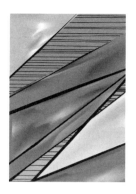

References

Alexander, K., & Alexander, M. D. (2011). *American public school law* (8th ed.). Belmont, CA: Thomson West.

Altschul, I., Oyserman, D., & Bybee, D. (2006). Racial-ethnic identity in mid-adolescence: Content and change as predictors of academic achievement. *Child Development, 77*(5), 1155–1169.

Amatea, E. (2008). *Building culturally responsive family-school partnerships.* Boston, MA: Allyn & Bacon.

Amatea, E. S., Daniels, H. D., Bringman, N., & Vandiver, F. (2004). Strengthening counselor-teacher-family connections: The family-school collaborative consultation project. *Professional School Counseling, 8*(1), 47–55.

Amatea, E. S., Mixon, K., & McCarthy, S. (2013). Preparing future teachers to collaborate with families: Contributions of family systems counselors to a teacher preparation program. *Family Journal, 21*(2), 136–145.

Amatea, E. S., Smith-Adcock, S., & Villares, E. (2006). From family deficit to family strength: Viewing families' contributions to children's learning from a family resilience perspective. *Professional School Counseling, 9*(3), 177–187.

American Counseling Association. (2014). *ACA code of ethics.* Alexandria, VA: Author.

American Mental Health Counselors Association. (2010). *Principles for AMHCA code of ethics.* Retrieved from: http://ethics.iit.edu/ecodes/node/5125

American School Counselor Association. (2005). *The ASCA national model: A framework for school counseling programs.* Alexandria, VA: Author.

American School Counselor Association. (2009). *The school counselor and student mental health.* Alexandria, VA: Author. Retrieved from http://schoolcounselor.org/asca/media/asca/PositionStatements/PS_StudentMentalHealth.pdf

American School Counselor Association. (2010). *Ethical standards for school counselors.* Alexandria, VA: Author.

American School Counselor Association. (2012a). *The ASCA National Model: A framework for school counseling programs* (3rd ed.). Alexandria, VA: Author.

American School Counselor Association. (2012b). *ASCA school counselor competencies.* Retrieved from http://www.schoolcounselor.org/asca/media/asca/home/SCCompetencies.pdf

American School Counselor Association. (2013). *The school counselor and safe schools and crisis response* [Position statement]. Retrieved from https://www.schoolcounselor.org/asca/media/asca/PositionStatements/PS_SafeSchools.pdf

American School Counselor Association. (2014a). *ASCA mindsets & behaviors for student success: K-12 college- and career-readiness standards for every student.* Alexandria, VA: Author.

American School Counselor Association. (2014b). *The school counselor and confidentiality* [Position statement]. Retrieved from https://www.schoolcounselor.org/asca/media/asca/PositionStatements/PS_Confidentiality.pdf

American School Counselor Association. (2014c). *The school counselor and group counseling* [Position statement]. Retrieved from https://www.schoolcounselor.org/asca/media/asca/PositionStatements/PS_GroupCounseling.pdf

American School Counselor Association. (2014d). *The school counselor and multitiered systems of support* [Position statement]. Retrieved November 21, 2015, from https://www.schoolcounselor.org/asca/media/asca/PositionStatements/PS_MultitieredSupportSystem.pdf

American School Counselor Association. (2016). *Ethical standards for school counselors.* Alexandria, VA: Author. Retrieved from: https://www.schoolcounselor.org/asca/media/asca/Ethics/EthicalStandards2016.pdf

American School Counselor Association. (2018). *Role of the school counselor.* Alexandria, VA: Author. Retrieved from https://www.schoolcounselor.org/administrators/role-of-the-school-counselor

American School Counselor Association. (n.d.-a). *Appropriate and inappropriate roles for school counselors.* Alexandria, VA: Author. Retrieved from http://www.schoolcounselor.org/asca/media/asca/home/appropriate-activities-of-school-counselors.pdf

American School Counselor Association. (n.d.-b). *Information for administrators.* Retrieved November 20, 2015, from http://www.schoolcounselor.org/administrators

Anyon, J. (1981). Social class and school knowledge. *Curriculum Inquiry, 11*(1), 3–42.

Arredondo, P., Toporek, M. S., Brown, S., Jones, J., Locke, D. C., Sanchez, J., & Stadler, H. (1996) *Operationalization of the multicultural counseling competencies.* AMCD: Alexandria, VA.

Assistant Secretary for Planning and Evaluation, U. S. Department of Health and Human Services. (2008). *What challenges are boys facing, and what opportunities exist to address those challenges?* [Fact sheet: Mental health]. Washington, DC: U.S. Department of Health and Human Services. Retrieved from http://aspe.hhs.gov/hsp/08/boys/factsheets/mh/index.shtml

Association for Counseling Education and Supervision. (2011). *Best practices in clinical supervision.* Retrieved from: http://www.acesonline.net/wpcontent/uploads/2011/10/ACES-Best-Practices-in-clinical supervision-document-FINAL.pdf

Association for Specialists in Group Work. (2000). ASGW professional standards for the training of group workers. *The Journal for Specialists in Group Work, 25,* 327–342.

Astramovich, R. A., & Harris, K. R. (2007). Promoting self-advocacy among minority students in school counseling. *Journal of Counseling & Development, 85,* 269–276.

Astramovich, R. A., Hoskins, W. J., & Coker, J. K. (2013). *Organizing and evaluating data driven school counseling programs.* Dubuque, IA: Kendall Hunt.

Bandura, A. (1997). *Self-efficacy: The exercise of control.* New York, NY: Macmillan.

Barrio-Minton, C. A. (2007). Assessing suicide risk in children: Guidelines for developmentally appropriate interviewing. *Journal of Mental Health Counseling, 29*(1), 50–66.

Bathje, G. J., & Pryor, J. B. (2011). The relationships of public and self-stigma to seeking mental health services. *Journal of Mental Health Counseling, 33*(2), 161–176.

Bemak, F., & Chung, R. (2008). New professional roles and advocacy strategies for school counselors: A multicultural/social justice perspective to move beyond the nice counselor syndrome. *Journal of Counseling & Development, 86,* 372–281.

Benson, P. (2004). Emerging themes in research on adolescent spiritual and religious development. *Applied Developmental Science, 8*(1), 47–50.

Bernard, J. M., & Goodyear, R. K. (1998). *Fundamentals of clinical supervision* (2nd ed.). Boston, MA: Allyn and Bacon.

Bernard, J. M., & Goodyear, R. K. (2004). *Fundamentals of clinical supervision* (3rd ed.) New York, NY: Pearson.

Bethell, C. D., Carle, A., Hudziak, J., Gombojav, N., Powers, K., Wade, R., & Braveman, P. (2017). Methods to assess adverse childhood experiences of children and families: toward approaches to promote child well-being in policy and practice. *Academic Pediatrics, 17,* S51–S69. https://doi.org/10.1016/j.acap.2017.04.161

Biaggio, M., Orchard, S., Larson, J., Petrino, K., & Mihara, R. (2003). Guidelines for gay/lesbian/bisexual-affirmative educational practices in psychology programs. *Professional Psychology: Research and Practice, 34,* 548–554.

Bidell, M. P. (2005). The Sexual Orientation Counselor Competency Scale: Assessing attitudes, skills, and knowledge of counselors working with lesbian, gay, and bisexual clients. *Counselor Education and Supervision, 44,* 267–279.

Bikos, L.H., Haney, D., Edwards, R. W., North, M.A., Quint, M., McLellan, J., & Ecker, D. L. (2014). Missionary kid career development: A consensual qualitative research investigation through a social cognitive lens. *The Career Development Quarterly, 62,* 156–174. doi:10.1002/j.2161-0045.2014.00077.x

Blount, A. J. & Mullen, P. R. (2015). Development of an integrative wellness model: Supervising counselors-in-training. *The Professional Counselor, 5,* 100–113.

Borders, L. D., & Usher, C. H. (1992). Post-degree supervision: Existing and preferred practices. *Journal of Counseling & Development, 70,* 594–599.

Bordin, E. S. (1979). The generalizability of the psychoanalytic concept of the working alliance. *Psychotherapy: Theory, Research & Practice, 16,* 252–260. http://psycnet.apa.org/doi/10.1037/h0085885

Bosworth, K., Espelage, D., & Simon, T. (1999). Factors associated with bullying behavior in middle school students. *The Journal of Early Adolescence, 19,* 341–352.

Brock, S. E., Lazarus, P. L., & Jimerson, S. R. (2002). *Best practices in school crisis prevention and intervention.* Bethesda, MD: NASP.

Brock, S. E., Sandoval, J., & Lewis, S. (2001). *Preparing for crises in the schools: A manual for building school crisis response teams.* New York, NY: Wiley.

Broderick, P, & Blewitt, P. (2015). *The life span: Human development for the helping professionals.* Upper Saddle River, NJ: Pearson Education.

Bronfenbrenner, U. (1979). *The ecology of human development: Experiments by nature and design.* Cambridge, MA: Harvard University Press.

Brown, D., Feit, S., & Forestandi, R. (1973). Career education: The counselor's role. *School Counselor, 20,* 193–196.

Brown, K., & Bradley, L. (2002). Reducing the stigma of mental illness. *Journal of Mental Health Counseling, 24*(1), 81–87.

Bryan, J. (2005). Fostering educational resilience and academic achievement in urban schools through school–family–community partnerships. *Professional School Counseling, 8,* 219–227.

Bryan, J., & Henry, L. (2012). A model for building school-family-community partnerships: Principles and processes. *Journal of Counseling & Development, 90,* 408–420.

Bucher, R. (2008). *Building cultural intelligence (CQ): Nine megaskills.* Upper Saddle River, NJ: Pearson Education.

Burnham, J. J., & Jackson, C. M. (2000). School counselor roles: Discrepancies between actual practice and existing models. *Professional School Counseling, 4,* 41–49.

Burns, M. K., & Gibbons, K. (2013). *Implementing response-to-intervention in elementary and secondary schools: Procedures to assure scientific-based practices.* New York, NY: Routledge.

Calia, V. F., & Corsini, R. J. (1973). *Critical incidents in school counseling* (1st ed.). Englewood Cliffs, NJ: Prentice-Hall.

Campbell-Whatley, G. D., & Comer, J. (2000). Self-concept and African-American student achievement: Related issues of ethics, power and privilege. *Teacher Education and Special Education: The Journal of the Teacher Education Division of the Council for Exceptional Children, 23*(1), 19–31.

Capuzzi, D. (2002). Legal and ethical challenges in counseling suicidal students. *Professional School Counseling, 6*(1), 36–46.

Carey, J. D., Harrington, K., Martin, I., & Hoffman, D. (2012). A statewide evaluation of the outcomes of the implementation of ASCA National Model school counseling programs in rural and suburban Nebraska high schools. *Professional School Counseling, 16*(2), 100–107.

Carter, R. B., Spera, S., & Hall, M. H. (1992). A guidance and counseling needs assessment for a rural, multi-cultural K-8 school. *Education, 113*(1), 19.

Center for Mental Health in Schools at UCLA. (2008). *Responding to a crisis at a school.* Los Angeles, CA: Author. Retrieved from http://smhp.psych.ucla.edu/pdfdocs/crisis/crisis.pdf

Centers for Disease Control and Prevention. (2010). Youth risk behavior surveillance—United States, 2009. *Surveillance Summaries, 59*(5), 1–142. Retrieved from http://www.cdc.gov/mmwr/pdf/ss/ss5905.pdf

Chen-Hayes, S. F., Ockerman, M. S., & Mason, E. C. M. (2014). *101 solutions for school counselors and leaders in challenging times.* Thousand Oaks, CA: Corwin Press.

Child Welfare Information Gateway. (2012). *Acts of omission: An overview of child neglect.* Retrieved from https://www.childwelfare.gov/pubPDFs/acts.pdf#page=2&view=Definitions

Clifton, L. (1983). *Everett Anderson's goodbye.* New York, NY: Henry Holt.

Cohen, D. J., Clark, E. C., Lawson, P. J., Casucci, B. A., & Flocke, S. A. (2011). Identifying teachable moments for health behavior counseling in primary care. *Patient Education Counseling, 85,* 8–15. doi:10.1016/j.pec.2010.11.009

Colistra, A., & Brown-Rice, K. (2011). *When the rubber hits the road: Applying multicultural competencies in cross-cultural supervision.* Retrieved from: http://counselingoutfitters.com/vistas/vistas11/Article_43.pdf

Committee for Children. (2011). *Second Step: A violence prevention curriculum.* Seattle, WA: Author.

Constantine, M. G., & Sue, D. W. (2007). Perceptions of racial microaggressions among black supervisees in cross-racial dyads. *Journal of Counseling Psychology, 54*(2), 142–153. doi:10.1037/0022-0167.54.2.142

Cook-Sather, A. (2006). Sound, presence, and power: "Student voice" in educational research and reform. *Curriculum Inquiry, 36*(4), 359–390.

Corrigan, P. (2004). How stigma interferes with mental health care. *American Psychologist, 59*(7), 614.

Council for Accreditation of Counseling & Related Educational Programs. (2009). *CACREP 2009 standards.* Alexandria, VA: Author. Retrieved from http://www.cacrep.org/wp-content/uploads/2017/07/2009-Standards.pdf

Council for Accreditation of Counseling & Related Educational Programs. (2015). *CACREP 2016 standards.* Alexandria, VA: Author. Retrieved from http://www.cacrep.org/wp-content/uploads/2018/05/2016-Standards-with-Glossary-5.3.2018.pdf

Crowe, A., & Averett, P. (2015). Attitudes of mental health professionals toward mental illness: A deeper understanding. *Journal of Mental Health Counseling, 37*(1), 47–62.

Culbreth, J. R., Scarborough, J. L, Banks-Johnson, A., & Solomon, S. (2005). Role stress among practicing school counselors. *Counselor Education and Supervision, 45,* 58–71.

Dahir, C.A., & Stone, C.B. (2012). *The transformed school counselor* (2nd ed). Belmont, CA: Wadsworth.

DeKruyf, L., Auger, R. W., & Trice-Black, S. (2013). The role of school counselors in meeting students' mental health needs: Examining issues of professional identity. *Professional School Counseling, 16*(5), 271–282.

Dimmitt, C., Carey, J. C., & Hatch, T. (2007). *Evidence-based school counseling: Making a difference with data-driven practices.* Thousand Oaks, CA: Corwin Press.

Dinkmeyer, D., & Carlson, J. (2006). *Consultation: Creating school-based interventions* (3rd ed.). New York, NY: Routledge.

Doka, K. J. (Ed.). (2000). *Living with grief after sudden loss: Suicide, homicide, accident, heart attack, stroke.* Amityville, NY: Baywood.

Dollarhide, C. T., & Miller, G. M. (2006). Supervision for preparation and practice of school counselors: Pathways to excellence. *Counselor Education and Supervision, 45,* 242–252.

DuBois, D. L., Portillo, N., Rhodes, J. E., Silverthorn, N., & Valentine, J. C. (2011). How effective are mentoring programs for youth? A systematic assessment of the evidence. *Psychological Science in the Public Interest, 12,* 57–91.

Durlak, J. A., Weissberg, R. P., Dymnicki, A. B., Taylor, R. D., & Schellinger, K. B. (2011). The impact of enhancing students' social and emotional learning: A meta-analysis of school-based universal interventions. *Child Development, 82*(1), 405–432.

Eisel v. Board of Education of Montgomery County, 324 Md. 376, 597 A. 2d 447 (Md Ct. App. 1991).

Emerson, S., & Markos, P. A. (1996). Signs and symptoms of the impaired counselor. *The Journal of Humanistic Education and Development, 34,* 108–117.

Erford, B. (Ed.). (2007). Accountability. In *Transforming the school counseling profession* (2nd ed., pp. 236–277). Upper Saddle River, NJ: Pearson.

Erford, B. T. (Ed.). (2019). *Transforming the school counseling profession* (5th ed.). Columbus, OH: Pearson.

Erickson A., & Abel, N. R. (2013). Leadership in providing school-wide screenings for depression and enhancing suicide awareness. *Professional School Counseling, 16*(5), 283–289.

Executive Office of the President. (2014, December). *2014 Native youth report.* Retrieved from https://files.eric.gov/fulltext/ED565658.pdf

Farmer, L. B. (2011). *Counselors' self-perceived competency with lesbian, gay, and bisexual clients* (Unpublished doctoral dissertation). Virginia Polytechnic Institute and State University, Blacksburg, VA.

Figley, C. R. (1995). Compassion fatigue: Toward a new understanding of the costs of caring. In B. H. Stamm (Ed.), *Secondary traumatic stress* (pp. 3–28). Lutherville, MD: Sidran Press.

Filmore, J. M. (2014). Lesbian, gay, and bisexual counseling competency: The difference between LGB education, clinical experience and personal relationships on student competency (Unpublished doctoral dissertation). Northern Illinois University, DeKalb, IL.

Finkelhor, D., Mitchell, K. J., & Wolak, J. (2000). *Online victimization: A report on the nation's youth.* Alexandria, VA: National Center for Missing and Exploited Children.

Fiore, L. (2011). *LifeSmart: Exploring human development.* New York, NY: McGraw-Hill.

Flannery, K. B., Fenning, P., Kato, M. M., & McIntosh, K. (2014). Effects of school-wide positive behavioral interventions and supports and fidelity of implementation on problem behavior in high schools. *School Psychology Quarterly, 29*(2), 111–124. http://dx.doi.org/10.1037/spq0000039.

Flom, B.L., & Hansen, S. (2006). Just don't shut the door on me: Aspirations of adolescents in crisis. *Professional School Counseling, 10*(1), 88–91.

Ford, J. D. (2005). Treatment implications of altered affect regulation and information processing following child maltreatment. *Psychiatric Annals, 35,* 410–419. https://doi.org/10.3928/00485713-20050501-07

42 United States Code. The Public Health and Welfare. § 290dd-2; 42 C.F.R. Part 2

Gable, R., Mostert, M., & Tonelson, S. (2004). Assessing professional collaboration in schools: Knowing what works. *Preventing School Failure, 48*(3), 4–8.

Georgiades, K., Boyle, M. H. & Fife, K. A. (2012). Emotional and behavioral problems among adolescent students: The role of immigrant, racial/ethnic congruence and belongingness in schools. *Journal of Youth and Adolescence, 42,* 1473–1492. doi:10.1007/s10964-012-9868-2

Gong, Y., Deng, C., Yagi, D. T., Mimura, T., Hwang, M., & Lee, D. (2013). Career counseling in Asian countries: Historical development, current status, challenges, and prospects. *Journal of Asia Pacific Counseling, 3*(1), 9–33.

Goodyear-Brown, P. (2010). *Play therapy with traumatized children: A prescriptive approach.* Hoboken, NJ: Wiley.

Grabosky, T. K., & Ishii, H., & Mase, S. (2013). Counseling in Japan. In T. H. Hohenshil, N. E. Amundson, & S. G. Niles (Eds.), *Counseling around the world* (pp. 97–106). Alexandria, VA: American Counseling Association.

Graham, S. R., Carney, J. S., & Kluck, A. S. (2012). Perceived competency in working with LGB clients: Where are we now? *Counselor Education and Supervision, 51*, 2–16.

Grayshield, L. (2006). Barriers and best practices for American Indian students. *New Mexico Review, NMSU*, Las Cruces, NM, Vol. XIV.

Grey (1973). Youth and the occult. *The School Counselor, 20*(3), 167.

Griffin, D., & Steen, S. (2011). A social justice approach to school counseling. *Journal for Social Action in Counseling and Psychology, 3*(1), 74–85.

Gruman, D. H., Marston, T., & Koon, H. (2013). Bringing mental health needs into focus through school counseling program transformation. *Professional School Counseling, 16*(5), 333–341.

Guajardo, M. A., Guajardo, F., Janson, C., & Militello, M. (2016). *Reframing community partnerships in education: Uniting the power of place and wisdom of people.* New York, NY: Routledge.

Guo, Y., Wang, S., & Combs, D. C. (2013). Counseling in Taiwan. In T. H. Hohenshil, N. E. Amundson, & S. G. Niles (Eds.), *Counseling around the world* (pp. 145–152). Alexandria, VA: American Counseling Association.

Gurwitch, R., & Schonfeld, D. (2011). *Support traumatized students.* Retrieved from: https://www.schoolcounselor.org/magazine/blogs/september-october-2011/support-traumatized-students

Gysbers, N. C. (2012). Embracing the past, welcome the future: A brief history of school counseling. In *ASCA National Model: A framework for school counseling programs* (3rd ed., pp. vii–ix). Alexandria, VA: American School Counselor Association.

Hatch, T. (2013). *The use of data in school counseling: Hatching results for students, programs, and the profession.* Thousand Oaks, CA: Corwin Press.

Hatch, T. (2014). *The use of data in school counseling: Hatching results for students, programs, and the profession.* Thousand Oaks, CA: Corwin Press.

Hays, D. G. (2017). *Assessment in counseling: A guide to the use of psychological assessment procedures* (6th ed.). Alexandria, VA: American Counseling Association.

Herlihy, B., Gray, N., & McCollum, V. (2002). Legal and ethical issues in school counselor supervision. *Professional School Counseling, 6*, 55–60.

Hohenshil, T. H., Amundson, N. E., & Niles, S. G. (Eds.). (2013). Introduction to global counseling. In *Counseling around the world* (pp. 3–8). Alexandria, VA: American Counseling Association.

Holcomb-McCoy, C. (2005). Investigating school counselors' perceived multicultural Competence. *Professional School Counseling, 8*, 414–423.

Holcomb-McCoy, C. (2007). *School counseling to close the achievement gap: A social justice framework for success.* Thousand Oaks, CA: Corwin Press.

Illinois Coalition Against Sexual Assault. (2015). *Crisis centers.* Retrieved from: http://www.icasa.org/crisisCenters.aspx?PageID=501

Illinois General Assembly. (2015). *The consent by minors to health care services act.* Retrieved from: http://www.ilga.gov/legislation/ilcs/ilcs3.asp?ActID=1539&ChapAct=410%26nbsp%3BILCS%26nbsp%3B210%2F&ChapterID=35&ChapterName=PUBLIC+HEALTH&ActName=Consent+by+Minors+to+Medical+Procedures+Act

Jackson-Cherry, L., & Erford, B. (2010). *Crisis assessment, intervention and prevention.* Upper Saddle River, NJ: Pearson.

Janson, C., & Maxis, S. (2015). School counselor as active collaborator. In J. Ziomek-Daigle (Ed.), *School counseling classroom guidance: Prevention, accountability, and outcomes* (pp. 222–250). Thousand Oaks, CA: Sage.

Janson, C., Stone, C., & Clark, M. (2009). Stretching leadership: A distributed perspective for school counselor leaders. *Professional School Counseling, 13*(2), 98–106. https://doi.org/10.5330/PSC.n.2010-13.98

Jimerson, S. R. (2001). Meta-analysis of grade retention research: Implications for practice in the 21st century. *School Psychology Review, 30,* 420–437.

Johnson, J., Rochkind, J., Ott, A., & DuPont, S. (2010). *Can I get a little advice here? How an overstretched high school guidance system is undermining students' college aspirations.* Retrieved from: http://www.publicagenda. org/files/can-i-get-a-little-advice-here.pdf

Johnson, K. & Stephens, R. D. (2002). *School crisis management: A hands-on guide to training crisis response teams.* Alameda, CA: Hunter House.

Johnson, K. D., & Hannon, M. D. (2014). Measuring the relationship between parent, teacher, and student problem behavior reports and academic achievement: Implications for school counselors. *Professional School Counseling, 18*(1), 38–48.

Kaffenberger, C., & Young, A. (2013). *Making DATA work* (3rd ed.). Alexandria, VA: American School Counselor Association.

Karatekin, C. (2017). Adverse childhood experiences (ACEs), stress and mental health in college students. *Stress and Health, 34,* 36–45. https:// doi.org/10.1002/smi.2761

Karst, P. (2000). *The invisible string.* Camarillo, CA: DeVorss.

Kataoka, S. H., Zhang, L., & Wells, K. B. (2002). Unmet need for mental health care among U.S. children: Variation by ethnicity and insurance status. *The American Journal of Psychiatry, 159,* 1548–1555. doi:10.1176/ appi.ajp.159.9.1548

Kerr, M. M. (2009). *School crisis prevention and intervention.* Upper Saddle River, NJ: Merrill/Pearson.

Keys, S., Bemak, F., Carpenter, S., & King-Sears, M. (1998). Collaborative consultant: A new role for school and community counselors. *Journal of Counseling & Development, 76,* 123–133.

Knox, K. S., & Roberts, A. R. (2005). Crisis intervention and crisis team models in schools. *Children & Schools, 27*(2), 93–100.

Kwok, D. K., Winter, S., & Yuen, M. (2012). Heterosexism in school: The counselling experience of Chinese tongzhi students in Hong Kong. *British Journal of Guidance & Counselling, 40*(5), 561–575.

Ladany, N., Mori, Y., & Mehr, K. E. (2013). Effective and ineffective supervision. *The Counseling Psychologist, 41,* 28–47. doi:10.1177/0011000012442648

Lamb, D. H., Presser, N. R., Pfost, K. S., Baum, M. C., Jackson, V. R., & Jarvis P. A. (1987). Confronting professional impairment during the internship: Identification, due process, and remediation. *Professional Psychology: Research & Practice, 18*(6), 597–603. doi:10.1037/0735-7028.18.6.597

Lambie, G. (2007). The contribution of ego development level to burnout in school counselors: Implications for professional school counseling. *Journal of Counseling & Development, 85*, 82–88.

Lambie, G. W., Davis, K. M., & Miller, G. (2008). Spirituality: Implications for professional school counselors' ethical practice. *Counseling and Values, 52*, 211–223.

LaVigna, G. J. (2012). The efficacy of positive behavioural support with the most challenging behaviour: The evidence and its implications. *Journal of Intellectual & Developmental Disability, 37*(3), 185–195.

Lawson, G., & Venart, B. (2005). Preventing counselor impairment: Vulnerability, wellness, and resilience. *VISTAS: Compelling Perspectives on Counseling*, 243–246.

Lee, S. M., Baker, C. R., Cho, S. H., Heckathorn, D. E., Holland, M. W., Newgent, R. A., et al. (2007). Development and initial psychometrics of the counselor burnout inventory. *Measurement and Evaluation in Counseling and Development, 40*, 155-168.

Lee, S. M., & Yang, E. (2013). Counseling in South Korea. In T. H. Hohenshil, N. E. Amundson, & S. G. Niles (Eds.), *Counseling around the world* (pp. 137–144). Alexandria, VA: American Counseling Association.

Lee, V., & Goodnough, G. (2007). Creating a systemic, data-driven school counseling program. In B. Erford (Ed.), *Transforming the school counseling profession* (2nd ed., pp. 121–141). Upper Saddle River, NJ: Pearson.

Lemberger, M. E., Brigman, G., Webb, L., & Moore, M. M. (2013). Student Success Skills: An evidence-based cognitive and social change theory for student achievement. *Journal of Education, 192*, 89–100.

Lenz, A. S., & Smith, R. L. (2010). Integrating wellness concepts within a clinical supervision model. *The Clinical Supervisor, 29*, 228–245. doi:10.1080/07325223.2020.518511

Lewis, J. (1996). Children teaching adults to listen to them. In M. John (Ed.), *Children in charge: The child's right to a fair hearing* (pp. 209–215). London, England: Jessica Kingsley.

Lim, B. K., & Lim, S. (2013). Counseling in China. In T. H. Hohenshil, N. E. Amundson, & S. G. Niles (Eds.), *Counseling around the world* (pp. 77–86). Alexandria, VA: American Counseling Association.

Lim, S. L., & Nakamoto, T. (2008). Genograms: Use in therapy with Asian families with diverse cultural heritages. *Contemporary Family Therapy, 30*, 199–219. doi:10.1007/s10591-008-9070-6.

Limberg, D., & Lambie, G. W. (2011). Third culture kids: Implications for professional school counseling. *Professional School Counseling, 15*(1), 45–54.

Linde, L. E. (2015). Ethical, legal, and professional issues in school counseling. In B. T. Erford (Ed.) *Transforming the school counseling profession* (4th ed., pp.146–172). Upper Saddle River, NJ: Pearson.

Lusky, M. B., & Hayes, R.L. (2001). Collaborative consultation and program evaluation. *Journal of Counseling & Development, 79*, 26–38.

Maag, J. W., & Katsiyannis, A. (2010). School-based mental health issues: Funding options and issues. *Journal of Disability Policy Studies, 21*(3), 173–180. doi:10.1177/1044207310385551

Machado, A. (1978). Proverbios y cantares XXIX. Campos de Castilla [Proverbs and songs XXIX. Fields of Castilla]. In B. J. Craig (Trans.), *Selected poems of Antonio Machado*. Baton Rouge: Louisiana State University Press.

Marlette, J. (1973). Hand scheduling versus the computer. *School Counselor, 21,* 149–151.

Maslach, C. (2003). *Burnout: The cost of caring*. Cambridge, MA: Malor Books.

Mason, E. C. M., Ockerman, M. S., & Chen-Hayes, S. F. (2013). Change-Agent-for-Equity (CAFE) model: A framework for school counselor identity. *Journal of School Counseling, 11*(4). Retrieved from: https://files.eric.ed.gov/fulltext/EJ1012301.pdf

McBride, C. M., Puleo, E., Pollak, K. I., Clipp, E. C., Woolford, D., & Emmons, K. M. (2008). Understanding the role of cancer worry in creating a "teachable moment" for multiple risk factor reduction. *Social Science Medicine, 66,* 790–800. doi:10.1016/j.socscimed.2017.10.014

McCormick, M. P., Cappella, E., O'Connor, E. E., & McClowry, S. G. (2015). Social-emotional learning and academic achievement. *AERA Open, 1*(3), 1–26. doi:10.1177/2332858415603959

McKnight, J., & Block, P. (2010). *The abundant community: Awakening the power of families and neighborhoods*. San Francisco, CA: Berrett-Koehler.

McMahon, H. G., Mason, E. C., Daluga-Guenther, N., & Ruiz, A. (2014). An ecological model of professional school counseling. *Journal of Counseling & Development, 92,* 459–471.

McMahon, M., & Patton, W. (2000). Conversations on clinical supervision: Benefits perceived by school counsellors. *British Journal of Guidance and Counselling, 28*(3), 339–351.

Mental Health Foundation. (2018). *A–Z*. Retrieved from https://www.mentalhealth.org.uk/a-to-z

Mikell v. School Admin. Unit No. 33, 972 A.2d 1050 (N.H. 2009).

Monteiro-Leitner, J. D., Asner-Self, K. K., Milde, C., Leitner, D. W., & Skelton, D. (2006). The role of the rural school counselor: Counselor, counselor-in-training, and principal perceptions. *Professional School Counseling, 9*(3), 248–251.

Nakamura, N., Chan, E., & Fischer, B. F. (2013). "Hard to crack": Experiences of community integration among first- and second-generation Asian MSM in Canada. *Cultural Diversity and Ethnic Minority Psychology, 19*(3), 248–256.

National Association of School Psychologists. (2011). *NASP position statement: Grade retention and social promotion*. Bethesda, MD: Author.

National Center for Education Statistics. (2010). Status and trends in the education of racial and ethnic groups (NCES 2010-015). Washington, DC: Author. Retrieved from: http://nces.ed.gov/pubs2010/2010015/index.asp

National Education Association Healthy Futures. (n.d.). *After a crisis*. Retrieved from http://http://healthyfutures.nea.org/wpcproduct/school-crisis-guide/

National Suicide Prevention Lifeline. (n.d.). *Best practices*. Retrieved from https://suicidepreventionlifeline.org/best-practices/

Neimeyer, R.A. (2005). *Lessons of loss: A guide to coping.* New York, NY: Routledge.

Neukrug, E. S., & Fawcett, R.C. (2015). *The essentials of testing and assessment* (3rd ed.). Stamford, CT: Cengage Learning.

Newsome, D., & Gladding, S. (2010). Counseling individuals and groups in schools. In B. T. Erford (Ed.), *Transforming the school counseling profession* (pp. 209–230). Upper Saddle River, NJ: Merrill Prentice Hall.

No Child Left Behind Act of 2001, Pub. L. No. 107-110, § 115, Stat. 1425 (2002)

Ockerman, M. S., Mason, E., & Hollenbeck, A. F. (2012). Integrating RTI with school counseling programs: Being a proactive professional school counselor. *Journal of School Counseling, 10*(15). Retrieved from: https://files.eric.ed.gov/fulltext/EJ978870.pdf

Osborn, C. J. (2004). Seven salutary suggestions for counselor stamina. *Journal of Counseling & Development, 82,* 319–328.

Payne, R. K. (2013). *A framework for understanding poverty: A cognitive approach.* Highland, TX: aha! Process.

Pedrotti, J. T., Edwards, L. M., & Lopez, S. J. (2008). Promoting hope: Suggestions for school counselors. *Professional School Counseling, 12,* 100–107.

Phillips, J. C. (2000). Training issues and considerations. In R. M. Perez, K. A. DeBord, & K. J. Bieschke (Eds.), *Handbook of counseling and psychotherapy with lesbian, gay, and bisexual clients* (pp. 337–358). Washington DC: American Psychological Association.

President's New Freedom Commission on Mental Health. (2003). *Achieving the promise: Transforming mental health care in America. Final report* [DHHS Publication no. SMA-03-3832]. Rockville, MD: U.S. Department of Health and Human Services.

Rance-Roney, J. (2009). Best practices for adolescent ELLs. *Supporting English Language Learners, 66*(7), 32–37.

Ratts, M. J., Singh, A. A., Nassar-McMillan, S., Butler, S. K., & McCullough, J. R. (2016). Multicultural and social justice counseling competencies: Guidelines for the counseling profession. *Journal of Multicultural Counseling and Development, 44,* 28–48.

Reardon, S. F. (2011). The widening academic achievement gap between the rich and the poor: new evidence and possible explanations. In G. J. Duncan & R. J. Murnane (Eds.), *Whither opportunity? Rising inequality, schools, and children's life chances* (pp. 91–116). New York, NY: Sage.

Reid, L. M., & Dixon, A. L. (2012). The counseling supervision needs of international students in U.S. institutions of higher education: A culturally-sensitive supervision model for counselor educators. *Journal of International Counselor Education, 4,* 29–41.

Remley, T. P., & Herlihy, B. (2013). *Ethical, legal and professional issues in counseling.* (4th ed.) Upper Saddle River, NJ: Pearson Education.

Remley, T. P., & Herlihy, B. (2016). *Ethical, legal, and professional issues in counseling.* New York, NY: Pearson.

Remley, T. P., Hermann, M. A., & Huey, W. C. (2010). *Ethical & legal issues in school counseling* (3rd ed.). Alexandria, VA: American School Counselor Association.

Remley, T. P., Rock, W. D., & Reed, R. M. (2017). *Ethical and legal issues for school counselors.* Alexandria, VA: American School Counselor Association.

Roberts, J., Abu-Baker, K., Fernandez, C. D., Garcia, N.C., Fredman, G., Kamya, H., . . . & Zevallos Vega, R. (2014). Up close: Family therapy challenges and innovations around the world. *Family Process, 53*(3), 544–576. doi:10.1111/famp.12093

Roe v. Wade, 410 U.S. 113 (1973)

Ruf, M., Schauer, M., Neuner, F., Catani, C., Schauer, E., & Elbert, T. (2010). Narrative exposure therapy for 7- to 16-year-olds: A randomized controlled trial with traumatized refugee children. *Journal of Traumatic Stress, 23,* 437–445. https://doi.org/10.1002/jts.20548

Rüsch, N., Angermeyer, M. C., & Corrigan, P. W. (2005). Mental illness stigma: Concepts, consequences, and initiatives to reduce stigma. *European psychiatry, 20*(8), 529-539.

San Antonio Independent School District v. Rodriguez, 411 U.S. 1 (1973).

Sandoval, J. (2013). *Crisis counseling, intervention, and prevention in the schools.* New York, NY: Routledge.

Sattler, J. M. (2014). *Foundations of behavioral, social, and clinical assessment of children* (6th ed.). San Diego, CA: Author.

Savickas, M. L. (1994). Donald Edwin Super: The career of a planful explorer. *The Career Development Quarterly, 43,* 4–24. https://doi.org/10.1002/j.2161-0045.1994.tb00842.x

Scarborough, J. L., & Culbreth, J. R. (2008). Examining discrepancies between actual and preferred practice of school counselors. *Journal of Counseling & Development, 86,* 446–459.

Schilling, E. A., Aseltine, R. H., & Gore, S. (2007). Adverse childhood experiences and mental health in young adults: a longitudinal survey. *BMC Public Health, 7,* 30. https://doi.org/10.1186/1471-2458-7-30

Sheridan, S. M., Eagle, J. W., Cowan, R. J., & Mickelson, W. (2001). The effects of conjoint behavioral consultation: Results of a 4-year investigation. *Journal of School Psychology, 39,* 361–385.

Singleton, G. (2015). *Courageous conversations about race: A field guide for achieving equity in schools.* Thousand Oaks, CA: Corwin.

Sink, C. A., & Devlin, J. M. (2011). Student spirituality and school counseling: Issues, opportunities, and challenges. *Counseling and Values, 55,* 130–148.

Sirin, S. R. (2005). Socioeconomic status and academic achievement: A meta-analytic review of research. *Review of Educational Research, 75*(3), 417–453.

Soleimanpour, S., Geierstanger, S., & Brindis, C. D. (2017). Adverse childhood experiences and resilience: addressing the unique needs of adolescents. *Academic Pediatrics, 17,* S108–S114. https://doi.org/10.1016/j.acap.2017.01.008

Sorensen, J. R. (1989). Responding to student or teacher death: Preplanning crisis intervention. *Journal of Counseling & Development, 67,* 426–427.

Stamm, B. H. (2010). *The concise ProQOL manual,* Pocatello, ID: Author.

Stoltenberg, C. D., & McNeil, B. W. (1997). Clinical supervision from a developmental perspective: Research and practice. In C. E. Watkins Jr. (Ed.), *Handbook of psychotherapy supervision* (pp. 184–202). New York, NY: Wiley.

Stone, C. (2013a). Suicide: Err on the side of caution. *ASCA School Counselor, 51*(1), 6–9.

Stone, C. (2013b). Suicide contracts, assessments, and parental/guardian notification: Err on the side of caution. *ASCA School Counselor, 51*(2), 6–9.

Studer, J. (2005). Supervising school counselors-in-training: A guide for field supervisors. *Professional School Counseling, 8,* 353–359.

Sue, D. W., & Sue, D. (2016). *Counseling the culturally diverse: Theory and practice* (7th ed.). New York, NY: Wiley.

Sutton, J. R., & Pearson, R. (2002). The practice of school counseling in rural and small town schools. *Professional School Counseling, 5*(4), 266.

Tatar, M. (2009). Teachers turning for help to school counsellors and colleagues: Toward a mapping of relevant predictors. *British Journal of Guidance & Counselling, 37*(2), 107–127. doi:10.1080/03069880902728564

Thompson, R. A. (1995). Being prepared for suicide or sudden death in schools: Strategies to restore equilibrium. *Journal of Mental Health Counseling, 17,* 264–278.

Topdemir, C. (2010). *School counselor accountability practices: A national study.* Unpublished doctoral dissertation, University of South Florida, Tampa, FL.

Toporek, R., Ortega-Villalobos, L., & Pope-Davis, D. (2004). Critical incidents in multicultural supervision: Exploring supervisees' and supervisors' experiences. *Journal of Multicultural Counseling and Development, 32,* 66–83.

Toste, J. R., Heath, N. L., & Dallaire, L. (2010). Perceptions of classroom working alliance and student performance. *Alberta Journal of Educational Research, 56*(4), 371–387.

Trusty, J., & Brown, D. (2005). Advocacy competencies for professional school counselors. *Professional School Counseling, 8*(3), 259–265.

Tsukuda, N. (2001). *Country report: Career guidance in Japan.* Retrieved from www.spc.org.sg/9thARACD/CAREER%20GUIDANCE%20IN%20JAPAN.doc

Tuason, T. G. & Arellano-Carandang, L. (2013). Counseling in Philippines. In T. H. Hohenshil, N. E. Amundson, & S. G. Niles (Eds.), *Counseling around the world* (pp. 117–126). Alexandria, VA: American Counseling Association.

Tucker, C. (2009). Low income African-American caregivers' experiences of being referred to mental health services by the school counselor: Implications for best practices. *Professional School Counseling, 12*(3), 240–252.

Tyson, L. E., & Pedersen, P. B. (Eds.). (2000). *Critical incidents in school counseling* (2nd ed.). Alexandria, VA: American Counseling Association.

U.S. Department of Education. (2009). *Race to the Top program: Executive summary*. Washington, DC: Author. Retrieved from http://www2.ed.gov/programs/racetothetop/executive-summary.pdf

Vontress, C. E. (1979). Cross-cultural counseling: An existential approach. *Journal of Counseling & Development, 58,* 85–144. https://doi.org/10.1002/j.2164-4918.1979.tb00363.x

Weinrach, S. G. (1973). Integration is more than just busing. *School Counselor, 20,* 276–279.

Werblow, J., Urick, A., & Duesbery, L. (2013). On the wrong track: How tracking is associated with dropping out of high school. *Equity & Excellence in Education, 46*(2), 270–284.

Whaley, A., & Davis, K. (2007). Cultural competence and evidence-based practice in mental health services: A complementary perspective. *American Psychologist, 62,* 563–574.

Whiston, S. C. (1996). Accountability through action research: Research methods for practitioners. *Journal of Counseling & Development, 74,* 616–623.

Williamson, A. A., Modecki, K. L., & Guerra, N. G. (2015). SEL programs in high school. In J. A. Durlak, C. E. Domitrovich, R. P. Weissberg, & T. P. Gullotta (Eds.), *Handbook of social and emotional learning: Research and practice* (pp. 181–196). New York, NY: Guilford Press.

Witmer, J. M., & Young, M. E. (1996). Preventing counselor impairment: A wellness approach. *The Journal of Humanistic Education and Development, 34*(3), 141–155.

Wolak, J., Mitchell, K. J., & Finkelhor, D. (2006). *Online victimization: 5 years later.* Alexandria, VA: National Center for Missing and Exploited Children.

Wood, C., & Rayle, A. (2006). A model of school counseling supervision: The goals, functions, roles, and systems model. *Counselor Education and Supervision, 45,* 253–266.

Wright, J. (2007). *RTI toolkit: A practical guide for schools*. Port Chester, NY: Dude Publishing.

Yeo, L. S., Tan, S. Y., & Neihart, M. (2013). Counseling in Singapore. In T. H. Hohenshil, N. E. Amundson, & S. G. Niles (Eds.), *Counseling around the world* (pp. 127–136). Alexandria, VA: American Counseling Association.

Young, A., & Bryan, J. (2015). The school counselor leadership survey: Instrument development and exploratory factor analysis. *Professional School Counseling, 19*(1), 1–15.

Young, A., & Kaffenberger, C. (2011). The beliefs and practices of school counselors who use data to implement comprehensive school counseling programs. *Professional School Counseling, 15*(2), 67–76.

Young, M. E., & Lambie, G. W. (2007). Wellness in school and mental health systems: Organizational influences. *The Journal of Humanistic Counseling, Education and Development, 46,* 98–113.